NORTHBROOK
AUTHOR

"This book is a rich gift from two very perceptive writers, Terry Ashby Larkin and Marjorie Ashby Steiner. Sisters both biologically and spiritually, they juxtapose the darkness of death and tragedy with the light of faith, the light of God's presence. Their stories are a stunning reminder of the importance and power of paying attention, being consciously aware, and staying open to "moments of grace." Herein we're able to journey with them through the personal catharsis that writing one's story can produce."

—Marianne Novak Houston, facilitator/consultant with the Center for Courage and Renewal in Seattle and author of the recent poetry collection, *On the Street.*

"Terry's NDE and Marj's LIGHT experience with the passing of her daughter have given them wisdom that many of us have not yet been given. In this book, they generously share that wisdom in a way that we can use in our own lives. I highly recommend it as a book you will place as one of your favorites in the genre of spirituality. Beautifully written, accessible, and enjoyable!"

—Mary Leary

THE LIGHT GAP:
God's Amazing Presence

*Our Journey to Understand LIFE Through
LIGHT and Near-Death*

Terry Larkin & Marjorie Steiner

BALBOA
PRESS
A DIVISION OF HAY HOUSE

Balboa Press books may be ordered through booksellers or by contacting:

Balboa Press
A Division of Hay House
1663 Liberty Drive
Bloomington, IN 47403
www.balboapress.com
1 (877) 407-4847

Because of the dynamic nature of the Internet, any web addresses or links contained in this book may have changed since publication and may no longer be valid. The views expressed in this work are solely those of the authors and do not necessarily reflect the views of the publisher, and the publisher hereby disclaims any responsibility for them.

The authors of this book do not dispense medical advice or prescribe the use of any technique as a form of treatment for physical, emotional, or medical problems without the advice of a physician, either directly or indirectly. The intent of the authors is only to offer information of a general nature to help you in your quest for emotional and spiritual well-being. In the event you use any of the information in this book for yourself, which is your constitutional right, the authors and the publisher assume no responsibility for your actions.

Any people depicted in stock imagery provided by Thinkstock are models, and such images are being used for illustrative purposes only.
Certain stock imagery © Thinkstock.

Print information available on the last page.

ISBN: 978-1-5043-6653-3 (sc)
ISBN: 978-1-5043-6654-0 (hc)
ISBN: 978-1-5043-6666-3 (e)

Library of Congress Control Number: 2016915586

Balboa Press rev. date: 10/04/2016

In Loving Memory

To

Anne Marjorie Steiner

1976–1996

All who knew her cherished her soul in life and now in death.
Her memory will be forever preserved in our hearts!

Contents

Introduction

We came from God's love through the miracle of birth into the loving arms of our parents. The miracle of birth brings love, seen in the face of every parent gazing into the eyes of their newborn. As a newborn, we could sense already awe and love through the touch of our parent as the birth unfolded before them, producing a totally unique human being. We were launched into a world of enchantment with a built-in sense of wonder about our new surroundings. At what age did we look around and find our enchanted world had diminished? We were born in love, but fear is what we *learned*, and it started early in life.

Every one of us has felt lost and alone at one time or another in our lives, and it brought fear. So many personal stories fade into our background with little thought as new and pressing challenges or joys shape our daily lives. Too often, our fearful minds spin a web of complexity that makes the hardships of the world seem unbearable with little hope of escape. What if life wasn't meant to be hard or fearful? Love was meant to dominate our lives by threading only the unconditional love God has for us into daily living.

We are about to take you through the adventures of our lives, hoping to open a window into a simpler, calmer, and more peaceful existence. Our spiritual journeys were the *unlearning* of fear and accepting love back into our hearts. The meaning of our lives is to experience love in others and ourselves!

Terry's Voice

Life is so fragile. I was hearing the beautiful sounds of two young children laughing in the back of my van. It was like any other day. I was busy thinking about getting to the city pool. Children would be waiting there for me to blow the whistle and say, "Dive in. Three laps, everybody. Get warmed up. I'll be ready to see the eight-and-under group first. We will work on breaststroke today!" But their coach never showed up that day. My van and a tree changed that beautiful laughing sound. All I could hear were the agonizing sound of my two young boys screaming, "Mom!" I still hear that horrifying sound sometimes, thirty-four years later. The day would bring changes to every one of my senses. I know I added many more senses than I had the day before. Life gave me five senses; death gave me pause to recount. Death found me completely unprepared. Memories—are they stored in our bodies, or is it outside of our bodies? Brain function—can we think logically when our brain is lying in a body below? I would find some answers that day.

I remember the unbelievable calm and peace I felt when I realized I was looking at my lifeless body below as doctors and nurses were frantically trying to revive me. How could I be seeing that? My spleen ruptured a few hours after arriving at a hospital, where doctors, using only x-rays, were trying to find out what was happening in my body. I had to process this information while gazing down at myself. I had no idea that anyone had ever had a view of themselves above their body. No one was talking about near-death experiences (NDE); I had never heard the term. My story will relate the long process, piecing together my memories on my own and trying to make sense out of them. I had a tremendous fear that even my family would think I was absolutely nuts, so my inner thoughts were asking some pretty hard questions. I couldn't even imagine asking someone else. I can clearly look back now and smile at my naivety.

Today, if I close my eyes in one of my quietest moments, I see and feel a love and light that envelops my body. Memories of entering into a GAP of light so brilliant white I wish I had a palette full of dazzling white paint, so I could share that amazing brightness with all of you! But it took a journey of many years to understand the messages absorbed in my body while time seemed to be suspended. Seeds of truth were planted, but there would be the pain of growth leading to the light I feel today. We will travel back to Shelbyville, Tennessee, to the year 1982. Maybe I can share that light in a different art form, a painting of living vibrantly through words. I want you to experience the joy of bursting and bearing fruit as I relive the experiences of many years.

Marj's Voice

At the death of our almost twenty-year-old daughter in 1996, I turned to God for answers. Why did this accident happen? Why did this happen to Anne, a wonderful, vibrant person? I demanded of God, "I have to know," and God responded! I will take you on our journey, starting with a beautiful sunny day as my husband and I were celebrating our twenty-eighth wedding anniversary. Our day was to be full of celebration. Jim was officiating at the wedding of a young man we watched grow up from childhood. But before that day of celebrations could fully unfold, we received a phone call from our son. Anne had died. She had traveled to Norway and then to London and would now never return. My knees gave way as I sank to the floor. I called out, "Anne, Anne, you can't leave." It was a parent's worst nightmare. I will share our time in London as we traveled with our two sons to the accident site to try to make sense of the circumstances.

The day after our return from London, a spiritual experience overtook me in a way I did not think was possible. As I stood in my kitchen talking on the phone to Anne's clarinet teacher about a dream she had about Anne, I was suddenly consumed by LIGHT. I had been crying almost twenty-four hours a day, and in a second I was experiencing only joy and love. I was wordlessly receiving messages so fast that I could not take it all in. Time stopped, but as I looked back on the experience, my phone conversation was not interrupted as one might expect.

Our family's world had been turned upside down. Keeping going after such a shock was a great challenge. However, I was experiencing what Dickens wrote about in *A Tale of Two Cities*[1]: "It was the best of times, it was the worst of times, it was the age of wisdom, it was the age of foolishness, it was the epoch of belief, it was the epoch of incredulity, it was the season of Light, it was the season of Darkness, it was the spring of hope, it was the winter of despair ..." Epoch and incredulity ... My LIGHT experience was an instant in time that has become a reference point that started a new era in my life. I was in a different state of being, unable to believe or fully understand what I had experienced, but I knew that the LIGHT was a huge gift.

I will relay my story of how difficult it was to keep going after such a shock and how I began to find balance. Unusual "coincidences" kept happening. I now know there is no such thing as coincidences. They are moments when God is present and acting in our lives, supporting our growth. You will read about mountaintop experiences and time spent in the deep valleys of despair.

Both Voices

An incredible white LIGHT had consumed both of us!
*It was a light GAP full of **God's Amazing Presence**.*

How did we get to a new and different place in our lives? This book is about our discovery, finding God's Amazing Presence, bringing light into darkness and thereby returning to love. But we were asking a whole lot of questions along the way. Perhaps you will recognize some of them.

> What in the world happened to us?
> Why did God create us with complete free will?
> Are we the ones that have gone crazy? Or does the world just not understand life?
> Is God sending messages through people into the world? Are we listening?

---

[1]   Charles Dickens, *A Tale of Two Cities* (NY: Dover Publications, 1999), 1.

Where is God *really*?

Does any one church have all the answers?

Why do bad things happen to good people?

Does God *really* answer some prayers and not others?

Why doesn't happiness just stay put in our lives?

Why does health seem to be a journey and not a destination?

Are there ancient texts giving us answers to life's dilemmas?

Is everybody confused, or is it just us?

Can brain scientists tell us what happened in my brain that day?

Can medical professionals be questioning common beliefs too?

How about the experts? Do they get confused?

Many people are happy with the simplicity of we'll never know answers. Our life experiences have painted a different picture because a seed of discovery was planted in both of us. We began to unravel our lives by realizing what entanglements we had woven into a fear-based life. Our culture seems to be based on fear for amazingly complex reasons. Fear takes on many disguises: anger, violence, desire, grief, apathy, guilt, shame, anxiety, craving, condemning, evil, and so much more. What if simple God-realized love could dissolve the tangled mess so that a beautiful patterned web can emerge? What if our view of that web was filtered in beautiful shimmering light? For us, love emerged with new meaning. We experience love as kindness, compassion, acceptance, non-judgment, and grace threaded through other people all over the world. Each of us can do our part to cast out the darkness in others through our love. Our tangled world needs a lot of us to offset fear turned into hate.

Throughout our book, we will be using the concept of a light gap in the forest. The rain forests on earth are the best place to observe this process, but it is also just as evident in the national forests that have been preserved in our country. The top layer of trees in a forest is called the canopy. It is the roof of the forest. The canopy can be so dense that only a trickle of light reaches the floor of the forest. Down below on the forest floor are seeds that are waiting for the intense heat of the sun to begin to sprout. Seeds can remain in the soil for hundreds, perhaps thousands, of years, waiting for the right conditions to begin new life. The variety of seeds that lay waiting can regenerate the forest over time as the right conditions present themselves. One tree hit by lightning, high winds, or old age can take down many trees as it falls. It opens up a space on the forest floor with direct light and provides the opportunity for new growth.

Our lives can mirror this process. In our book, we will share how tragedies are often like the trees falling in the forest. Seeds germinate within us so ideas we have not acted on can emerge to change beliefs that free us to *be*, instead of constantly *doing*. New ways of thinking about our circumstances emerge, sprouting acceptance and forgiveness. All these start new growth that regenerates our lives. Most important, a space is made for us to hear the ever so quiet voice of God talking directly to us, supporting us through the chaos we are feeling in our lives. Often, it is in the middle of destruction that the depths of our spiritual gifts are recognized for the first time. We deepen our understanding of reality. We will take you into some extraordinarily difficult times of our own lives. Our LIGHT experiences helped us begin a journey of rebuilding and discovery. In the telling of our stories, we hope you find your own way to an expanded view of God, to new hope with joy, love, and light in your life.

Chapter 1

The Mystery of Death

Friday, July 16, 1982

My life was very ordinary in 1982. I was thirty-two years old, living in the sleepy, small town of Shelbyville, Tennessee. The setting is a rural countryside dotted with beautiful horse plantations. The National Walking Horse Competition takes place in Shelbyville every year. My husband, Doug, and our two young children made our transition here from Denver, Colorado, a year prior to this. Business brought Doug to accept a new position in his career. We had enjoyed the challenge of new sights and sounds, helping our two boys, four-year-old Jason and two-year-old Jeremy, adjust to a new environment.

We were enjoying wonderful new friends and finding southern hospitality enjoyable while we slowly got used to hearing a "new language"! Growing up in Michigan, there were chuckles as people enjoyed hearing our boys sounding very "northern" in their speech.

My life was busy like any young mother. Having graduated with a degree in early childhood education, I had volunteered to help create a new educational daycare setting where parents could count on a preschool experience being incorporated into their children's days. Children's World was created, and I was busy writing curriculum for a kindergarten program to integrate as well.

Meanwhile, I had also agreed to help a group of interested parents create an age-group swim program in Shelbyville. They really wanted to grow swimmers who could compete with other area schools participating in middle and high school swim meets. I grew up swimming in a lake. I rode my bike to a lifeguarded beach all during my youth. I don't even remember not knowing how to swim. I had been trained in college classes on how to instruct all of the swimming strokes. I took advanced swimming in college for an easy credit, and then realized I could go on and add to the Junior Life Saving Certification I received in high school at that beach. But I had absolutely *no* experience coaching. I was still perfecting my skills in that arena.

Death was the furthest thing from my mind. In fact, I'm not sure I ever thought about death in any concrete way. I grew up in a progressive but typical Presbyterian church outside of Detroit in a very rural setting. We had joined the First Presbyterian Church of Shelbyville and felt comfortable there. I only remember thinking about death once in my youth, but I did not understand the significance. That story actually surfaced not too long after my near-death experience (NDE) in a wondering sort of way.

At twelve years old, I suffered a concussion after slipping off of a diving board; I was sent backwards, hitting my head on the board and landing in the lake water. I can still visualize a white light reaching out and pulling me up to the surface of the water. But, for all of my youth, I thought it was the lifeguard! I had a crush on the lifeguard. He was extremely kind and so interested in kids' lives. I was often at my childhood beach with my two best friends from ten in the morning until four in the afternoon. It wasn't until many years later when I heard that he came out in the boat and pulled me in. I was crushed hearing that—he didn't dive in the water to save me? I was unconscious, so who pulled me up? I have memories of being in shock, and I was eventually hospitalized with a serious concussion for nearly a week. I never put meaning to this event until after my NDE.

Swimming was comfortable for me. Summers were hot in Tennessee. The water was refreshing in the outdoor pool, and I enjoyed coaching all ages. My son Jason was now five and swimming in the eight-and-under group. Jeremy was now three. He loved all the parents and younger kids who kept him by the pool while I coached. I was heading to my job as coach on a sunny Friday morning, July 16, 1982. I traveled out in the country on a two-lane highway to Bell Buckle because I needed to pick up some flyers to give to my swimmers and discuss some fall plans for Children's World. I spent time talking, but as I climbed back in my van, I did not put on my seat belt. I found myself enjoying the giggling sounds coming from my boys in the back of the van. I was heading back to the Shelbyville pool ... when in a few tragic moments my life would totally change.

A man driving a pickup truck in front of me was traveling slowly. I decided to pass him. All of a sudden, he turned to the left into my path. I swerved to the right to miss him, but we collided, and I went smack into a tree that was close to the road. Accidents happen in such quick moments, and we react instinctively. It's hard to recall my thoughts as it was happening. I hit the tree before I even realized what had taken place.

I know I was unconscious, but I don't know for how long. I awoke to screams from my boys calling, "Mom, Mom!" This is etched in my memory. It is something that never leaves, and it resurfaces at odd moments. I could not move. I kept going in and out of consciousness. I wish today I knew who the angels were who came to my car. I can picture a friendly face of a man. They took the boys out of the back. I have a memory of a lovely lady sitting by a tree in front of her house with my children. The kind ambulance drivers made sure I saw my boys sitting under the tree in the grass as I was put on the stretcher ready to be placed in the ambulance. Nowhere except in a small, close-knit town would someone find my husband, Doug, and have him arrive just as they were putting me into an ambulance. He shared later that Jason and Jeremy had been calmed by a very kind lady sitting on the grass with them when he arrived. I feared that Jason and Jeremy would retain trauma, but all of those thoughts came much later. My largest memory is people staring at me through the window telling me not to move. Little chance—I could not move. I must have been asking if the boys were safe, because they kept assuring me the neighbor lady had my boys. Luckily, I never had to see that van again. I know Doug was afraid it would be too traumatic for me to see it.

I don't remember the ambulance ride, but I do have a few faded memories of being in the emergency room at the Bedford County Hospital in Shelbyville, Tennessee. I remember seeing Doug when they had me on a stretcher on the road, but I don't remember anything he said to me. So much had to be told to me later as I was recovering.

Back in the eighties, there were no MRIs to figure out what was happening with a body. They knew I was bleeding internally, but it appeared to be slow. I do remember agonizing pain when they had to move me on to an X-ray table. I faded in and out of consciousness periodically. My head hurt so badly; it felt like hammers were knocking in it somewhere. The pain in my abdomen caused me to be conscious only part of the time. They stitched up my chin, which evidently came down on the steering wheel. Who knows where and what I hit exactly. I had no seat belt on, and airbags were only in the imagination of an inventor. They were concerned about a brain concussion and were focused on that. But, amazingly enough, they found no broken bones. I was moved to a room, but I have no memory of that.

My next memory was hearing these words: "There is slow internal bleeding." I remember a searing, out-of-control pain, screaming, and then blackness … very black.

All of a sudden, I was feeling like myself again. The next memories were *extremely clear*. I was processing what I was seeing. But I had a lot of questions. Thoughts were very calmly going through my head. I remember internal conversation going on in my head like it was yesterday, even though memories of my life in 1982 have faded greatly. As I was researching for this book, I needed to go back and piece together the periphery of my life—parts I filed away in my deep subconscious mind. What about my memories during my NDE? They are like a crystal-clear pool of water with intact memory. What a contrast. As I relive that day for you, these are the words I was thinking and saying. The thoughts swirling in my head …

I don't remember arriving at the hospital. I'm in a bed in a room. Oh yes, the accident. When and how did I get here? Oh, that's my doctor. I recognize him. Dr. Rich is our family doctor. How did they find him? Can I piece together memories? I do remember a pain and then blackness. Pain and screaming, I remember that. But now I have no pain. In fact, I'm feeling wonderful, peaceful, and calm. How can that be?

Wait a minute ... am I down there? That's my body! How can I be looking down at myself? Who are all of these people running around like crazy? Why are they running in and out? There are so many of them. What are they doing? Hey, everyone, I'm right here! My thoughts and words don't seem to be changing their actions. And yet, I believe I am using my voice.

Later thoughts: I was remembering and thinking very rationally without my body. No, memories are not stored inside my head.

I realize I am hearing their words and shouts, and I am sensing a lot of confusion. I recognize my doctor, but I'm still questioning thoughts as I am making sense of the scene. He seems to be yelling at everyone that is coming in. He's looking totally stricken. Interesting. Why?

Why am I feeling so calm? I have no pain. "Hey, everyone, I'm not in any pain!" I hear something about my spleen rupturing. I hear, "It's a huge tear. She's losing a lot of blood." I'm thinking, where does it go?

I am so peaceful.

My view was enlarging in a way we don't see.

The areas around me are huge. *I'm not really confined in the room. Oh, and the boys are fine. I know that. I know what house and set of friends have my children. I am happy they are safe. Doug is talking to them but leaving in a hurry.*

Later thoughts: How did I know that the kids were fine? I just did.

Wait, all of the people are leaving one at a time. Why? They are gone, all except Dr. Rich. My body is still lying there. I'm studying my body. It looks so small now. The expanse of this room is absolutely huge. My doctor is holding my hand. He is talking. "I'm sorry, I didn't know! I'll wait here to be the one to tell Doug." Tell Doug what? Why are you so sad? I'm feeling great. Wait, he is holding my hand, but I don't feel it.

Reflecting back: I don't ever remember having a conscious thought like *I guess I'm dead.* I've long wondered why I wasn't thinking that. I still don't know.

I have reflecting, calm thoughts as I watch the scene below. *Hmm, my husband, Doug, isn't there in the room. I don't see him now. The doctor is waiting for him, but he keeps talking to me and holding my hand. My body is so motionless. I hear his words, but I don't feel his touch.*

The hospital room started to be quite foggy looking and there was a huge amazing white light above me. The scene below me was getting smaller and smaller, disappearing into a fog. Eventually I was completely in a white foggy-looking space. Time was moving, but time was standing still. There was no definition of time. I was peaceful, serene, and I remember an enveloping love that has no words. I was not worried or scared in any way.

It wasn't very dark, although the cloudy look was darkish. But above me was an incredible white light. There was no definition to my space at all. There is no turning to look at something; I saw it all at once, all at the same time. The foggy look began to swirl in a cone shape. The brilliance of the white light ahead was almost blinding, but there was no awareness of my eyes or any body part. In and around the cone-shaped foggy clouds were streams of very light colors. There were blues and purples mixed with greens and yellows in hues that we don't see on earth. We would call them pastel, and yet they were too bright to be in that spectrum. It was beautiful but not a rainbow. These colors were floating in and out of the fog streaming into the light. As I got closer to the point of this cone, it seemed larger, more like an opening. But the incredible light was getting brighter and brighter as I traveled toward the opening. I was already receiving a very profound message that I brought back with me: love is all there is! There were no words; a knowing had been absorbed inside my being. The feeling of this love was incredible. This love message was the first and the most prominent in my memory from the whole time I was in this realm.

I began hearing sounds. It wasn't singing exactly. It was more like chimes, not any chimes I had ever heard before. There was a voice quality to it but more like humming and chanting with no words of any kind, swirled in musical tones. I loved these sounds. They were beautiful. I wanted to get closer to them.

Since I was a little girl, music has always been huge in my life. There were records always being played in our family room. I have wonderful memories of my older sisters playing piano as I sat and listened to them with envy. My turn would come. My parents made sure all five siblings had piano lessons and played an instrument, all with private lessons. I had my turn in that too. I chose to play a flute, and I loved piano lessons. But like many dutiful teenagers, I gave them up because I was just too busy for such things. I was playing in the band and orchestra. It would be much later as an adult that I would regret that decision to stop piano! We all sang in the church choirs from the time we were five on through high school. I loved to sing. My mother had a beautiful alto voice, and I loved to hear her sing. Choir directors at the Orchard Lake Presbyterian Church just assumed all of the Ashby girls would be altos as well. I kept saying, "But no, I can hit all of these high notes easily!" They insisted I was an alto. I didn't move to soprano until high school. And all of my adult life, in every church, in all of our moves, I have always sung in the choir. I still do. There are only two years in my life that I did not sing in a choir. I was too sick to do it. That story will come out later in my growth story. I love singing. I did keep playing the flute all through college, and I still play to this day. Amazing music and sounds can take me back to my NDE. For years I searched to hear this music again. First it was my record stack. Then I had my eight-track stack. Then it was my cassette stack. And now it's my CD stack and downloaded music on my phone. Even today my CDs are like a mountain of steps, searching to find just the right sound. Music … it's God's celestial orchestra. I've come pretty close to those sounds. Many thanks to Dr. Wayne Dyer and James Twyman for producing the powerful frequencies that bring my being back to that light.[2] I will share that experience as my journey unfolds.

> *The sounds carried me toward light. The sounds are locked into my being and were never lost. After the beautiful colors were mixing with the sounds, I was moving closer and closer to the end of this conical shape. It sounds odd to say that an incredible white light was drawing me into a small space. But that smallness absolutely dissolved in an instant into dazzling, alluring, and brilliant white. I was wrapped in the most loving love. I merged into an incredible white light being that enveloped me. There were not arms, but it is a way that my five senses can describe how seeing, feeling, hearing, and knowing all meld into one. I'll have to say that now I wonder why I didn't experience smell or taste. I will have to check that out next time! There was love, information, messages, and my earthly life all coming to me at once. I can remember this so vividly. It's a place I always seek. Love is all there is, love is all there is!*

I need a new expanded vocabulary beyond my English to describe how all senses go together. I think I could spend hours on the Internet, reading every thesaurus, listing every adjective for the meaning of this concept, but what I always find going inward is *love*. There was information and reflection but not condemnation or judgment in any way. In years to come, I would *need* to move as close to this realm as I could come in my earthly home to try to figure out the second message that I received on this journey. *We have the ability to heal ourselves!* God perhaps already knew I would need that knowledge in years to come. The search would continue for a very long time.

---

2   Dr. Wayne W. Dyer and James F. Twyman, *I AM Wishes Fulfilled* Meditation CD.

I had heard the messages: Love is all there is, and we have the ability to heal ourselves. I also heard I came back for a special reason. Now, as I reflect back on all of this, I cannot imagine that I didn't want to just *stay* there and not return. So many people who have had an NDE talk about a conscious decision to come back to their body for some reason. I have no memory of a conscious decision to come back. I know now God had a reason to send me back. The words were even in the knowing state when I returned. *I came back for a reason! I came back for a reason? What?*

I learned over time how to relive my experience, but the method of how was long in coming. This message was an addition to the others I had heard. *I came back for a very special reason.* I came back into my body racked with pain. While the time away from my body seemed quite long, the time heading back was more like the snap of someone's fingers. Click and I was there! Next was this conscious thought:

I am back in my body, and oh, the incredible pain!

Somehow, the look on my doctor's confused face was happier though; at least my earthly brain must have thought that. But memories of this time frame are very fuzzy for me. Around me were doctors and nurses, but I had no view from above. Once again I moved in and out of consciousness, only this time at some point I saw Doug. He said, "They are rushing you into an ambulance and taking you to another hospital." They couldn't give me too much medication; they needed me awake so they could monitor what was happening. *Black out* again. This is where my memory stopped cold.

I have absolutely *no* memories after this. My husband told me I was in Baptist Hospital in Nashville. Eventually doctors would tell me they had to clean out all of the blood inside, where it was in all the wrong places. There was nothing left of the spleen to fix. They replaced almost as much blood as a human being has in a body. It took me a long time to come around, and I'm pretty sure at that point I was well sedated for a lot of the time. They told Doug the surgery went well and they were expecting me to recover completely, all wonderful news. I have been pondering recently … why do I have such crystal clear memories of the time spent during my NDE when I can't remember Baptist Hospital at all, not even one detail of my time spent there?

I went home eventually, and my precious two boys greeted me with love and hugs to last a lifetime, at least that's what Doug shared with me. I can't remember it. I struggle wondering why I don't have a visual picture of that. My gentle and loving older sister, Lynne Anne, said she would come and help me as I recovered. I remember being pretty emotional during this time, but I was still in quite a fog. She just knew how to take over and have fun doing it. I still marvel at her unselfish act of kindness. She had children of her own at home. I know we had many meals brought to us by very special people. How would I ever repay the friends that kept my kids while I was in the hospital so Doug could be with me and eventually return to work? There were times when I'd be lying in bed, and all of a sudden, a wave of love would come through me and make me smile. I wondered what it was. It was a feeling, not an event. It took many weeks before I started having little flashbacks in memory. There were little pieces making limited sense. But my body was actually recovering at a very rapid rate, and my surprised doctor commented on how quickly my body was healing. Today as I write my memories, I have very few memories of my life then. It's still a mystery to me why I don't remember much during the first three or four months of my life after returning home.

I do remember several visits back to my doctor. He marveled at how well I was doing and how quickly I was recovering. For me, there was never a doubt. I knew I would recover and that I would push myself hard. I had my sons and my husband to take care of, and they were more important than how I was feeling.

After several months, I was getting stronger. I could vividly remember looking down at my body, but I was telling *no one* about it. There were pieces of my experience that took a long time to process. A picture, like a movie, was emerging in my mind. But I was telling no one. Goodness, I thought I was losing my mind to think this actually happened. Maybe I was quite sheltered in my life, but I had never heard of *anyone* who had died and came back. It was 1982. I found no books, and no one talked of such things.

What were my visions, memories, and flashbacks telling me? I knew that people would think I was nuts if I started repeating what I remembered. I also realized that I had never experienced the death of a really close person to me. My grandmother died when I was nine. I remember really crying at the funeral, but that was such a faded memory. And my grandfather, whom I really loved, died while I was in Germany. My parents didn't talk about death either. At this point in life, they were aging but vibrant and alive. I was *stalling*. There was an emotion inside, a feeling that would come over my body when I tried to remember. It was beautiful. So, why was I not telling Doug?

It was several months before I finally told Doug my sketchy memories of the time. He was wonderful. I should have known he would believe me. He always supported me in everything I did. I'm not at all sure he understood or had a real concept of what happened. In fact he will tell you he didn't at first. I was busy forming a new school. I had two kids that needed a loving mother present in each moment. I had come back into this realm to give love and take care of my family. I escaped my NDE memories by being busy in my life. I was in the right profession for me; I loved children, and I loved teaching them. Love experienced was pouring out of me. But there was a knowing in my body reaching out for more information. There would be no putting it aside for long.

I remember so vividly the day I finally decided I was going to make an appointment with my doctor and ask him what happened. This was a good four or five months after my surgery. My checkups were always so positive. "What amazing healing, Terry," he would say. Why ruin a good thing? I told myself! But finally I had to know. So I started the conversation by telling him that I had some memories about my accident, and I needed to know what all really happened. I was pretty sketchy on the details, but I told him that I remember seeing him holding my hand, looking very sad and that I heard him talking to me. I shared words he said to me. His eyes opened pretty wide, but I continued to tell him that I realized I was viewing all of this from above. I told him I could see my body—and how could I have seen that from above? His mouth dropped open, and he said, "You ... *remember* that? How could you have ..." He started to say something else, but he never finished that sentence. His mouth fell open, and his eyes were wide in disbelief. I don't think he knew what to say. He confirmed, "Yes, you nearly died, *but* ... you came back!" He started talking fast. He told me about my spleen rupturing and that the bleeding was totally out of control. They hadn't figured out where I was bleeding internally from the X-rays. I finally asked, "Was I gone?" He answered, "Yes." He quickly recovered and seemed to regret he had said this. I started to say there's more to my story, but I thought he was mortified. I did not want to make him feel more uncomfortable. I had the confirmation I needed. I thought I was making him feel guilty. And that was the last thing I wanted, though surely that was what he was thinking. I doubted he could even grasp what I was saying either. I was never convinced he wanted to hear any more. He left. I left. I wish I had gone back a second time within a short period of time, but I didn't. Instead, I tucked my memories a little further back inside of me. Instead of processing further, I put all of these thoughts in my own prayers at church. I found I could tune out and not listen to the minister's prayers or sermons. I was hearing God's words in a new and different way.

Life moved on, and we had a full life for sure. I had two boys that were the delight of my life. I loved my life of teaching. I became pregnant with my third child. In a way, I began to think, this must be the reason I lived. I was meant to have a third child. Our marriage was wonderful, and we were happy with healthy and loving boys.

I died, and I figured it was only an amazing gift for me. Today, when I reflect back, I realize how naïve that thought was.

Little did I realize that there were others who had experienced NDEs. I just didn't know about them yet. Sitting in church, I began to always have my own little church going on inside my head. I would listen to scripture, but now it seemed to be telling me another story. I began to interpret Jesus's life very differently than I had before.

There were times when music brought an energetic feeling in my body, and for a fleeting moment, I would *feel* God's celestial music. I loved letting myself move back into that feeling of love I had experienced. The love message was a knowing, and I enjoyed sharing it. I just kept quiet and let my inner self feel that joy as I remembered. It would be quite a while before I realized that by keeping all of that inside, I never shared a huge love I could have with so many people.

I came back for a reason. I figured that it was accomplishing something worthwhile. I loved being a mom and wife. I was working hard at Children's World. I had a full life. Wasn't that it? I know now how naïve that thinking was. But I always had this empty feeling like there was something else.

The possibility of death came to me again. I came close to losing my oldest son, Jason, due to a fall in Shelbyville. I was scared to my core. I pleaded with God and brought *all* of my experiences up to Him. I couldn't believe He would have brought me back to then lose my son. Jason pulled through, but my eyes were opened a little wider. Death was beautiful, and life could be beautiful. It was a paradox. Living life was more complicated. I didn't understand where death fit in. I needed to open my eyes! I did begin telling the rest of my family, but it was always in very sketchy ways. What I failed to realize then was that if I had just opened up, love would have been shared, and my life could have been very different. Upon reflection, God was very patient with me.

We soon made the decision to move back to Michigan. Doug's company was making a big change, and the Shelbyville plant closed. By this time, I was really beginning to search for answers but seldom talked about my experience. It was naïve to think I could run away from God.

When I had my death and dying experience, I was not shown what heaven looked like. I had decided it might be because I had not formed a vision for myself of what heaven would be like. I was young in my thirties, and while I attended church all my life, even at a very early age, I was questioning how all of the lessons I was learning could be true. Too many of them just made no sense to me, even as a child. I had not come close to understanding what God had to say to me because my soul had only been slightly awakened in my youth. After my NDE, I was struggling to fit back into my world. I had changed. My views of God and life had changed. I came back with understanding mixed with questions. As in a forest light gap, I was the restless seed floundering around in darkness, reaching for the light of understanding. In the ten years following my NDE, this list describes my thoughts.

- *Love* is all there is! I was still learning what that meant, but I could feel it. Conflicting messages from others kept me searching.
- There was no pain, no sadness, only a euphoric feeling of peace after death. I no longer feared death at all; it was freeing me to *live*. I wondered why so many people feared God. I was still hearing in church settings that we should fear God. Really? Why?
- White light that I could still visualize *completely guided me.* Can I get back in that white space? It took me way too many years before I realized that the answer was yes.
- Beauty in color beyond our comprehension helped me find places in nature where I could be in God's presence and be close to the love in color.
- Colors radiating in hues remembered are unbelievable, but our Earth has amazing vistas that God created too, and I was always searching for them.
- Sounds were in my memory … not singing in words … lovely bell/chime sounds. I was searching to hear them.
- I came back for a reason. I still did not understand why I was back.
- I did not see people in my NDE. I had only experienced God. Why? Is my memory truth? I had read the Bible since a child, but did I believe all I read?
- Even early in life, I had wondered if translations had altered meanings. More questions came.

I had so many more experiences yet to happen in my life. God had a plan. I see that clearly now. At this time, I was living in fear of telling my story. I didn't know how to interpret it. How could I share it? But there were scholars out there in the bodies of theologians, scientists, and medical researchers that were visionaries. It was a world I had not discovered yet, but I have now, and it's powerful. I never lost sight of the message that I came back for a reason. I could feel God's love in my body. Fear of death was gone, but I was still living in fear of what others thought of me. It's clear now that coming back was not about my accomplishments. It was not a successful swim team. It was not a successful school. It was not my teaching career. It was not even about three children we loved dearly. What was God sending me back to do? I was busy trying to do the *right* thing by pleasing everyone around me. Surely they all knew the answers. I didn't know I could change any of that thinking or *perhaps* even change my life.

I grew to love the phrase coined by Dr. Wayne Dyer, "Don't die with your music still inside of you."[3] I was slowly dying, and my "music" was tucked away about as far away as it could get. It was deep inside where it felt protected. My journey took me to the place where I discovered so much more. My journey was not about moving back to my home state of Michigan. I was closer to family, and I felt a little more at home, but the journey would continue in totally unforeseen ways.

Life began to change for me. My heart was in total joy as I began to realize deep in my soul answers were bursting forth. Yet, who around me understood my internal truths intertwined with external conflict of how others around me perceived the world? Life experiences would be bringing more answers.

God opened my eyes when I was ready to see.

---

[3]   Dr. Wayne Dyer, *10 Secrets for Success and Inner Peace* (Carlsbad, California: Hay House, 2001), 19.

Chapter 2

Marj's LIGHT Experience
A Story of God's Amazing Presence

On, June 15, 1996, Jim and I were celebrating our twenty-eighth wedding anniversary.

It was a beautiful sunny day. We were excited to be gathered with our wonderful friends, Jules and Diane, in Madison, Wisconsin. Their son was to be married in the late afternoon, and Jim, my husband and a Presbyterian minister, was performing the wedding for Eric and Paula.

Friday night, many had gathered for the wedding rehearsal, and it had brought reunions with youth we had known since their childhoods. There was excitement, laughter, and fun for all. Toasts were offered to the future of tomorrow's bride and groom. Saturday, our actual anniversary, we had a wonderful breakfast where we were staying, and then Jim and I headed out for a leisurely walk in a nearby woods that opened to an expansive prairie. Afterwards, I met up with our niece, Elizabeth, and she and I spent the morning planting a garden for her mom and dad. They were in Oxford where Bob had been teaching for the year at the University of Oxford in England, and they were coming home in late summer. Lynne Anne, my sister, had planted a garden near the community pool for years, so it was a gift that the two of us could surprise her—a bountiful garden upon their return. I called Jim to say that we were not quite finished, so we would finish up, and then Elizabeth would drive me over to the bed-and-breakfast for a quick shower and then to the later afternoon wedding. "Yes, I promise I will be there on time!" I had said. He knew me well …

But I did not show up! As I was getting dressed, the phone rang in our room. It was our oldest son, Michael, who was living in New York. The police had tracked down our two sons. They were trying to find us. Michael and Scott had been given the task of calling us and giving us the message: their baby sister, our nineteen-year-old daughter, had died in an accident in London, England! That possibility is a parent's worst fear when they send them off on a trip. Anne had just finished her sophomore year of college, and she had gone to Norway with the St. Olaf College band. She was stopping on the way home to see her best friend, Val, who was going to school at London University. The next day, she was to visit my sister Lynne Anne and her husband in Oxford.

"Mom, Anne has had a terrible accident in London."
The shock was unbearable!

"But she is going to be all right … right?

"No, she has died."

With Elizabeth at my side, I sank to the floor. "No, it can't be right. No! No!" I began to sob and shake.

The wedding had been beautiful, but in Jim's mind was concern. After the wedding, he received a message from Elizabeth telling him there was an emergency and to come back to the bed-and-breakfast. As people were off to the reception, Jim came back. With tears flowing, I said to him, "Jim, Anne is dead."

We were in a horrible daze. Tears kept falling. The memory of the next couple hours is fuzzy. We decided to get home as fast as we could. We called our friends after the reception and told them what had happened. We packed up our things and drove home. Michael booked a ticket for Chicago, Scott left DePaul where he was studying, and they headed home, a place that would never be the same. Oh, how we needed each other.

The next day, Winnetka Presbyterian Church immediately came to our aid. The pastor, Martha Greene, was at our side, helping us make decisions that were impossible to make. Michael, his future wife, Heather, and Scott arrived home and were so helpful. Close friends gathered, and we sat on the back deck of the house. It was another beautiful day, the beauty of which we could not take in. It was now Sunday, and I was booked on a Monday flight to attend a science conference for teachers at the Smithsonian Institute in Washington, DC. I called the curriculum director of our school district to tell her I would not be there. I could hardly talk. I sobbed my way through the conversation, and within a half hour, my wonderful, caring principal, Sandy Karaganis, was calling. She gave me tremendous support. Others in the district were able to carry on at the conference. I am forever grateful for the support the community and our families and friends surrounded us with.

We were in a deep fog. Many friends guided us through the maze of decisions that needed to be made. We only had enough money for one or two of us to go, but we needed each other desperately. The church made it possible for our whole family to go to London to make sense of what had happened. Even the US government helped. Only one of us had a passport. I frantically searched for the documents we needed to get tickets. I sobbed my way through conversations with numerous officials in Washington and London. They allowed us to get the passports at the embassy in London.

By Monday, we were on our way to London. I had not slept since Saturday night. Jim seemed to be doing better on that score than I was. Each of us was in our own world, just surviving. We could hug and receive comfort, but words were few. Martha drove us to the airport, and as we were boarding, she handed me a small package and told me, "Take one of these when you get on the plane." I was asleep in minutes and remember nothing until the wheels hit the ground in London. The American embassy picked us up in their limousine.

When we reached the embassy, we were greeted and directed with such warmth and respect and care. We were assigned a person who would help us with anything we needed at any time of day. The passports were issued. Photographs can lie. I used that passport for a number of trips, and I was always amazed at how my picture looked like it had been taken on any normal day.

We were driven to the hotel where we were staying. One of the church member's husbands worked as an executive of a large hotel chain. He contacted the hotel in London and told the manager of our situation. The hotel gave us a small apartment to stay in. It provided us a living room where we could sit and be away from all the chaos we were feeling and relax as best we could. Our daughter's friend Val, who Anne was visiting, was joined by her mother to help her cope with the situation. With a space of our own, we could sit and talk and cry together. We were told that no one paid for the apartment. The manager's response was, "You need a place to stay, we have space, so we welcome you with heartfelt condolences and love."

Jim, Michael, Scott and I spent a week meeting with the authorities in the mornings, talking with the inspector assigned to Anne's case, working with the US embassy, and yes, we had to go to the morgue and identify her body. "Anne, Anne, please don't leave us! Come back ..."

Anne was to go visit my sister Lynne Anne the next day. She and her husband were living in Oxford at the time. She took the train in to London to be with us. Lynne Anne and I have always been very close, and it was such comfort to have her there. We were all in great pain, helping each other cope. Mornings we spent with American embassy personnel and the city of London police inspector. Anne had fallen—or there had been foul play—from the eighth floor of her friend's dorm room while Val was at the library studying. She had fought for her life for four hours in a nearby hospital. The inspector was sure that someone else was involved. In the afternoons, we sat at café tables, reminiscing, telling stories, laughing, and crying. Yes, somehow we discovered that there was still humor in the ironies of what we were experiencing.

We had not given any thought prior to this time about what we wanted to do if one of us died. We decided that we would have her body cremated, so there was no point in taking her body back to the States in a casket. In the conversation with the crematorium, the women asked if we wanted an organist to play while Anne's body was cremated, and how many guests would be arriving. What? Well, it turns out in England they have a service in the next room while the body is being cremated. We decided no, we would not sit there, but at the appointed time, we sat in a private little park across the street from our hotel. We spent the time together, each in our own way praying and honoring her for the richness she brought to us, and sent love to our very special Anne.

The next day, we were told to come and pick up her ashes. We took a taxi and walked into the funny little place to pick up the box. I had asked them to wrap it, so that people would not know what it was as we took it home on the plane. When the man handed me the box, it was warm! That startled me. I could not imagine them not cooling the ashes first. *Or ... that's a silly thought.* I dropped the idea. We went out to get into our taxi. England's taxis have a running board, and you have to step high to get in. I was carrying the box, but I needed to have someone hold it as I got into the taxi. One of the boys was behind me, so I passed it on, and then it was passed into the taxi to someone else. Scott or Michael said, "This is crazy carrying Anne in a box!" The tension broke, and laughter struck.

As we got back to the hotel, the boys were not going to carry "Anne in a box" through the lobby. "But no one will know it is ashes," I said. But they insisted, so they had the taxi driver go around to the back entrance, and they carried Anne through the service entrance and up the back stairs. Funny what happens when you are under such stress.

We had one day left before our flight home, with no more official business to do. Lynne Anne planned a day of hiking on the little paths between towns in the Cotswold area. It was a beautiful day and such a relief to get out of London. The Cotswold villages are in south-central England, an area of rolling hills, and amazing houses and fences built of Cotswold limestone. It is picture-perfect territory. You can walk from town to town on little paths made from hundreds of years of people walking. As we began walking, we ran into a flock of sheep. They were all lying down and not at all disturbed by our presence. One sheep was standing by the path, and Jim began bah-ing at the sheep and having a conversation with her. Later, as we came into Bibury, in the river was a swan with eight baby cygnets. We took pictures and enjoyed watching the peaceful scene before us. This walk was the most peaceful time we had while in England. The next day, we boarded a plane for Chicago.

Upon arriving home, we began to make arrangements for Anne's memorial service. In 1996, Jim was serving as interim pastor at the Presbyterian Church in Henry Illinois, 140 miles from our home. We were in the process of putting three children through college when Jim was ready for a job change. We made the choice to anchor our job situation with my teaching job rather than move. While he was working in Henry, he came home on Wednesday night after his meetings and stayed until Saturday morning. His constant companion was our dog, Zeke, so the two of them were traveling partners. We had been gone for almost two weeks, so Jim needed to touch base with the church. He would leave as soon as we had our meeting with our minister, Martha Greene, to plan Anne's memorial service. At our meeting, we determined that music was going to be important. Anne had gone from a struggling clarinet player in junior high to a fabulous player with lessons from her teacher, Kathy Pirtle. They had a very special relationship, so she was the person I wanted to ask to play at Anne's service. After our meeting to plan, Jim left to touch base with his church, so I was now on my own for the first time.

I went right home and began the process of contacting Kathy, Anne's clarinet teacher. I could not find her telephone number. It was summer, and I had always contacted her through the high school. Anne had her private number … That evening good friends came over to visit, and I voiced concern that I could not find the number. Denise asked, "Who are you looking for?" When I told her, she exclaimed, "Oh, I have that number! We just won a raffle from her

Orion Ensemble's fundraiser. I will go right home and call you back with her number." What was the possibility of that? By the time I got the number, it was ten o'clock at night, but I could not take the chance of missing her. The service was in two days. So I called her.

Kathy greeted me with, "Oh, it is great to hear from you. How is my favorite clarinet player?" The news was shared, and we both dissolved into tears. "Of course I will play. I am going to call my accompanist, and I will call you right back. But don't worry, I will play no matter what." I waited until midnight, but she did not call back, so I went to bed.

I was about to experience a life-changing event.

In the morning, I had to talk to the inspector in London, and because of the time difference, I was to call at 5:00 a.m. There were unusual circumstances surrounding the accident, and the inspector was continuing his search for evidence. I picked up the phone to call London. The line was dead. That was the last straw. I was not doing well as it was. I ran around the house like a crazy lady, picking up each phone over and over. I don't know how I thought that would help. I sat down and got myself under control and picked up the phone one more time. And there was the dial tone. I called London, and the minute I put the phone down, Kathy, Anne's clarinet teacher, called. "Where were you last night? The phone rang and rang. No one answered." Later in the day, Scott called, and he too said he had tried to check in on me that night to see how I was doing, and there was no answer.

As Kathy and I talked, she reported that she had had a dream about Anne. "Tell me about it," I said, surprised. Kathy dreamed that Anne's funeral was in Florida, and she only had a car and two hours to get there. She was frantic. Then Anne's voice came to her, and Anne said, "Don't worry about me. I am okay."

"What do you mean Anne's voice was talking to you?" I asked.

"I taught Anne for four years. It was her voice. She was talking to me." I really couldn't fully comprehend what that comment meant right then. But the words began to heal something within me. I immediately knew how to interpret Kathy's dream. It told me about the last time our family was all together. We were attending our nephew's wedding. Key words were *Florida, two, car,* and *frantic.*

Let me explain. Anne's cousin John was getting married in February 1996 in Florida. Our whole family was going to go. Anne wanted to be at the wedding. But St. Olaf College was on winter break on that date, and the band, of which Anne was a member, was going on a Midwest tour during the same week as the wedding. In September, she had spoken to the band director about being excused from the winter break tour so she could go to the wedding. The band director said no, the band was getting ready for the Norway trip. If she did not go on winter tour, she could not go on the summer trip. That was the college's policy. However, *two* weeks before the wedding, Anne called me, and she was *frantic.* She had figured out that when the band was in Chicago for a concert, she could get a friend to pick her up after the concert in their *car* and get her to O'Hare Airport for a flight to *Florida.* She would miss just two concerts and be back for the home concert in Minneapolis. "Everyone is going to be there, and I just have to be there too." We talked it all over, but she continued to be frantic. It was not like her. Finally, I suggested that she talk to the band director again. She would have to be very clear about why she needed to go to the wedding. She did, and this time he said yes. Our family, grandparents, aunts and uncles, and cousins all had a fabulous time ... and that was the last time her brothers and the extended family saw Anne alive. Later when we went up to St. Olaf in the fall after her death, the president of the college was very surprised that the band director had let her go. He said they have too many tours and just have to be firm in their policies.

While I was listening to Kathy tell me about her dream, a huge light filled my kitchen. It consumed me! I could see nothing but light. I felt infinite love that had no beginning or end. There was no sense of my body, only the LIGHT I was experiencing. I had been crying almost twenty-four hours a day, and now the light consuming the room brought a sense of complete joy! It was like being drunk with joy. I felt wrapped in love. Time stopped. As I think back, there was no gap in the conversation. I can't even describe accurately what it felt like. I could not see anything other than being in LIGHT. There was a quality to the light that defies words. In this light, there was a voiceless voice. *Thoughts* and *information* were coming into me. I was not going toward anything; something seemed to be coming to me. It was like the videos you see of traveling through space at a very fast pace, with planets and stars and space pieces whizzing by. I think it was information coming in, but I could not take it all in. I now think I have been remembering the messages, slowly over time. Perhaps I have been guided by the messages. Was it my higher self, an angel, or God voicelessly speaking to me? I do not know. There was a conversation going on in the light. One of the messages was that I was going to write a book. Me? Write a book? About what? Not me! It scared me to death. Anne loved to write, and I thought she would write a book someday. She was discovering the power of journaling and writing. She had received an award for an essay she wrote in college her first year. I had always thought that Anne was going to do something special. It was a kind of intuition. I even knew exactly when she was conceived … I just knew. But now she was gone. What about our time together? What about her contributions to our world? What about the children that might have been? What about her writing? Now what?

Dazed but so full of joy, I went on with my conversation with Kathy Pirtle. There was no confusion; that came later. It seems impossible that no time passed as I was having this LIGHT experience. But she did not sense my "absence." She asked me what music I would like her to play. I was not making decisions well, so I just asked her to tell me what she had in mind, and I would tell her whether I liked it or not. She had decided to play "Sheep May Safely Graze" by J.S. Bach and "Carnival of the Animals, the Swan" by Camille Saint-Saens. She had chosen music that told us what we had done the day after Anne's body was cremated! What are the chances of that? What was going on here?

The feeling of joy and love and peace from the LIGHT experience lasted the whole day. Friends came to visit in the afternoon, and I enthusiastically said, "Come on in. Let's have tea!" I sounded like nothing had happened. They must have thought I had lost it. In a way, it did feel like I was going crazy, but I *knew* I was not. The message coming my way was, "I am with you." I was experiencing God's Amazing Presence. I still had to get through the memorial service, and I was incredibly sad. But I began to be stronger. There was definitely a healing aspect to the LIGHT experience.

At Anne's memorial service, I was numb, kind of on automatic pilot. With Jim's job as a youth pastor and my job in public education, our lives had been quite public. Our skills and our faith kept us moving. The front of the sanctuary held a beautiful collection of flowers—daisies and gifted flowers making it look like a garden. Kathy's beautiful music filled our hearts with peace. The minister's words brought comfort. Our sons both spoke, telling stories of growing up, of wonderful vacations in Eagle River, of playing together, of teasing, of the joy that Anne had brought into their lives. The church was overflowing with people who had come to say good-bye to Anne and to be with our grieving family, now reduced by one. Anne's grandparents, aunts and uncles, and cousins came to hold us up. Our church family, Anne's childhood friends, community friends, school friends and colleagues, and students from my classes were there. A whole contingent of college friends and her band director came from St. Olaf. All enveloped us with love and support. We were well fed, physically and spiritually, but still numb and so sad. We had to figure out a new way to live life.

It was over ... or so I thought. I had heard Anne's words in Kathy's dream, "Don't worry about me. I am okay." She must be alive somewhere. A shift from belief to knowing was beginning. Kathy's choice of music—how could that coordinate with our experience in London? There was no way she could have known. Questions and more questions ... I had to find out what I had experienced in the LIGHT.

Chapter 3

Terry's Spiritual Milestones
The Amazon Changed My Life …
Time

Time … we wonder where it goes. We sit and wish time would pass quickly. Time stands still in agonizing moments. We reflect back and ask, where did all that *time* go? We look ahead and ask, will that *time* ever come when … we can all fill in the blanks. When I was above my body, time was suspended, and yet people and events around me were flashing by. I was suspended in glorious white light in a state of timeless bliss. My earthly body had not caught up with my heavenly soul in understanding time. How could I share that amazing feeling of love there? Time wasn't the same, words can't describe it, but I had learned to *feel* it back in 1982. I also knew I came back for a reason. This goal seemed to be a blank page in my memory, and that bothered me for ten years. I didn't recognize back then that it was not what I would be doing but what I was *becoming*. I would expand my knowledge concerning time, opening a larger pathway of brilliant light flowing my own personal GAP.

Little did I know that I would again experience the suspension of time. I knew that my consciousness level had been expanded in incredible ways during my NDE, but I had yet to realize that deep inside of me was the ability to see and hear God. All of this happened in an environment that was totally new to me, a unique ecosystem teaming with life, where I learned and understood for the first time how totally complex and beautifully intricate God's creation of life really is. I was privileged to travel deep into the Amazon River basin outside of Iquitos, Peru, in 1992. Let me take you back to 1991.

I left Tennessee and moved back to Michigan, our home state, with my family in 1986. I loved living near the sandy beaches on Lake Michigan. Our love of nature took us traveling back to cherished locations in upper Michigan. I had three amazing, lively, and spirited boys and a wonderful husband. I had begun to learn meditation in my very limited form and was finally absorbing some spirituality literature, limited at the time. God's touch was in my life, coming through in quiet times with my thoughts. I was teaching kindergarten, surrounded by amazing people and realizing how much of God's love I could transfer to small little bodies so full of potential. Life was good. My NDE was tucked *far* away inside of me. Thinking, feeling, and pondering inside my head, that's all I would allow. Fear is a nasty emotion. I had *no fear* of death any longer because God was pure love. So why was I so afraid to speak out and share my experiences?

One fall evening, our son Jeremy, now in sixth grade, announced at dinner that we had to hurry up and eat because we needed to get to a meeting. He was terribly excited to explain that there would be a group of students going to the rain forests of Peru, and he planned to be one of them! My husband and I looked at each other in the way only parents can to communicate a silent message. "Do you mean there's a rain forest exhibit in Peru? How will you get there? Will you be going on a field trip? Where?"

We attended the meeting that night, and my *life changed forever*, because I would travel with this group! The students spent the year learning rain forest ecology, studying the culture, and preparing to be taken to a location where few students had ever travelled. A new chapter of my life began. I had no way to know I would be experiencing God again through incredible experiences.

This group became the first group of middle school students to travel to the Amazon basin in Peru, South America. All were from Zeeland Public or Christian School. Three teachers from Zeeland,

Michigan, were far ahead of the thinking that existed at the time. University professors traveled along with us, amazing individuals volunteering their time to share their expertise. Our local ABC station, Grand Rapids Channel 13, sent a photographer and reporter along with us. Many people thought the organizers were nuts taking a group of students this young so far away and into a country that most people considered highly unstable. I never even considered fear. My NDE had allowed me to really *live* my life, no fears in sight, boldly moving forward in search of new knowledge. We were all out of our comfort zones for sure, landing in a camp with no electricity or plumbing.

Our students were making quite a scene. I felt like I had stepped back in time three or four centuries once we left Lima, Peru, and landed in the gateway city of Iquitos. Peruvians were used to seeing adult tourists, but who were these *kids*? Our guides explained that most foreign tourists were terrified of the city and much preferred sleeping on a boat. People went straight to the boats heading down the Amazon. Our group stayed overnight in Iquitos. I instantly felt comfortable. Why was that? Was it no fear of death?

We saw only a few cars in those early years in Iquitos. Transportation was by a three-wheeled motorbike able to carry two or three people at a time. Riding on them was a wonderful experience, although weaving in and out of people walking, carrying loads of produce in various interesting ways on roads where no one paid attention to right and left sides of the road was quite an experience. I was constantly asking questions of our guides. We had ridden in an open-window wooden bus with no glass to block our views. We were seeing life in a third world country up close. There were open markets with live animals of every sort and medicinal bottles for sale that looked like ones we had all seen in museums. And *what* was in those bottles? Young kids were in the streets selling goods and running up to the windows of our bus with gigantic smiles. Other children were seen in school uniforms, wearing a white shirt with dark pants or a skirt, carrying a few books. We had exchanged letters and pictures with a school in a remote area and then visited them. Exchanging smiles and experiences was life changing for both cultures. Finding humble, loving, and caring groups of people living a very simple life with few if any modern conveniences made a very deep impression on my soul. These are all God's beautiful creations.

It took immersing myself in a totally different culture to be able to learn, with compassion, the effect the human population has on every ecosystem in our world. The indigenous tribes living in the Amazon basin for centuries learned to live in harmony with the rain forest, using the forest's resources wisely, preserving God's amazing creations. But our very "civilized" modern inventions and way of life would change the lives of the native people along the Amazon very quickly. Think of our own country and how swiftly the ways of Native Americans had their way of life wiped out in a blink. Here I was in 1992, landing in a world so completely different from our own. I had not been prepared for this most unique land of God's creation. It was easy to see the beauty, but it could easily be seen as a place that needed to catch up with the rest of the world. I had studied the complex issues. Experiencing the happiness in families along the Amazon River brought me to the realization that we can love life anywhere if we choose to find a community that exists with people appreciating life. Iquitos became a city where people moved to "make a better living." As in every culture experiencing this move to bigger cities, human challenges joined them as they moved closer to Iquitos. As humans, our natural instincts tell us we need "more" all of the time. Personally, when I returned home, I admired a simpler life.

Many of our students were only twelve and thirteen and very tall in comparison with Peruvians. Fingers were pointing and minds speculating in whispers. We learned later from our guides that they were all speculating on how bodies could grow this big in so few years. Was it the milk we drank? Did the kids use bleach on their hair? And *where* were their parents?

Leaving the city, we traveled down the Amazon for about four hours. I delighted in the slow-moving, thatch-covered boats. I realize now how it helped my mind to slow down and reflect in the quiet, and God was always right there with thoughts for me.

I spent many wonderful hours talking and absorbing information from the native guides who grew up and lived in the Amazon. Our university professors traveling with us also had amazing stories of research in the Amazon. They were gifts to me, teaching me as much about *life* as they were about the animal and plant kingdoms. The people encountered in Peru—local families, our guides, the children and parents we met in villages—to this day, they remain part of some of the most cherished memories of my lifetime.

We stayed within the camp structure of Explorama Lodge, in the Amazon basin, with three locations, each unique. Today, Explorama has four camps to choose from and is still going strong in the ecotourism business.[4] Life there has changed since 1992. I saw huge changes by my last workshop in 2002. I was seeing the changes happen in front of my eyes, and emotionally inside, I could feel the pain of change, the thrill of change for some, and the challenges faced because of them. The area is now preserved and offers wonderful opportunities for all to enjoy the Amazon. Their expertise is astounding. Change is inevitable, but they have been able to adapt and help preserve the biological wonder and culture—for research as well as pleasure.

Seeing and observing plant and animal life from the canopy of a rain forest is to walk into an ecosystem never observed anywhere else. Learning canopy ecology from 115 feet above, studying birds and bats that I never imagined existed, and experiencing insect life that had to be the largest and most unique seen in my limited lifetime was amazing enough. Fishing for piranha and tropical fish I'd seen only in aquariums and quietly observing mammals interacting in their own environment gave me an understanding of God's creation I had only imagined. But it was the people living amongst this complex environment that moved me to internalize new spiritual experiences.

Thoughts from my NDE came flooding back to me when times were quiet. It was an energy feeling I had learned to recognize, and it was rejuvenating my whole body. Something was happening here

---

[4] www.explorama.com.

that was right for my soul. God was present in the Amazon, making sure I *woke up* to the knowledge shared during my NDE. As you will read shortly, I had no idea what a powerful experience I was about to have that would *change my life completely* and help me internalize the amazing power of God that lives within us.

I fell in love with the forests. Plant life and gardens were joys I grew up with as a child. I even cherished and hoarded my grandfather's copy of the 1954 *Life* magazine that had the very first color photographs of this mysterious place called the Amazon. I still have that copy! I read every word of it as a child. I had forgotten my childhood dream of one day visiting this place. But more than the beauty, I fell in love with the culture and the people.

I came back from this first experience excited to approach my own school board of Holland Public Schools in Michigan to be the teacher sponsor, giving more students in Holland this same amazing experience. In 1993, Holland and Zeeland combined, taking 110 students to the Amazon. The local people again shared a life that would forever change mine.

I continued traveling to the Amazon, visiting many locations, staying longer each time. Medicinal plants fascinated me. Native guides showed the plants to us as we hiked. Meeting native healers personally was powerful. I was absorbing as much of their knowledge as I could. This was directly feeding my need to understand my NDE message about healing ourselves. My NDE thoughts of healing never left my mind. I was sure they must possess a piece of the puzzle. We began taking students into a whole new culture in the highlands of the Andes in Peru, hiking the Inca Trail. This trail took us to the Inca ruins of Machu Picchu. Experiences in this ancient city would further my understanding of the *powerful* piece of God inside of me, connecting in spirit with long-ago departed souls. Eventually I would hike this trail eleven different times with students, each year building knowledge from local inhabitants, the Quechua.

Our Amazon Children's Workshops expanded into another location in the opposite direction from Iquitos called Yacumama

Lodge.[5] I heard more stories, experienced different communities, and met more amazing individuals. Yacumama is a marvel of environmentally sound engineering, styled after indigenous houses. It too is operating today, offering beautiful and comfortable accommodations displaying authentic indigenous artifacts. It was here that I would experience my first shaman demonstration. I was learning more each time I saw one. I had a very powerful experience during a demonstration of a Shaman in 2002. All of this learning was very significant, as you will see in our continuing journey. While workshops continued in the Amazon and Machu Picchu, we began leading student workshops into many ecosystems. We traveled into Costa Rica. For me personally, meeting Cabeto Lopez was amazing. He was the instructor explaining a light gap, which was so significant for Marj. We eventually went into a new ecosystem, the Savanna's of Kenya, Africa. The diverse cultural experiences on the continent of Africa cemented in my soul the knowledge that God is at work *everywhere*. He is in each person all over the world.

This program for middle school students exploded. Within several years, a nonprofit organization called Children's Environmental Trust was formed. CET was founded by Zeeland teacher Jim Cronk and my husband, Doug Larkin. I took on the role of program director. Along with other staff members, we continued traveling with students from schools all over the United States and Canada. On September 11, 2001, terrorists destroying the Twin Towers in our own country changed life for all of us. I was no different. CET closed, and my heart was broken. God already had a plan; I just didn't know it at the time. Out of every deep sorrow grows new and better life. Global Explorers emerged, eventually becoming No Barriers Youth through the efforts of an incredible human being, Julie Ivker Dubin, who had been the program director full-time for CET. No Barriers Youth has been recognized globally as providing our youth of today with very rich and meaningful experiences. These youth who have had such

---

[5]   www.yacumamalodge.com.

rich experiences will be bringing much-needed peace to our ailing planet.

While in Iquitos, we always took our groups to the large open markets. Local inhabitants came from long distances throughout the Amazon basin to buy and sell their goods. Live animals were sold for food or pets, along with animal parts of every sort. It was quite an education in survival versus humane treatment of animals. We would see families traveling in dugout canoes or rafts strung together with logs, with a small dwelling perched on top. It might take them up to a week to get to Iquitos with nothing more than paddles moving them *up* river. No motors graced these rafts like our boats carrying us to our camps. These motors were very small in comparison to those found in the States.[6] While in this market, our students came across a baby sloth for sale.

"You bought a baby sloth? What were you thinking?"

Unfortunately, those were my unfiltered words when I heard that one of our groups had purchased a sloth in the open market in Iquitos. Can you imagine what a vendor was thinking as he encountered us? There's nothing like 110 bright matching shirts, water bottles strapped on our waists, cameras dangling from our necks, traveling in groups of twelve with guides through the city streets of Iquitos. All of our leaders had to make quick decisions about purchases that may or may not have been wise use of our students' money. Never had we seen such unique fruits and vegetables, and everything from large mounted insects to anaconda skins.

Of course they immediately fell in love with this darling creature and somehow convinced their leader that the sloth would have a better chance of survival if we carried him upriver and placed him back into the forest. Their thoughts were pure, but we also feared he would have little chance for survival. He was separated from his mother, who was likely someone's meal. The students quickly named

---

[6]   Today, faster boats of metal take you the same distance in two hours.

him "Static Cling" because he would cling so tightly as they passed him around from one student to the next. I can visualize myself holding and watching that baby sloth. He was darling, but all I could think about was how in the world would he survive. I also realized our students' parents would question our sensibilities for sure!

Now that you know the details of where I was at the time, here is what was happening in my spiritual life. I had pondered the question frequently about where and how I would find God once I was back in my earthly body. How could anything compare with the experience of being *with* God? In my mind, it seemed that every religion had different versions of God, and they all thought they were the *true* one. I was asking myself, how could that be? I wouldn't realize until 1993 that my journey of finding God came by "letting" God be my guide. It happened through an animal with no voice at all, a baby sloth. Join me in the Amazon; you'll *love* it. You are safe from large, fierce, biting insects and brightly colored snakes slithering on branches. There is no jaguar in sight, only a calm, slow-moving, cuddly baby sloth on the pages of our book! But be careful; you might find God too!

Not one of our travelers came back the same person as when they left. But then neither did I. I loved the challenge it presented with each very unique group I led into these experiences. I was the one blessed by each human soul I met. But it was the soul of a tiny baby sloth that literally brought huge changes to my life. This experience took me so off guard I grew to expect the unexpected from that day on.

I will let you know ahead of time; it is very difficult for some to think experiences like these actually happen. The events are true. I hope you'll read with an open mind.

Meet Static Cling: time … God in motion

The sloth rode to Explorama on my group's boat. As I reflect back now on that event, I can see Static Cling trying to move from my arms to a pole on our boat. It was all made out of lumber from the tropical forest, with a thatched roof and a stunning glass-free view of the Amazon River. I was totally knowledgeable about the habits of a sloth, but this was my first true experience with one out of his natural environment. So far, this was not at all what I would have expected! My first sighting of a sloth had been in 1992, and he was right in his tree, in his natural environment, sleeping. Everything fit right then, but Static Cling was different. I watched that very S~~L~~O~~W movement of his arm. I was *shocked* how very slowly he actually moved. We all found ourselves rooting for him to make some progress, shouting, "Come on, you can do it! Keep *reaching*!" Kids were yelling and wanted to move his arm for him. I encouraged them to wait, thinking he could do it on his own. I sat looking into these amazing brown eyes, thinking …

> Linear time froze for me at that moment. I saw how S~L~O~W my reaching for God had been. I was waiting for God to reach for me. (I needed to rethink that one!) Kids were watching and calling to him. I only heard silence. Only Static Cling was moving, so slowly that my mind froze watching him. I saw the kids only in a fog, their words frozen with excitement on their faces. And my thoughts blasting through my brain about God and time like a movie showing a flower opening in fast motion. It seemed like a long time, but I suspect it was not. I snapped back into the moment. So many thoughts became "knowledge" while time froze, all with no words. I was in awe, and I quickly looked to see if the riders on my boat had noticed anything odd. But it was like I had never left. Time, did it stop? What did this mean?

The students and I continued to stare, watch, and erupt in laughter. The slowness was unbelievable. It was a true insight for us to experience that. He was trying, yet that was as fast as he could move. A lot like me.

> I was in God's light again! I felt the all-encompassing love I had experienced in my NDE years ago. I could feel God's presence as time was suspended. God was inside of me, patiently waiting for me to hear and feel and understand. I recognized the feeling, yet knowledge came without words. Why didn't I think of that before? The understanding of God residing within me took a long time to take hold in linear time. I was agonizingly S~L~O~W in processing the meaning of my NDE.

Just as the first toe on our sloth reached the pole, we found ourselves in complete joy for Static Cling! It was going to take an agonizingly long time for his second arm to reach the pole. He had no mother to teach him. Experience was going to help him learn. Experiences were the critical steps I needed for my insights to become real.

> So often we expect instant miracles. It makes us think we've been let down because we think answers from God aren't coming to our questions or requests. We recognize miracles if they are quick and recent; perhaps slow can be just as profound. The sloth could not feel the grace of security until at least the other arm reached the pole. My life, my journey to understanding God's grace inside of me, was a long upward climb; it must have been the one-arm approach. There was so much to process and learn, as well as experience.

Back on the boat, Static Cling finally found the security to *let go* of my arm with his other arm, still two legs dangling in midair. It was actually pretty hilarious to watch. I too was still dangling in my understandings; God must have been having a good belly laugh—"NDE and she still doesn't get it!"

> I had to let go of some of the beliefs that I had learned as a child, just as Static Cling had to let go of my arm. Grounding beliefs I absorbed from church or family started me out in life in some form. This is our security blanket to grow into adulthood. For myself, I had beliefs about God I thought were strong. Until I could let go of things that did not make any sense, my ability to see more was slowed. I didn't recognize it then. I would soon realize that God had been sending

people to help me. My sister Marj was one of them. *I just needed to believe it before I would see it.*

Dr. Wayne Dyer helped me internalize belief through his book entitled *You'll See It When You Believe It!*[7] Dr. Dyer is an author who made a profound difference in my life. He helped me through my journey from belief to knowing through many books and lectures. The learning during my NDE moved to *belief* while I was in the Amazon. My eyes were opened, and I began *seeing* so much more. I saw amazing wildlife in the forest, but it would be the people who would truly open my eyes. I had many amazing spiritual experiences there, and I will share these as my story continues. They taught me what I knew already. We are *all one.*

> Two feet *dangling* underneath his body suspended in the air must have been terribly frightening to our baby sloth! Don't we all feel like we've been dangling, with only threads to hold us up at times? Feeling very frightened? I know I have. I can see myself dangling and wishing someone or something would hand me support right then! But what I kept doing was praying to God for some amazing miracle to arrive, not realizing I had to do the reaching. Would things still go *wrong* after a profound experience? I can remember myself saying angrily, "Come on, God. You aren't helping me here!" Soon I would be the one dangling and holding on with only threads in my life.

Yes, it happened. Static Cling's foot reached the pole and all on his own! We were all cheering with excitement for him! He was strong enough to do it all on his own! No one had taught him how; somehow inside of him was a strength given to him by whom? Instinct? God?

---

7   Dr. Wayne W. Dyer, *You'll See It When You Believe It!* (New York: William Morrow and Company, Inc., 1989).

What a *bolt* of lightning came into my body There was a power right inside of me. I was searching everywhere else outside of me! I was still waiting for others to tell me the answers in church. I found God in the most amazing places around the world, in the hearts of people I met and loved, and authors with insights that were all placing seeds inside of me to grow and nurture.

We were still cheering on Static Cling.

God had been patiently cheering me on, giving me grace to go to that next step. But I had been looking for that last link all around me instead of realizing that I *am* a piece of God. He is right within me, giving me amazing power to change my thoughts and change my life. Yet I had a lot of work to do to find out just how much power lies within each and every one of us on the planet through the grace of God. Was there more to prayer than I thought?

The sloth was hanging on to a piece of familiar tree. It was a post made into a pole from a tree. This was the closest he could come to his home in a tree at the moment, a piece of the *familiar.* I was very *familiar* with prayer. But I was also very often just saying words and joining others in their words. No real feeling was involved. Prayer was my bridge for learning yet to come. Remember that dangling feeling? The concept of God within me providing power—what are others going to think if I voice that? I kept silent until I could face my fear and not have support handed to me. Eventually I would reach for it myself.

The greatest challenge for my sloth would be arriving into the wild safely. Could he adapt to *different* surroundings? Would he find just the right tree to feed on? Was I adapting to my *new* surroundings? Life beyond an NDE was my *new* surroundings! I needed just the right food too. Yes, nutritious food for my body, and I needed nutrition for my mind also!

I had learned something about *time* in my NDE. Life as we see it now in linear time seems like all there is. We live life doing all the *right* things, we die, and *if* we are good enough, then we go to heaven. That was the end of the story. I heard lots of stories and discussion, but an NDE experience was telling me a new and very different story. And now a tiny sloth brought God flooding back in, once more reminding me of it all.

> God is *love*. That is all there is! Unconditional *love*. This was the biggest message I could voice. I came back with that years ago, and it always lived inside of me. When I was quiet, I kept hearing this message. God doesn't judge you; He loves you and helps you be love. God doesn't condemn you; He loves you and helps you be love. God is only love. My life here on earth was to *be* that love and enjoy it without fear. God's Amazing Presence had been poured inside of me once more.

THE LIGHT GAP

> My GAP was finally large enough to allow amazing new growth in me, just like in a forest. God came flooding in with new thoughts as I let his light in. I internalized these beliefs. I began learning more from God in quiet in small doses every day.

Let's return to the Amazon and rain forest plant ecology for a moment. In any newly formed gap in any forest, incoming growth is different. It is similar, but the plants have adapted to having more light. Nature changes and adapts to its new environment. But it only does so with the *help* of all of the other plants and animals that have now made this place their new home. These plants and animals have had to adapt as well. The gap will regrow but not without all interconnecting plant and animal life. Once this knowledge is learned in ecology, biologists can begin the task of rebuilding a beautiful forest.

As human beings, we need to learn to change and adapt with our new knowledge. I was never the same again. New and different growth began in me. I needed others, and I needed knowledge. We'll never be able to comprehend all of God's mysteries. Near-death experiences and encounters with beings of light are giving us vital information. Can we be open to hear the message God is sending to us now?

The sloth was going to need *courage* and a whole lot more help if he was ever going to survive in his new forest home. We could not know if he would survive. I needed that same *courage* to reach out and learn from the angels God was sending into my life. I first needed to recognize that they were *there*. I was gaining amazing strength from my time alone with God. It led me to totally change my eating habits and get myself in shape physically so my emotional self could handle all of the new information that was coming at me at an amazing speed, in linear *time*. This came in the form of people with new ideas, videos, newspaper articles, books, and computer sites. My sister Marj is a very special angel that was been placed in my life. She is my mentor, and I gained strength from her. She is always one step ahead of me, finding just the right information to read. A book or lecture would literally be right in front of me at just the right time.

We have found loving, caring, compassionate, and nonviolent people believing in God all over the world. God had asked me to be a messenger to others. I had been too busy saying a messenger of *what*? God had been providing me with *courage*. It took so much *time* to realize that I was the one who would be harnessing that power and it would come from *within* me. Meditation … I had a lot to learn about my heightened sense of intuition. I also needed a community to help me.

We could not know if Static Cling was able to survive in the wild on his own. This is his picture upon release into the water, a sloth's specialty ... he can swim well, quickly and easily, which gave at least some comfort as he sought refuge. Did he swim to a place where there would be help? Perhaps. Did he have guidance? I know he had God's intuition right inside of him! Sloths are great swimmers, much faster in water than on land.

Releasing Static Cling

Many photos exist of this little guy because author Susan E. Goodman and photographer Michael J. Doolittle traveled with us for a week. I was delighted to have them follow my group that year. Eventually, Susan wrote about our students' adventures in a book called *Bats, Bugs, and Biodiversity, Adventures in the Amazonian Rain Forest*. It was later released in 1999 as *Ultimate Field Trip #1 Adventures in the Amazon Rain Forest*.[8] Susan and Michael were

---

[8]   Go to www.susangoodmanbooks.com to see the book and a picture of Static Cling being held by a girl named Sarah on her website.

another gift to me, amazing and talented people that I grew to love and appreciate more each day. They never knew what happened to me with the sloth. I was too shy to tell them. If you find a copy of that book, just look for the darling sloth on page seven. Susan E. Goodman has gone on to write many true stories of students and their "Amazing Field Trips!" all with Michael Doolittle's photographs. I love them all. His photography is amazing, and they appear in many magazines and books. See how you inspired me as an author, Susan? And, Michael, you were my son's inspiration to go to RIT in photography! All of us connected through God's amazing plans.

After being in the Amazon during the summer of 1993, I walked into a bookstore in Grand Rapids, Michigan, and saw the cover of a book that really took me back. My heart stopped for a moment. There was a woman reaching for light. I found *Embraced by the Light*, by Betty J. Eadie.[9] I caught my breath as I read the words on the back of the book. I had no idea anyone had ever had the experience of dying and going into light like I had done. Her experience was different, but here was her story in print for me. That book was the beginning. My search for spiritual meaning had already begun; now it was time to find meaning in my *own story*. She was describing her experience, and I wanted to reach out and ask her questions! I finally accepted that I was not crazy. It was the beginning of a journey to learn more about near-death experiences. I had never heard this word before. Memories began flooding back in amazing detail, especially during quiet moments. I began learning how to meditate, being driven by an internal force. I had no idea how. I knew no one that practiced meditation, but I would learn how! God was well placed inside of me, and I was ready to learn more.

As I write this book, my stuffed, very real-looking sloth sits in my writing space along with the amazing painting that our artist, Lois Mulder, painted of Static Cling for us. She captured his eyes in a way that helps me when I get stuck on something. I used the stuffed sloth in my classroom. Children laughed when I said it was my favorite

---

9   Betty J. Eadie, *Embraced by the Light* (NY: Bantam Books, 1992).

animal. They always said, "Really? Why?" I loved explaining to them why his slow, deliberate movements shaped his existence just right for himself. I shared how slowing down their own lives to reflect and think could help them to make wiser and more loving decisions. Children's eyes tell a lot too. I learned my intuition kicked right in when I took time to look. Eyes. Look deeply into the eyes of someone you love; you'll find God staring back at you! That is why I decided to share my intimate sloth story with you. I wanted to help you "see" and "hear" a message of love for all of you, not from me, from God. But I love you too!

Nothing prepared me for the next huge learning in my life. It was 1996. I was at my parents' home with my husband, Doug, and we were just leaving on Sunday night after a weekend with them. We had our coats on, heading out the door. The phone rang, and before I answered it, I *knew* who it was and why she was calling. A dreaded feeling I never want to feel again. How did I already know? I knew Anne was dead before I picked up the phone.

It was my sister Marj calling to tell our parents that her daughter Anne, age nineteen, traveling in England, was dead. My heart stopped, and I swallowed hard before answering. Marj was emotionally in another world. I remember her yelling at me. "You don't understand, Anne is dead!" I told her I did understand, I know. Can you imagine that I even said, "I know." That was a guilt that I lived with for a long time, something I had to live with until I could make sure I shared every single moment of my NDE with her. We all loved Anne more than we could express, and I couldn't imagine the horror the whole family was going through. We all grieved beyond belief. But I added guilt on top of my grief. God brought me back to live again after death, but I couldn't help save hers? Why? What had I failed to see and understand? My agonies were different from those of others. It was because months earlier I had such a bad feeling concerning Anne. And yet I was busy getting her involved to go to the Amazon with us. It didn't make sense. I knew she had plans to travel to Europe. I didn't know then what a premonition felt like. I knew there was something, but I didn't know what. I even made a phone call to my husband's brother in Minneapolis to please arrange to get together with Anne at St. Olaf because I was too far. It never worked out, but I now know that I couldn't have changed what happened. Now I know that premonitions are very real. There are times I wish I didn't know what they felt like.

After traveling with Marj into Peru in 1997, our spiritual growth would again be launched into new heights. Our journey was continuing. Artist Lois Mulder captured the depth in Static Cling's eyes as she painted him. He represents our slow journey in life as we reach to understand God's incredible love for us.

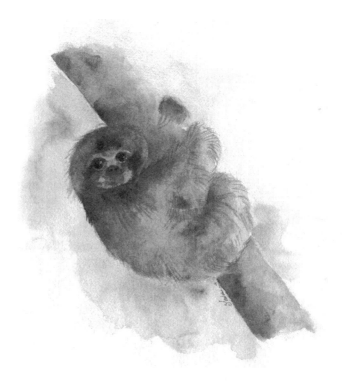

Painting by Lois Mulder

Chapter 4

Marj Finds Balance

In the summer of 1996, I joined a club that I had never wanted to be a part of—parents who had lost a child. Life must go on … but I felt totally spent.

When Anne was a baby, I had three reoccurring "events." I really don't know what to call them—they were like thoughts but with a different quality to them. I never forgot them. Our house was next to a parking lot for the church. The church building was next to that alley. We had to carefully watch for cars because it was a blind spot, and we could not see them coming. Whenever I started out to town, I went up on the sidewalk to be safe, walked the length of the building, and rounded the corner. One day I was walking to the store with Anne in the stroller. As I was rounding the corner, the message came into my consciousness, "Someone is going to die, and you are being prepared." I thought, *Oh?* I thought of my mother because she had heart trouble. So I called her when I got home from the store. All was well, and I let it go. This happened two more times over a period of a few months. The message came in exactly the same place and circumstance—Anne in the stroller, me pushing the stroller as we rounded the corner. Same message. It got my attention for sure, but I reasoned it was a fluke. Nothing was happening to threaten death. I pondered it over time when it came to mind, but nothing happened. I was not worried. I thought well … maybe I was not aware of worrying about someone's death. But nothing happened. Fast-forward to the winter before Anne died. I was attending a different church. As I was in the chancel area, which is the area near the communion table, three different times I heard a message, "Someone is going to die, and you are going to have to choose which church to have the service in." This time I worried about Jim. He was driving each week to and from work 140 miles away ... an accident? Mom now had pulmonary fibrosis and was struggling. Would she have a heart attack? It was unnerving. But I just let it go. I don't tend to worry, and I could not control it anyway. Never in these experiences did I ever think of Anne! Were these premonitions?

> We don't yet see things clearly. We are squinting in a fog, peering through the mist. But it won't be long before the weather clears and the sun shines bright! We'll see it all then, see it all as clearly as God sees us, knowing him directly, just as he knows us! (1 Corinthians 13:12)[10]

Grieving is like being in a fog with sadness as your companion. Life has to go on, and the people around you, not directly affected by the death, appear to be going about their life with all their strengths and power. The grieving person used to be doing that too, but now the desire to leave this place and join your loved one is so strong, as is your desire to sit down and quit.

I don't remember much about the two weeks that followed Anne's memorial service. I was so thankful that it was summer. I did not have to deal with guilty feelings about not being at work. I missed my classroom children. It had been so great to see some of them at Anne's memorial service. I was thankful for the parents' insight that allowed them to bring them to the service rather than avoid the questions they would have to address. Colleagues at school finished putting things away in my classroom, but I had finished most of the

---

[10]   Eugene H. Peterson, *The Message: The Bible in Contemporary Language, New Testament with Psalms and Proverbs* (Colorado Springs: NavPress Publishing Group, 2002), 268.

work before I left for the wedding in Madison. I do remember that I did not want to be out and about where I would meet people I knew. I was still in the shock of Anne's death, tears flowing. It felt bizarre.

Luckily, it was almost time for our family to head to Eagle River, Wisconsin, for our annual two-week vacation. We had planned to have the whole family together for the first week. Scott, Michael, and Heather had arrived. We were exhausted and grieving, but nature began to provide its magic. Anne's presence was painfully missing. As I am writing this, I know that she was present with us in some form, but I did not know for sure at the time. We spread Anne's ashes in all of her favorite spots: our hiking trail, the double swing, the hammock where Anne spent hours reading, the lake front where we spent hours of fun laughing and splashing, boating and swimming, and the outdoor patio on the edge of the hill overlooking the lake where we met each late afternoon to talk and relax together with our hosts. We were stopping at each of these spots to tell stories. We had been coming to the same cottage for twenty-five years, all the children's growing years, as guests of the Townsend family. Familiar activities sustained us as we continued to hike, canoe, swim in the lake, and watch the sunsets. I look at pictures from that time and realize how pictures can lie. How could we look healthy and happy?

When the kids left to get back to their jobs and lives after the first week, Jim and I were lost. One day, I stayed in bed the whole day, which was very unlike me. I couldn't move. I lay there stunned— all day! That wasn't going to help anything, so the next day I was determined to do better. I picked up a book that was given to me by a friend just before we had come up to the cabin. She had said, "I have a book that I think might help you." The book was called *Parting Visions*[11] by Melvin Morse, MD. He is a pediatrician. He had been working with very young children, two- and three-year-olds, who were dying of diseases such as cancer and leukemia. The children were talking about seeing grandparents that had died. They were

---

[11] Melvin Morris, MD, with Paul Perry, *Parting Visions: Uses and Meanings of Pre-Death, Psychic, and Spiritual Experiences* (New York: Villard Books, Random House, 1994).

drawing pictures of tunnels and light. He stated that they were too young to be affected by our culture's stories. So he set up a study to which he could bring the entire required scientific rigor to his research. His findings began to bring me hope that Anne existed somewhere in another form. I had always believed in life after death, but it was not yet a *knowing*. Anne's words in Kathy's dream had been running through my head, perhaps not running through my heart yet. "Don't worry about me. I am okay." Melvin Morse's book set off a determination to find out what I had experienced when the LIGHT consumed me in my kitchen. Is there really a heaven?

That first year was so hard! I had been given a head start with the amazing healing power of the light. I was still so sad, so lost … but I was learning to identify that God was walking this journey with me.

When we returned from Eagle River, I faced a summer schedule of full-time tutoring young children with learning challenges. I could not abandon them; they were counting on my help. Jim and our dog, Zeke, went back to Henry, Illinois, to the church he was serving. We needed each other, but the demands of jobs were real. We now only had one child in college to support instead of two, so the money was not quite as tight, but I needed to get back to some sense of normal. So I began my tutoring work with the best gusto I could muster. As it turned out, my tutoring work really was a God-sent gift for me and for the children. The professional side of me took over, and I found I was happier at work. The kids fed me. I was happy doing this work. But the minute the workday was over, I dissolved into tears. I cried my way home each day. Once at home, I went out into my garden to pull weeds and yelled at God. The why of Anne's death haunted me.

It occurred to me that there was a better way of handling these after-work challenges. I needed to get my mind off of the circular thinking about missing Anne, asking why, and thinking about the possibility that if I had been a better mom, none of this would have happened. The thinking wasn't even rational. It was not my fault that Anne died. I started to get books on CD from the library and listened to them as I drove home. Elisabeth Kubler-Ross, a Swiss-American psychiatrist, became my companion. I read her book called *Death and Dying.*[12] Then I listened to M. Scott Peck's book *The Road Less Traveled*[13] and many of his other books. The right books just started falling into my lap. I would look on a shelf, and a book would catch my eye. This practice did help me become more positive, and my practice of listening to books on my way home has continued for years. I was still talking to God constantly, trying to understand. I kept telling God that I needed to know what happened.

As we struggled to normalize our lives, amazing things just kept happening. In late summer, a friend of Anne's called us. Kristin, a friend from high school and the church youth fellowship group, had been out of the country when Anne died. She asked if she could come over and talk to us. As we were sitting in our living room talking and reflecting, Kristin reported that she had had a dream about Anne. *Another dream?* "Tell me about your dream."

She told us the story. "I dreamed that Anne was in the tower room at the church where we always met. Everyone was there, and Anne was there. I said, 'Anne, you can't be here, you're dead.'" Anne took her hand and said, "Don't worry about me. I am okay." Then she said the dream shifted, and she saw Anne up in the mountains in a spiritual circle of people, holding hands, healing. Kristin went on to say that she had always thought her dreams were important in her childhood, but when she began to study science, she let that idea go and had not thought much about them after that. Wow! You can't imagine how 'blown away" I was when I heard this dream. To hear again the words, "Don't worry about me. I am okay," sent shivers up and down my spine. How can they be the same words? Now I have identified that those shivers going up and down my body are a signal that my thinking is on track or that something that has been said is

---

[12] Elisabeth Kubler-Ross, *On Death and Dying: What the Dying Have to Teach Doctors, Nurses, Clergy, & Their Own Families* (New York: Scribner Simon & Schuster, 1969).

[13] M. Scott Peck, MD, *The Road Less Traveled: The New Psychology of Love, Traditional Values and Spiritual Growth* (New York: Touchstone, 1978, 1985, 2003).

leading me to a better understanding of how God works in our lives. They work as a guide for me.

The next incredible experience began to bind Terry and me together in deeper, more significant ways. Mid-August, those of my siblings and the kids that could make it were going to meet in West Virginia for a camping/rafting trip. Jim, Michael, and Scott were not going to be able to go, but Anne and I had planned on going. When I built my tutoring schedule for the summer, I had ended their work so that they had two weeks before school started to be with family and more time to play, and I too had time to play. Now, I was thinking, *No, no, no.* Anne loved to camp, and she loved to be with all her aunts and uncles and cousins. I had been really looking forward to that time to be with Anne and the whole crew.

A memory floated in. When I was driving Anne to St. Olaf College for her sophomore year the previous fall, we packed all of her stuff for the year in our little Honda Civic Hatchback, along with our tent and sleeping bags, with the bikes on the back. What an amazing time for us to be together after such a busy summer.

But now, when it came time for the planned West Virginia trip, I called my siblings and said I was not going. I just did not have the strength to go. I was afraid I would cry too much and ruin their fun. My brother and sister and families offered to pick me up at the border of Michigan and Indiana. No excuses. As we drove east, Terry and I began to talk. Talking a lot is not unusual as we get together with each other. Terry began to tell us that she had had a near-death experience (NDE) years ago. I had never heard this story. We talked all the way to West Virginia. I was so intrigued with her story. I *knew* what *I* had experienced, but often it felt like I was going crazy. I also *knew* I was not going crazy. I was a changed person. I had heard of NDEs but did not know much about them and had been intrigued. Now, here was my own sister talking about an NDE! Terry and I talked about the feelings that we had while in the light. Even though our experiences were not the same, there were similarities, especially the fact that the experience of *joy* and *love* were never going to be forgotten by either one of us. The door had been opened for years of conversations, reading books, sharing, and growing together at a time when there were not too many people that we could talk to and the need to process was great.

We arrived at the New River and made camp. I was to sleep in the camper with Terry and two of her boys. The youngest had pitched a tent with his same-age cousin, and they were excited to be tenting together. Others were in tents too. It soon began to rain cats and dogs. After we ate dinner in the camper, all twelve of us gathered under the rather small front tarp off of Terry's camper. It was quite crowded, but we just squeezed in tight. We began to talk and sing. My heart lifted. We had all sung in the church choir as we were growing up, and as adults we sang in church choirs. Bill and his wife, Norma, are professionally trained singers, and their two boys had been taught to sing harmony from infancy. That night we sang our hearts out with all our favorite anthems, ending in attempting the "Halleluiah" chorus! We did pretty well, and none of the other campers complained. Ten inches of rain fell, and some of the tents ended up in huge puddles of water by morning. Well, family gathering is a healing force. Anne couldn't come, or did she? Did she in some other form? The possibility was becoming real.

In October, St. Olaf College organized a beautiful service for Anne and another Chicago-area student who was struck by lightning as he was clearing the soccer field in a thunderstorm. He had died on the same day as Anne. The college could not have been more helpful and comforting. Her roommates and friends spoke of their times together with Anne and the St. Olaf band played. After the service, Anne's friend and the person she was going to room with the next year asked if she could speak to me the next day. So we made an appointment to sit on the benches on campus. The conversation with Chelsea led to her telling me that she had had a dream about Anne. My eyes got as big as saucers. *Another dream?* Chelsea said that in the dream she was in Norway at a banquet for the St. Olaf band, and everybody was there, and Anne was there. Chelsea kept saying, "Anne, you can't be here. You are dead." Anne reached under the table and took Chelsea's hand and said, "Don't worry about me. I am okay." Chelsea said that she was so discouraged at Anne's death that she was having trouble getting up to go to work. But once she had the dream, there was a healing effect, and she began to recover.

Each of these three people had to have the dream, remember it, and tell me the dream. None of these people knew each other. I was the common link. The second two were told in the same words, just a different context. What were the chances of all this? After the third dream, I was having an experience as portrayed in the movie *Close Encounters of the Third Kind*. I *had* to find out what I had experienced. I was being driven to find answers. Over the years, I have had many experiences of messages. I would suggest that things in twos are from this earth realm; things in threes are from the divine realm. I experienced messages in threes.

The day I talked to Chelsea at St. Olaf was Anne's birthday. For a number of years, on birthdays and holidays, Anne's absence was intensified. Our little family called each other for comfort. The first Thanksgiving and Christmas were happy/sad times. Traditions helped to smooth over the sharp edges. We were aware of the love we had for our two sons and Heather, and they for us. This was now our family, and we supported each other. For the first few years, those that could met for an hour or two to celebrate Anne on her birthday. Our extended families extended our lifeline. The first business trips our sons needed to take out of the country, I held my breath until they returned safely. People have asked me if I knew what I know now, would I have encouraged Anne to go on the band trip and to London to see her friend? At this point, I would say yes. Is it possible that our time of death is set at the time of our birth? I hear people say that is so. It is a mystery. I do not know the answer. I now keep an open mind. But I do know that hanging on too tightly would have caused great damage to the person Anne was—and perhaps to who she now is. Young adults need to explore, and we parents need to learn not to be afraid.

Winter set in, and I was well into the school year with my first-grade class. A number of mornings were very hard. The Greely School principal and superintendent were very generous in their support. My goal was to never miss a day. One cold day, I saw a beautiful sunrise out of my front window. Anne loved sunrises and sunsets! I dissolved into tears and could not stop crying. The sadness within me just kept pouring out. Anne and her roommates at school used to gather on the big hill at St. Olaf College and watch the beautiful skies and talk about life and about the important matters in their lives. *Anne ... come back.* I made it to Greeley but not until 11:00, and I looked terrible. It was tempting to just quit, but I had to go. As I walked into my classroom, twenty-three wonderful first graders, full of hugs, greeted me. One little girl named Emily bounded up to me and handed me a picture. She was a budding artist with accuracy and detail, but this day her picture was full of color, but I could not identify the content. First-grade teachers know to ask rather than comment. "Tell me about your picture," I said. "This is the beautiful sunrise I saw out of my window this morning. I made it for you!" *What were the chances of that?* Children have a way of knowing. Many of us have let go of that close connection. We forgot. They are naturally intuitive. Children are connected to God; they have not forgotten. Love poured out of my heart to Emily for the gift she had given me. Love poured out to my class the whole rest of the day and each day as I put one foot in front of the other.

I was learning that God works in the most amazing ways. I was being told, "I am with you always!" He is with me in all ways and at all times. I was also finding out that things were happening that I had once thought impossible. Amazing things continued to happen ...

In February 1997, Jim and I formed a grieving committee. It was my teaching experiences that gave me the idea of forming a grieving committee. Or, now I realize it is possible that I was listening to God whispering in my ear but not consciously. In the Winnetka schools, we had been studying the educational philosophy that has come from the community of Reggio Emilia in Italy. Attentively listening to how young children are forming their ideas and knowledge and recording their thinking is central to their preschool approach. I had been practicing this in my classroom. In my struggles with Anne's death, I recognized that we needed to be listened to attentively. So

Jim and I formed a grieving committee. We met about once a month until May. Michael could not attend over time since he was working in New York, but he was there for the first meeting. Scott was there, Anne's friend Val whom Anne was visiting in London, and Anne's friend Kristen who had one of the dreams. The committee consisted of some people we knew from the church, some longtime friends, and a few people that our pastor had recommended and we hardly knew—young people as well as some range-of-age adults. They were not afraid to let us cry. They held us softly in their hearts, as if we were little seeds in the dark but warm, rich soil trying to germinate. They listened to our stories, to my story of the LIGHT, the stories of the dreams, even if it sounded preposterous. My questions spilled out. They were open, with no agenda other than to support us. After about two meetings of us dissolving into tears telling our stories, we began to stabilize. The committee began to address the use of the memorial funds. Discussion began to address who Anne was, what made her special, and then the general question of what makes it so hard to grow up in our society. The grieving committee discussions began to restore my hope. I began to translate my insights into how I could make my life begin again. I will be forever grateful for this group's ability to listen to us, celebrate Anne's uniqueness, and reflect on our next steps.

There was another experience that served to clear my vision yet again. In February, I received a call from a science professor from National-Louis University who was working with the Chicago Botanic Garden, offering a trip for teachers to the rain forest in Peru! She had heard that I might be interested in going. What! An organization called Children's Environmental Trust (CET) was organizing the trip. Terry and her husband were part of the founders of this organization, as you read about in chapter 3. I signed up for the trip. I had been hearing Terry talk about these trips to Peru with junior high and high school young people for a number of years. I had been so busy working my two jobs to support the kids in college that I had not even considered that this was something that I could do. But Terry and I had been working toward making this experience possible for Anne. She was planning to go to Peru as a college assistant with a group of high school students from Minneapolis, but she ran out of time. Would I ever have done this, if not for the death of Anne? I doubt it. This trip was life changing.

In July, I found myself traveling up the Amazon River in a boat with twenty teachers, heading for Yacumama Lodge, located on the Yarapa Tributary of the Amazon River, near the tiny village of Puerto Miguel, 150 kilometers from Iquitos. This territory is the home to hunters and gatherers. One day we were in the "middle of nowhere" hiking in the amazing rain forest. Our accompanying Botanist, Cabeto, was describing the ecosystem we were exploring. He was explaining the life cycle of the familiar Philodendron plant. It is a vine. In the rain forest, the seed falls to the ground. On the floor of the forest, there is very little light. The tiny little seed-leaf vine has to grow up the tree, but it has only a limited amount of energy to make it to the light. So it grows up the *dark* side to *conserve energy*. It has tiny little leaves that don't even look like the Philodendron that we know. But when it reaches enough light, it grows the huge leaves that we all can recognize. Cabeto reached down and picked up the tiny little traveling vine and hung it on the bark of a tree as high as he could reach. *I was struck with understanding*—literally like a lightbulb experience! Energy was streaming through my body. It lasted for hours.

I had been living life at the level of this little vine, wandering around looking for the tree on which to climb to the light. Many experiences had taught me about God over my years of living. I was an active Christian. But I was conserving energy. I was walking in darkness even as I was so much a part of the church, involved in the stories Jesus taught to help me understand. The "darkness" of Anne's death, the three dreams that told me Anne was okay, the experience of the LIGHT consuming the room, had been like Cabeto taking that plant and saving it tons of energy by physically putting the vine up high on the tree, ready to grow into the plant it was meant to be. I was now *aware* that I was in the light of God. I had been catapulted into a whole new understanding, and I began thriving and growing into the person I was meant to be.

I began to take twenty-something students to the rain forest in Peru, organized by CET's wonderful programs designed to protect the environment and provide a service experience. We also hiked the Inca trail into Machu Picchu and learned about the Quechua Andes people. Another trip took students to Kenya to study the issues related to saving the large animals in the area between Tsavo East and Tsavo West National Parks. We helped the scientists evaluate the success of man-made ponds for the elephants. Later, after the impact of the Twin Towers disaster, parents were afraid to let their children travel. CET had to close and eventually was reorganized and became Global Explorers. With Global Explorers, I co-led two trips with high school students. The first was to the rain forest and Machu Picchu in Peru again. The second was to Tanzania where we worked with Jane Goodall's Roots and Shoots students with a reforesting project on the side of Mt. Kilimanjaro, and then on to Jane Goodall's research station at Gombe, beside Lake Tanganyika, where we followed researchers as we observed the behavior of the wild chimpanzees. These experiences opened my eyes to the wisdom of the indigenous peoples, the power of the beauty of nature and the animals in nature, and to the importance of saving our natural ecosystems. How powerful and helpful these experiences are for young people to get a better sense of themselves, to help them experience the joy of serving and doing their part, and to gain an understanding of how we are all interconnected. Today these educational experiences are still available through No Barriers Youth, formally called Global Explorers.

It has been twenty years, and I continue to grow and understand more how this life we are living is guided. I have grown in faith. Books have come my way that I would never have read if not for this experience; people have come into my life that I know were sent by God. Also came knowledge, experiences, meditation, and God's word that pushed my understanding. I read the Bible, and I now say, "Oh I know what that means!" Now I *know* that God talks to *all of us*, all the time. I am now *listening* and *hearing* in new ways. When I encounter new ideas about God working in our lives, I am not afraid. I can feel God's energy within. I still get sad sometimes. There is so much more to understand, so much more to learn. I still lose my way sometimes, but I am growing big leaves in the light, not wandering so often in the darkness of the forest floor.

It has been twenty years, and I continue to grow. I have learned that we must all reach for our own light source. For me, the inner voice of God is that light source. I am "opening up" into the person I am meant to be. I continue to experience reassurance that Anne is close by. My dear friend Marianne Houston visited us at our cabin in Eagle River a few years ago. As she sat with a cup of coffee, she experienced Anne's spiritual presence and was inspired to write this poem.

Coffee with Anne

I did not know you,
never saw your face
or heard your voice
or even the tootle of your clarinet
yet the warmth of the sheep cup
—memorial of the sad London trip—
held gently this morning over the two-eagle lake,
and the quiet warmth of your mom and dad
and their loving stories of you
have called you forth from your new home
to sit in comfortable and comforting silence here
with me.

I have just caught your ethereal smile
in the breaking sunshine on the two straight pines

and the lightness of your being
in the wind-moved, fall-tinged trees
across the lake.

In my bones I feel
the strength and swiftness
of your two young legs
Your happy contentment fills my spirit,
teaches me of the sheer curtain
between time and eternity.

Thank you.

I will tell your mom and dad
how much you love this land
and them,
and, if you don't mind,
carry your presence with me, forthwith,
wherever I may go.
R.I.P

—Marianne Novak Houston, Eagle River 2011

Chapter 5

Broadening Our Spirituality

To be nobody but
Yourself in a world
Which is doing its best day and night to make you like
Everybody else means to fight the hardest battle
Which any human being can fight and never stop fighting.
—e. e. cummings

Terry's Voice

It's fall of 1997, in Zeeland, Michigan. I had a long, tiring day teaching my kindergarten students. My oldest son, Jason, was away at college. Jeremy was busy practicing his guitar and drums, made lively by friends joining him in jazz tunes. It was his senior year in high school. Our youngest son, Jacob, was finishing up homework. Smelling dinner cooked by my husband, I was busy reading student journal writing from that day. Doug found me sound asleep. Deciding sleep might be more beneficial than food, I walked into the bedroom and fell into bed to take just a nap. Clunk. I was gone for the night.

But Doug found himself awakened in the middle of night by me screaming at him in an excited and animated voice.

"Wake up, wake up, Anne was here, it is *real*, she's alive, and she was just here! She looked wonderful.

She was sitting right here on our bed laughing and smiling. And you know what? She had Zeke with her! You remember, her dog died a few months after Anne died! He jumped up on our bed right next to her, right here! She was sitting right here on our bed. Anne and I talked about lots of things, and we both kept petting Zeke and laughing together. Wake up! She wants me to call Marjorie and tell her she's okay and about the green bag!"

Doug was sitting up staring with a blank look. He stated in a very sleepy voice, "Why don't you tell me all about it in the morning. I'll be more awake. But don't call Marjorie; it's the middle of the night!" It was a scene that seemed as real and natural as life had been during the day. I reluctantly went back to sleep, knowing my husband took a very long time to wake up during the morning hours, let alone in the middle of the night. I couldn't wait to tell him all about it in the morning. Then I wondered, why didn't our dog bark or join us? But Izzy was always curled up asleep with our youngest son, Jacob, way upstairs.

The next day, Doug was awake and ready to hear the details. I proceeded to tell him the amazing story, but as I was telling him, I realized I had a few missing details from last night. He called it a dream, and I sat wondering because, if it was a dream, it was the most realistic one I had ever had. My logical mind said it must have been a dream, but I just had this knowing love settling in my body. I had learned to recognize this following my near-death experience. It was my niece Anne. The last time I saw Anne was at a family wedding in Florida. We took a long walk out on the pier, and I was so excited to tell her that we had a primate researcher going to the Amazon with us in the upcoming summer. She was trying so hard to join one of our international student groups. She was majoring in animal behavior in college. But it was difficult. She was going to Europe with St. Olaf band, and she just didn't think she could make it work. She died before we could help get her there. How could such a beautiful young soul like Anne be taken away, but I lived?

Even in the years Anne came to Michigan, she really never did sit on our bed and talk. Running up and down the sand dunes in Saugatuck was more like it. It was the middle of the night, and she was talking to me with Doug asleep in the same bed? Not logical. But it was all so natural as I was remembering the experience. The picture of Anne that night is as clear to me today as it was then. Dreams fade, but this was real, and it never faded. The memory of Anne's death came flooding in, and sadness overcame me. But Anne had asked me to call her mom and tell her about the green bag and let her know she was okay! I knew I had to call my sister Marj and tell her! She was heading off to school to teach just like I was that day, and I was afraid to get her all sad again before leaving for school. It took me three days to call her. I just kept thinking I'd remember what was so important about the green bag. I couldn't remember why it was important. I was upset with myself. Why didn't I just get up and write it all down when I woke up! I worried I would put Marj back into sadness, but at the same time I knew she would be overjoyed to hear about a visit from Anne. I finally made the call.

******

Marj's Voice

Thanksgiving was coming up in a few weeks. As happened for a number of years, I became aware of tension in my body when the holidays were coming. I had had a long day at school because of a curriculum meeting, but that was not where the tension was coming from. It was the thought that Anne would not be coming home for Thanksgiving—ever again. But by the time I had gotten dinner on the table, I was thinking about our sons Michael and Scott, and Michael's fiancée, Heather, who would be coming. The phone rang, and it was my sister Terry. She said, "Mar, I have been afraid to tell you this. I don't want to upset you. But I decided I should tell you."

"What is it about?"

"I don't want to make you sad, but I had a dream. I dreamed that Anne was here with me. And Zeke was with her. She looked so strong and happy. She kept telling me that the green bag was important. She wanted me to tell you." I reassured her it did not make me upset. It had been more than a year, and I was not as easily caught off balance when someone talked about Anne. It was amazing what she was saying. Her message did the opposite of making me upset; it was another reassurance that Anne was safe somewhere.

After the phone call, I went to the basement to find the few boxes that were left that I had not sorted through. Anne had many bags that were green. Her duffle bags, her travel bag for cosmetics and toothbrushes, things like that. I looked at the travel bag carefully even though I had emptied the bag in the summer and used it when Terry and I went to the rain forest in Peru, sponsored by Terry's CET organization and the Chicago Botanic Garden. There was nothing there. *Let go, Marj Steiner*, I was saying to myself. *You have looked and looked.* I did not find anything that was unusual.

But I was beginning to realize how similar her dream was to mine! One night not long ago, I too had a dream. In my dream, Jim and I were in bed reading before going to sleep, which we often do. In the dream, I heard Zeke's chain in the hall, and then he came bounding up on our bed. Following Zeke was Anne! She was teasing Jim that she was going to plop on top of him, but she went to the end of the bed and plopped down in between us. Zeke settled in at our feet. We were talking, laughing, and having a wonderful time—just like we had done for years. The dream was so real and somehow had a different "feel" than other dreams. In the morning, I woke up with a wonderful feeling of closeness to Anne. The dream was so real. Terry's dream was not the same night but no more than a couple months apart.

However, that is not the end of the story. Late January, I was getting ready for a trip to Breckenridge as a chaperone for the church's high school youth group ski trip. As I was packing, I came across Anne's travel bag again. But this time, I saw a zipper along the bottom edge, and inside of that zippered pocket was all of Anne's jewelry that had been missing! I held it in my hands for a long time. It was the necklaces and earrings that she had worn for so long. I was soon on the phone with Terry. "You are not going to believe what just happened!"

Just this last spring, I came across the bag again when I was packing to go to Eagle River. I picked up the bag and looked it over carefully. There is no zipper on the underside of the bag! I do not know what to think ... I have the jewelry. I wonder ...

There was the beautiful light of God flowing through the GAP after such darkness during one of life's most tragic events. I remember the darkness as well as the light. The real message for me was that we could communicate with departed souls. It is the unseen that I had missed. Another example of an important concept; you'll *see* it when you *believe* it. Or put another way, we just have to be *aware* it is so.

******

Terry's Voice

It wasn't until after Anne's death in 1996 and Marj's LIGHT experience that I began to realize how much I needed to know more. Anne's death was devastating to me, but I knew my grief could not even touch the grief that was lodged in Marj. I had died, but I came back. "Why couldn't Anne come back?" I shouted this angrily to God. Telling Marj about my NDE opened the door for both of us to dig deeply and learn more about life and death. Seeing Anne vibrant in my bedroom, smiling and laughing with her deceased dog, Zeke, still brings a smile to my face. I used to call this the most vivid dream I've ever had. Now I know it was a visit of the spiritual being, Anne. For many years, I couldn't say this to people because I still had fears of being different and people thinking I was too "out there." I feared losing friends. Dreams are significant. But this was far more. I knew that my senses had been enhanced and expanded, my mind opened with a knowing that spiritual beings can and do live among us.

It was only about a year after Anne's death that our mother passed away. My mother was being cared for by hospice at home as she was dying. In her last few months, she began having visions of people around her, angels coming into her life. She began to tell me about them because my father would have *nothing* to do with any conversation about angels. She and I had some great conversations about how amazing the love of God was for her and that she should not be afraid. I had related all of the details from my NDE. But she still had fears about dying. I knew and believed the people she was seeing were very real. Angels were there to help her. One day she asked if I could see the man sitting over in the chair in the living room. I said no but asked her to describe him to me. She described in great detail a person, right down to what he was wearing. I asked what color his hair was. She started laughing and said, "I don't know." I looked at her with a questioning look. She said, "He doesn't have any; he's bald!" I asked her if he was talking to her. She said no, so I said, "Well, maybe he's waiting for you to talk to him." She simply said, "Oh I couldn't do *that*," and then calmly closed her eyes and fell asleep. It was so natural. She later talked of white angels above her bed at night. I found it very important for me to hear, listen, and validate what departing souls are saying to the living. We can learn so much.

I have had dreams that are significant. Perhaps this story can illustrate the difference between a dream and a spirit presence. My mother had been gone for thirteen years when my dad passed away. We had a water disaster in their house and had to totally remodel before the house could go up for sale. When we began this process, my dad was living, but he died shortly after. The house had been totally emptied. Construction workers were rebuilding walls, and there was a mess everywhere. My brother and I had been spending months making the drive to oversee the progress. In fact, we joked that our cars could probably drive themselves there. We knew well all that was happening and what the house was like. One night I had a dream. My dad came to me and asked, "Why did you leave the box of silver in the house?" When I awoke, I thought, *That's impossible.* All contents had long been removed. In fact, most of it was waiting in my own basement for the five children to finish sorting. But I called my brother Bill and asked if he'd drive the two hours with me to check. I told him about the dream. He laughed with me, but he said he would go with me to look. I knew he'd rather do *anything* other than make the drive again that day.

I guess by now Bill was pretty used to me telling him odd stories. Just a few weeks before this dream, I called to tell him the *impossible*; I had a phone call, and it was from Mom and Dad's old number, but no one was there. My caller ID confirmed as I looked back at it. Dad had been in a nursing home for over a year and half before he died. His phone had been disconnected for at least two years. Was he trying to get a message to us I that day? I wondered. I really did give that serious thought. And now here was a dream only a few weeks later. But he was not a presence in front of me talking about being alive and well like Anne had done. It was a dream.

Off we drove to Jonesville to look in the house even though we were both pretty convinced there couldn't be anything there. Well, sure enough, we found a box in a huge pile of construction garbage the workers would have thrown away. And in it was the silver, some unique jewelry, a wonderful old pocket watch, and a diamond that has become a symbol for me. Spiritual beings exist around us, and if we are open, they have messages for us. Eventually we found out that the diamond ring must have been our great-grandmother's due to the age of it. It's precious to me, not because it is a diamond but because it reminds me every day to always be present in each moment and thankful for *all* that is and has been over time. Someone out there might be trying to talk to me, and I never know just how it will manifest in our very complex world.

Marj helped me find Dr. Melvin Morse's book, *Where God Lives*, written along with Paul Perry.[14] This book brought understanding about my body's amazing vibrational nature, which I was experiencing. I would eventually realize the power this energy holds for health. Paul Perry would go on to devote a lifetime to research along with Jeffrey Long, MD, who coauthored *Evidence of the Afterlife: The Science of Near-Death Experience*, which I've used in my research.[15]

I still remember the day I couldn't stop reading, enthralled by Dr. Morse's children's NDE accounts from his private medical practice. There in front of me was a list of all the odd experiences I was having with electricity and electronics! I was laughing out loud reading pages to my husband, Doug. "Look, it's not just *me*! His research shows these are traits of people who have had NDE experiences. Maybe I'm not so crazy after all."

You see, I had become a joke with my custodian, by frequently burning out lights in my classroom. I couldn't keep a watch running for more than a few months at a time. Computers did odd things when I was near. I was even causing very *odd* results when doctors preformed electronic tests, such as an EKG. Running out in my neighborhood, I was trying to save time by meditating and running in the dark at 5:30 a.m. so I could get to my classroom ready to teach each morning. For several weeks daily, a large streetlight would go out as I got within ten feet of it, only to come on again after I was ten feet past it. One day I stopped right next to the light and asked God if he was trying to tell me something. This time I did yell it out loud. The light popped back on. That gave me a lot to think about! But I realize now that the vibration level in my body was very high as I was connecting with the divine. And I knew I could communicate. There is a two-way conversation if we open ourselves to hearing in new ways. It's not a voice; it's internal mind sharing. Some people

---

14   Melvin Morse, MD, with Paul Perry, *Where God Lives: The Science of the Paranormal and How Our Brains Are Linked to the Universe* (New York: Harper Collins Publisher, 2000).

15   Jeffrey Long, MD, with Paul Perry, *Evidence of the Afterlife: The Science of Near-Death Experiences* (New York: Harper Collins Publisher, 2010).

report they have heard a voice. I believe them. Any of this can happen to any of us. If doubt creeps in, however, we might be closing down the pathway. I am guessing there were many times my pathway was not open—but not any longer.

I had previously been unaware that science, including the medical profession, was researching near-death experiences. Dr. Morse and Paul Perry talked about how our brains are linked to the universe. I already knew this. But I needed to launch myself into research. Marj would be my partner in research. She was just as hungry for knowledge as I was. I began to realize even more that I needed to freely search my own thoughts and beliefs. I needed to release the fear of being an independent thinker. I wanted to search for the worldview that my NDE taught me, that we are all connected through God.

I am not my body. When I experienced death, I was able to use my mind to think through details I was seeing, hearing, and feeling. I was watching the shocked face of my doctor, angry and upset. I was feeling their emotions. My brain was inside of a head that was lying below, but I was remembering people. Scientists now agree our memories are not simply lodged physically in our brains but outside as well. New thoughts, new learning, and a newly regained life awoke within me as I landed back into my body. I learned I am a spiritual being occupying a temporary temple called a body. We are all having an earthly experience. Knowledge was absorbed in light through God. I have found that countless people have received the same messages from God in different and unique ways. The majority, like me, did not hear words. I learned that my incredible mind is infinitely connected with my soul. And it is connected with *you*. My life eternal transcends time. This gives the word *life* far more meaning than I had previously been taught.

I had been absorbed in the highest form of vibration, a white light full of such incredible love, earthly words can only portray a tiny window into the mysteries. There were gorgeous colors that are not earthly and sounds that resonate into the universe. It was magnificently beautiful, love traveling *within* sound. Have you considered why it is that musical sounds make connections in your brain immediately upon hearing them? I received knowledge that was absorbed into my expanded conscious mind through every sense. When I close my eyes, sounds, colors, and sights all travel together. The easy phrases to repeat were just the beginning of being able to express what was lodged in my heart and my soul. I was awakening to life as I opened my heart to God's messages. Memories were lying dormant inside of me, emerging ever so slowly over time. Repeated experiences have taught me to recognize the vibration in my body and have taught me what they mean. This happens when I find God validating truth through my thoughts or in others' words or actions.

Since God is pure love, our creator knows only love. When my heart and my mind are open with a loving outlook, I can hear and feel the presence of the divine. But when I am stressed or worried, my vibrations become lowered to the point I begin to feel distance from God. Bringing my thoughts into the present in any given moment helps me to remember this now. Daily meditation has helped me to keep my mind focused on love.

******

Marj's Voice

As I look back over my life with new understanding and better awareness of God's amazing presence, I realize that I experienced many synchronicities, coincidences, and messages that I did not connect to guidance from God. I now understand the truth of Wayne Dyer's statement, "You believe it, and then you see it." It is the reverse of what I thought earlier in my life; you see it, and then you believe. The more aware I am of "moments of grace," as Neale Donald Walsch calls them, the more often I experience them.

My grandpa and grandma Glasgow were very stabilizing people in my young life. I loved them dearly. We visited them in Jonesville, Michigan, often. I did not realize it at the time, but I had a glimpse into the mystery of death and experienced the closeness as I walked "in the valley of the shadow of death."

Grandma Anne had a heart attack two years prior to her death. She could no longer play the organ and direct the choir, which she had been doing since she was fourteen years old. I had fond memories of running up to the organ after the service and sitting on the bench with her as she played the postlude. Then she would let me help shut down the pipe organ. About two months before my grandmother died, we went down to Jonesville to visit. I took our little sewing machine from home (Grandma's was an old treadle machine) and my sewing to work on while I was there. Grandma had taught me how to sew. I was taking lessons and had entered a contest for a fashion show. I needed to get my suit done! I ran into a snag and got very frustrated. Grandma came to the dining room table where I was working to help me out. But I was a typical beginning teen and was too frustrated, and I rejected her help. I was in tears, and then Grandma burst into tears saying that she couldn't do anything anymore! I was shocked and felt so badly for hurting her feelings. I loved my grandma and didn't mean to hurt her. I ran upstairs and flopped on my bed sobbing.

That weekend was the last time I saw my grandma alive. I remember when we got the call that Grandma had had another heart attack. Dad came home from work, and my parents left for Jonesville as quickly as they could. A neighbor stayed with the five of us. Mom was so upset. She told me later that she was so afraid that she was not going to make it before Grandma died. About halfway there, a familiar piece of music came onto the car radio. All of a sudden, calm came over her. All she felt was love for her mother. She just knew her mother was gone. She noted the time, and when she arrived, it matched the time of Grandma's death.

Life in our family home continued, but I began to feel Grandma's presence. There was no vision to it but a form of just knowing. I didn't know what to think, but it was a new feeling! Could it be real? This feeling came just while I was at home for about a week. Did I believe it? Well ... I still remember it today, but I surely did not understand the significance of these feeling as I do today. Was she trying to tell me not to feel guilty about rejecting her help? I was feeling guilty and ashamed. With Grandma's presence, there was relief. And guess what? I did win first prize for my red suit!

During the months after our daughter's death, my mother was dying. Anne was just whisked away. Mom was dying by inches. As Terry said earlier, we siblings were taking turns visiting our parents on weekends. They both needed a break from Dad's faithful care. Mom was struggling to breathe because of her pulmonary fibrosis. I was struggling to find my balance, and being with Mom really helped. By Thanksgiving, Mom almost died but then rallied again. I am so thankful for that time we had together. For whatever reason, Mom was afraid to die. I could not understand why because she had been so faithful in her spiritual life, sharing love and kindness with all of us and with the patients she cared for as a nurse. She modeled her religious beliefs. My LIGHT experience had turned my belief in life after death into a solid *knowing*, and that death brought a return to a different form of life. With the reports of the dreams, three of Anne's friends had used the words "Don't worry about me. I am okay." I reassured Mom that there was life beyond this world. My reading was convincing me that God loves us *all* no matter what, and I shared my knowing that she too was going to be met with love and joy. Being with Mom in those months was so healing for me, even though it was so hard to see her suffering. It was such an effort for her to talk since she suffered from pulmonary fibrosis. I was grieving deeply. She too was in the grieving process, as she was letting go of her life. Our conversations were lifelines for both of us.

One Sunday, as Jim and I were getting into our car to return to Chicago, my sister Lynne Anne came running out to the car saying, "Hurry, something is happening to Mom!" Lynne Anne and Mom had been in the living room talking. It was too hard on Mom and Dad if we all left at once. We hopped out of the car, thinking Mom was dying. Lynne Anne said, "We were just talking, and Mom asked who was sitting in the chair over there!" Lynne Anne had replied, "No one else is here." "Yes there is. I can see him." "What is he saying?" Mom reported that he was communicating. "We are acknowledging that we see each other. I am supposed to listen." Over time, she saw this man many times, as Terry described. When I was talking to Mom about her experiences seeing him, I noticed that her eyes went up to the left as she thought about it. If I was asking her about her childhood or about our grandparents or about our childhood, her eyes went to the right as she gathered her thoughts. This led me to believe that she was accessing these memories from a different place in the brain. I find now that if I am thinking about being in the LIGHT, my eyes go to the left also. I tried asking other people about past experiences, and I found that their eyes looked up to the right. I have never seen anyone talk about this in all the books I have read.

As Mom got closer to death, she could hardly talk at all. She began seeing more beings around her. As Terry mentioned, Dad did not believe her at all. He would tell us not to encourage her! "You know there is no such thing." I *do* believe it was very real. It helped me to believe in what I was experiencing. Years later, Dad did tell me that he had a dream in which he saw Mom as an angel dressed in white.

One more story is significant. When I married my husband, Jim, he introduced me to his artist friend Sally. Jim graduated from college, and to help him decide whether he really wanted to go into the ministry, he took a job working with the youth in the La Port Presbyterian Church in Indiana. There he met Sally, the mother of six children. She and her husband ran a blueberry farm. He discovered that she was a graduate of Art Institute of Chicago. In visiting with her, she shared some of her incredible artwork that she was "painting" with strings and sticks because there was no money to buy art supplies. So he asked her what she needed and made sure that she got the supplies. From then on, she kept up with us and was our dear friend. She was what I call a mystic. Often I did not understand what she was saying, but my gut feeling was that she knew what she was talking about. One day we received an unexpected call. "I am coming up to spend the night with you. Okay?" "We would love to see you! Is there a special reason you are coming?" "No, we will just have a good visit." She arrived late afternoon. As I was getting dinner, she stayed in the kitchen with me and began to tell me a story. When her son was in high school, she had had a dream that her son was killed in an accident with the tractor. The tractor had a piece of equipment attached that harvested the grain. She said that she began to pray about this. The dream repeated itself, but the more she prayed fervently, the dream began to change. In the dream, he was not killed but only lost a limb. In the next dream, he was unconscious for days. When this boy was in high school, Sally and her husband had a rule for the children; they were never supposed to use any farm equipment when they had friends over. But one day, one of her high school sons got off the bus with a friend, and they walked across the field toward the house. The tractor was sitting there with a harvester attached. He wanted to show his friend how he helped his father cut the grain. So he started up the tractor. But things went all wrong. Something got stuck in the harvester, and in trying to fix the situation, he was injured badly but did not lose a limb and ultimately survived with no permanent injuries. Then she just stopped the story! I tried to ask her questions, but she went on just chitchatting. The next day, she went back to the farm. *That was strange*, I thought. I love to talk to her, but it left me wondering if there was a purpose to her story.

At the time of Sally's visit, our middle son, Scott, was five years old, and he was learning how to play hockey. About a week after Sally's visit, it was my turn to take Scott and his friend to hockey. I got them all into their hockey gear, their skate guards on their blades, so that I would not have to do all this at the rink. It was a time-consuming job! We ran for the car because it was pouring rain. We were rounding a curve on Wilmette Avenue on the way to the rink, and all of a sudden the car coming toward me was going too fast. His car slipped in the rain and did a 360-degree circle right in front of our car as he put on his brakes! As I slammed on my brakes, time suspended. We were in slow motion. The kids from the backseat came flying into the front and hit the windshield. It was before our car had back seat belts. The cars *just* missed, and the driver went on his way. The kid's gear, especially their helmets, saved the day. No one was injured. I was stunned and shaking!

Now ... was this the reason Sally had come to visit? Was this what her story was about? She never answered the question. Had she been praying for us, knowing that this might happen? Did her efforts change the outcome of that rainy morning? I pondered this for years. Now, my answer is that I think it is possible. I am very thankful.

******

Terry's Voice

In 2002, I had an experience that even today I am still trying to process completely. I wish I knew someone else who has experienced such an event. It would have made this story easier to tell, and yet it is significant in my growth. There is a touch of sadness in me as I relate this story. I had a very good friend, a fellow teacher bringing students to the Amazon and Costa Rica with CET. I met her early in my travels, having taken her daughter to the rain forest, and she traveled as a parent. As a teacher, she began taking her students with us. We were close in so many ways, mostly when we traveled together. I told her about my NDE very early, and she was a kindred spirit, understanding it all. We had lots of wonderful talks about life and death. I didn't know anyone quite like her. She developed brain cancer, and it eventually took her life. I visited her shortly before she died. We shared memories of our old and favorite place at Explorama Lodge. We called it Napo in the early days (1993), before it had individual rooms. We slept on mattresses on the floor covered in mosquito netting, women and girls on one side, men and boys on the other. We loved the authenticity of this place, and so I missed it when they remodeled to accommodate more travelers. We laughed that day I visited, weak as she was. We remembered a plaque we made together and hung in that lodge. She was the first close friend I lost to cancer. We agreed that she would *contact* me somehow if she could after she died. We hugged, and I was sure it would happen. That was the last time I saw her. A year went by. Another year, and I thought,

Well, maybe I don't understand communication from heaven. I had gotten very busy, and I suspected too busy. My pathways might have been shut down at times. I put it back into that memory space to cherish but not to think about often. Life moves on.

I was leaving for what I knew to be my last workshop with students to the Amazon, traveling to Explorama in 2002 with a group from Colorado. CET was closing. I was sorting through some things and found a picture of the two of us holding that plaque. I cried. Then I was determined that while I was back at Napo, changed as it was, I would search for that plaque she and I made together. I was devastated when I couldn't find it. Lots of them still hang on those rafters in that lodge, but newer ones were hanging there. I just kept thinking about her. In the evening after dinner, the sponsors of the kids I brought were busy getting the students off to bed. It gets dark at 6:00 p.m., and so it was pitch dark. Often the adults would meet back in the dining area for a conversation and wind down with a beer. They weren't down there yet, but I was sitting, studying the schedule for the next day. A couple came by and sat down near me. They were dressed in very old-fashioned khaki clothes and pith-type helmets that reminded me of the days of Teddy Roosevelt camping in the wild. I chuckled to myself but started up a conversation. I learned they had been coming here for years and that this was their absolute favorite camp. They loved sleeping on the mattresses on the floor. They were so interested in all of the medicinal plants the indigenous people used to cure themselves; we had a great conversation about that.

Thinking back, I don't know why I didn't ask where they were from, but I didn't. Or ask when they slept on those mattresses on the floor, knowing they weren't there anymore. They simply said they needed to get going off to the other camp. My mouth fell open. I wondered if they were leaving in the dark. I assumed a guide would be taking them. It was pitch black in the forest, and no one walks out in a jungle at night. We went with guides for night walks. But they headed out the back door by themselves. Now remember this is a very small place out in the middle of nowhere deep in the Amazon jungle. I pondered on this for a while. It finally got to me, so I walked up to a worker who had been there the whole time. I asked about the couple and were they really going out after dark with no guide? He looked at me funny and said, "What couple?" I said, "The ones I was just talking with over by my table." He knew me from many past workshops and said, "Terry, your group is the only one here in this camp right now. I saw you sitting over there, but there haven't been any people through today at all." It was all I could do to compose myself. I had no idea what to make of that. I was too embarrassed to talk to him more. All too quickly, the adults were drifting into the dining area. I went to bed that night thinking I was crazy once again.

The next day, I was thrilled to see the progress of the medicinal garden that had been planted there for research. It had grown so much over many years. After the tour of plants, we attended a shaman's demonstration that was held outside in an area meant for talks. I was so deeply entrenched in his words, the chants, the smoking incense; I really went into a deep meditative state—unusual for me in that setting with students. As I came out of it, I had this surreal feeling. I sent students to free time, their favorite time of the day. I kept feeling a presence. I sat by myself in that space, and all were gone. It wasn't a voice. Thoughts were creeping in my body. "Terry, it's me!" I spoke out loud, "Is this you?" She was laughing, "her" laugh that springs up in my memory every time I think of her. The couple ... did I get it? Oh my. My beautiful friend is alive somewhere too. She contacted me at last. Expect the unexpected. I told some people about this story right away this time. But only people that I knew had grown to expect to hear such unexpected things from me! Who knows what they thought.

I can only tell the story and let you decide for yourself what it means to you. My humble self knew. Time is not linear. Life is happening simultaneously all around us. Perhaps I had slipped into another time. Perhaps spirits slipped into my time. I filed away another very profound happening in my life. But it is always in warmth and love I remember it. As I write this story for this book, my body vibrates with her presence all over again. The vibration is love. Finally, now, I can say I was not crazy. I was just having an experience God wanted me to have. I *prayed* for understanding from God.

My former type of prayer was only a bridge in my learning. Something opens up when we meditate. Was I experiencing my own GAP, a space for God to move into thought? *Does God show up in the silence?* I was learning I needed to listen and then *trust* what I heard without fear. This was very new learning at the time and grew with me as years moved on. I now realize that through universal thought patterns we connect as humans. God is the same in all of us; he created our bodies to make sure connections happen between us. But if we lack the emotional *feelings* of love in these prayers, I believe that may block the pathway that God has put into us internally. I have experienced powerful change in my life when *feelings* of unconditional love accompanied my prayers. It is only recently that I've experienced the difference; words all by themselves may be very limited in bringing change.

Very powerful studies have proven that many individual prayers collect the energy to help the healing process. Is it the energy field within us when we pray? Is it the God within us projecting outward? Is it the total belief that it works? Is it because I placed feelings of love in my prayers? I'm sure you have ideas on this concept. I believe all of these concepts are part of the puzzle. Understanding that our thoughts have energy helped me realize how important it was to keep my thoughts positive. I used to pray with a running list of needs but never really acted on them for myself or included feelings of self-love. Every time I went to God in prayer, I thought He was outside of me somewhere. And He is out there, *everywhere*. I had experienced that, and the knowing was already well placed. So if He is everywhere, there is "no where" that He is not. So, He is also right inside *every* human being. I am a piece of God, given in grace, and He is in me too. And He is in you. That part of God had been lying dormant in me for far too many years. Meditation was very slowly showing me that in the silence, God's voice was there in ways I didn't understand yet. How could I go deeper without fear? It took holding on to the familiar, but I was questioning words I heard in prayers. I heard condemnation and judgment that just didn't fit. I heard how bad I was, with no consideration about what was in my heart. I was hearing views of a judgmental God that didn't feel right at all. I had to let go of beliefs that no longer fit. That is hard when there is always someone right there to tell you why you better "fear" and do what is "right" instead of choosing love. I chose love. The three messages that I remembered from my NDE were being filled in with more understanding.

- *"Love is all there is"* were the first words I uttered in reliving my NDE. Today I know they are still the most important words. The meaning is vast and encompasses some very complex realities about our world that I pieced together, the combination of science filtered with spirituality. I received amazing divine assistance as I journeyed inward. Angels in the form of other people were significant in this journey. Experiences continued to show up at the oddest moments. I needed to trust my intuition. Once I realized that my thoughts were creating my reality, I knew I better get busy and *change* my negative thoughts!

- *"We have the ability to heal ourselves"* turns out to be the most significant learning that I received. This concept will illustrate itself as you read on and into our chapter on health and healing. If you can find unconditional love in every creation of God, including yourself, good health can be the foundation beneath your footsteps. I had to journey more after my NDE as I experienced life back on earth. I was guided to "remember" and learn through the universe. God nudged me very hard at times to share the knowledge. My life as a teacher for thirty years was in preparation to teach some powerful concepts that can help bring peace, love, and health to many.

- *"We are all connected"* was a concept embedded in my body, a knowing after experiencing a totally new sense of *time* and *space*. Connectedness and trusting intuition helped me to find and uncover truths that I had experienced and yet couldn't comprehend. God meant for us to travel with others. We all need a spiritual guide. Marj is mine. I began a search for answers to some pretty basic questions about life; amazing human beings came with answers just as I needed them. And I found I have more spiritual guides to help me along my way.

A spiritual journey seems such an inadequate phrase to describe my life travels to find myself. Realizing that God was inside of me with an internal power that I could use in my earthly life is a concept that needs to be shared. I am no different from any other living soul. When we connect in love, we spread love to counteract a lot of fear, hatred, anxiety, and anger that is around us.

Back in Peru, I *yelled*, "We are all one!" But unfortunately it was in silence as I climbed up to the top of the Canopy Walkway, high off the ground, at Explorama Lodge along the banks of the Amazon River. Grounding myself in nature was perfect for me. This event followed my view into God through a sloth's eyes and after an encounter with spirits in a place I loved. I stood gazing at the sunlit haze early that morning and found my body vibrating in bliss, remembering God's incredible unconditional love for me. Gazing around at others there, connecting to people living a totally different life than mine, I knew beyond a doubt that all of us were connected through God. I wondered who in this environment might have had similar NDE experiences. I had heard some pretty amazing stories in Peru. Guides talked of meeting spirits that disappeared on trails. I did want to shout from those treetops high in the jungle teaming with incredible life. As a leader, I knew my students and fellow travelers might have questions I couldn't answer yet, and my instinct was still telling me it was safer to keep this inside. But I was there absorbing new knowledge every day and loving life! I had also learned that God meant for us to be happy and enjoy his beautiful creations without fear. And yet it was my own fear that kept all of this inside of me way too long.

******

Marj's Voice

Spiritual growth is like childbirth.
You dilate, then you contract, you
dilate, then you contract again.
As painful as it all feels, it's the necessary rhythm
for reaching the ultimate goal of total openness.
—Marianne Williamson[16]

Our experience tells us that spiritual growth never proceeds in a straight line. For both of us, as we continue growing, insights come some days, not others. Like the moon, it waxes and wanes, and at points it appears that growth is no longer proceeding—but then it pops up at an unexpected time. It is never absent. But our experience depends on our *awareness* that God is always communicating, communicating in all ways. The question is, are we listening? We found that going within via meditation and prayer made all the difference in the world. Over time, we gained confidence in the truth that we are always connected to God, every day and every night.

Going back to our beginnings helps give us perspective. Terry and I grew up in a family that attended church weekly. We learned Bible skills and the well-known Bible stories. Holidays were celebrated. Discussion was encouraged. Our beliefs developed rather naturally.

---

[16]   Marianne Williamson, *Look Within: I Can Do It Journal* (Hay House, Inc.), 26.

My memory of these times is one of being in a safe place with all those I loved. Creativity, imagination, and freedom also played an important part in our childhood. These capacities are important to developing the awareness and support of the spiritual dimensions of life.

Terry and I are a part of the Protestant Christian tradition. It is a path that has been meaningful in our lives and we trust will lead us into the future. It won't be without changes and challenges. Life is about change. We are just sharing our religious and spiritual formation so that you understand where we came from and where we are now. It is very important to add that we believe *there is no one, right way.* We honor all religious paths. We honor all spiritual paths. We honor all paths that are not named religious or spiritual. No one belief system has all the answers. We do believe, however, that everyone experiences the spiritual no matter what they call it, because it is built into each one of us.

As an adult, I appreciated the opportunity to study within a historical perspective, one that allows for the cultural imperatives of the historical times, as well as the fact that the Bible was edited many times over the centuries. I feel very fortunate that I was encouraged to think for myself. I believe that we are all theologians; we all are studying the nature of the divine in one way or another, even if we do not name it. All of our direct experiences with God are important, as are the experts who have tremendous expertise from academic study and application. Over my life, I have come to believe that Jesus's teachings are telling us how this world we live in is put together. Examples might be: what we give is what we will receive, or if you have clothed and fed the poor, you have clothed and fed Me since we are all connected. I believe that there are scientific laws for the interactions between humans in this earthly plane, as there are for the earthly environment, which science has discovered and described. Over the years, I have had many questions about some of the beliefs I was taught. I pondered and began to challenge them quietly. Now I am challenging them with respect. I did not know how much deeper my experience of God could go. Now I do. There will always be new rituality causes us to ask questions as we find the tivation and creative power to be something new.

irituality brings community and interrelatedness and lance to life.

irit calls us to explore the mysteries. There are infinite ssibilities.

piritual experiences are something out of the ordinary. We el the difference as we *feel* love or joy.

piritual connections with a friend or a stranger bring a nowing that the conversation was meant to be, which can nable healing.

of the belief changes for Terry and me was a strong interest rstanding all religions, including those of the indigenous . We believe that no one way is the only way or has all the s. To me, it just does not make sense that God would leave out s of people by choosing one particular religion. We say God saying that one religion has all the answers is not congruent all-loving God. I compare it to a jigsaw puzzle. If you do not he picture on the cover of the box, it is difficult to see what ished puzzle will look like until many pieces have been put er. Each religion has beliefs and traditions that provide very l insights into the true nature of God. Respectful dialogue ey to better understanding. Finding the common threads that ce love and respect will lead to peace.

nother change that I see beginning to develop, which will ide growth for the future, is the *weaving together of religion spirituality* into a life fabric that brings balance to our everyday and the everyday lives of our immediate communities and countries. Being a part of a religious community gives me a to celebrate God's constant presence in my life. It gives me a nework to think and rethink the mysteries of life. The opportunity ttend meaningful worship on a weekly basis renews my spirit. ing brings each of us insights. Community provides support as examine our particular beliefs and the beliefs of the historical

discoveries and insights into the mysteries of life on our planet. It is a place of infinite possibilities.

Before my LIGHT experience, I had not thought of spiritual without religion. As I became aware of new ways God was acting in my life, I realized that my background did not include what I had experienced with the LIGHT consuming me. In the LIGHT, the power of the love and joy was all consuming. It is hard to put into words!

My God experience became central. I certainly could read about such experiences in the Bible. Examples might be Moses and the burning bush or Mary being visited by an angel. Or closer to my experience, Saul experiencing a blinding light and, as a result of this experience, becoming Paul and changing his whole life, traveling and speaking to continue Jesus's ministry. But no one I knew was saying they had such a dramatic experience of God until Terry told me about her NDE. This probably reflects what I was willing to read prior to this time. Earlier, I would have been very skeptical of someone who was talking about such an experience. I would never compare my experience to these biblical people. However, *I did have an experience* that I had thought impossible! And what do you do with that experience? I began to read books that I probably would have never read without my LIGHT experience. The books just presented themselves to me. Friends gave them to me, friends recommended them, and I looked them up. Or I went into a bookstore, and just the right book was there on the shelf in front of me. They caught my eye. I was reading nonstop. This process continues currently. I began asking new questions. I couldn't read fast enough. I would hear scripture read in church, and I began to say to myself, "Oh, I know what that means!" I paid attention to what I was feeling and experiencing. Thanks to the cassette/CD player in my car, I listened to books as I traveled each day back and forth to the school where I was teaching. I excitedly talked about the books I was reading when I gathered for social occasions. I began telling others of my experience. I was afraid at first of what people would think, but most did not question or reject my story. They were interested. People told me their stories. Puzzle pieces were fitting into place.

New experiences helped me redefine my beliefs. I was much more open to new ideas. I was hungry for new connections that would help me understand what I had experienced. All this was going on at the same time I was going through the process of grieving the loss of Anne. Talk about opposites—a mountaintop experience while in the depths of despair daily. That was my experience for months.

The summer after Anne's death, I spoke earlier of the experience of going to the rain forest in Peru. My experience changed the direction of my thinking and feeling again. Somehow in my education or in my interpretations of what was being taught, I had the idea that we were more intelligent, more "with it" scientifically, than the indigenously connected peoples in the rain forest. They are still part of a hunter-gathering culture. Not so! I had unexpectedly found a hidden misunderstanding within me—that I, from the Western world, was somehow better. What I found were wonderful people! People more in tune with nature, more in tune with communication with the spiritual parts of life. For these people, *all* of life seemed to be spiritual. They had so much to teach me. I was experiencing more of the spiritual. I found that I needed to define the difference between spiritual and religious before I could again decide what I *really* believed about God and how that relates to living life.

Wisdom from a Rainforest by Stuart Schlegel helped me define spiritual versus religious. Terry found this book while attending a rain forest conference and gave it to me as a gift.

The direction of Stuart Schlegel's life was changed by his work in the Philippine rain forest. He went to the Upi Valley as a missionary, but after three years of work, found that he was being called to understand the way of life of the "forest people," the people whose way of life had not been disturbed by the American influence in the Philippines after WWII. He decided to go back to the United States, to the University of Chicago for a degree in anthropology. He returned as an anthropologist instead of clergy. He spent two years documenting the way of life of the Teduray people of Figel. These

people lived in the mountainous for in the Philippines. He found this con egalitarian way of life. His experience and beliefs profoundly. His distinction helped me to understand the difference. as "... whatever path we choose to jou meaningfulness ... our vision of what w All people are on a spiritual quest, wheth meaning in our lives is a part of being h the experiences and feelings of the divi are unlimited forms, infinite possibilities people who have developed words and institutionalize the experiences of spirit, religion ... is best applied to the traditions developed to protect and promote some part spiritual understanding."[17]

For now, I have defined spiritual or spi ongoing process. It is difficult for us to grasp until recently, we did not use the term often. about our spirit or our soul. It is a way that we t that animates all life. It is about the opportunity ways of being in relationship with our self, with and with God. It is knowing that *God is within* somewhere.

- Spirituality is like water to a fish. It is th live in.
- Spirituality is both a worldview and a proce
- Spiritual experience is like snowflakes, a one of us.
- Spiritual growth is an ongoing process.

---

[17] Stuart A. Schlegel, *Wisdom from a Rainforest: The Sp an Anthropologist* (Athens, Georgia: University of Geor 192–193.

Christian path. We grow in our faith and understanding as we share the ordinary ups and downs of life, as well as the tragedies of life. Where two or three are gathered, there is God also. As we really take seriously that *we are all one*, it will give us a better way to put beliefs into action. I hope religions will begin to look at the doctrines and their theological constructs and realize that there are inconsistences in the belief systems they are teaching. They will no longer try to control but will provide for a collecting of the wisdom we gain from our individual experiences of God. The picture being made in this new puzzle will provide a wider view. Our imaginations will be freed up to provide a vision of a better way of life that supports all.

Before Anne's death, I had never thought to meditate. Upon returning from my first rain forest experience in Peru, I was ready to sit quietly, ready to listen for the voice of God within me. Prior to this, I had never thought of meditating. But I didn't know how to go about it. I continued to be the one talking via prayer. I thought most of the answers came from the "experts." Studying the lives and suggestions of authors was helpful. It inspired me. Could I figure out the process of meditation? Communication, via what I was calling intuition or coincidences, was going on, but I was feeling there must be more.

Within that second year after Anne's death, I learned that a couple I had met at church, Hal and Betsy, were inviting people to their home once a week to teach and practice the monastic tradition of contemplative meditation. Richard Rohr, a current theologian and writer, defines contemplation as the "... deliberate seeking of God through a willingness to detach from the passing self, the tyranny of emotions, the addiction to self-image, and the false promises of the world." He calls contemplation "The Divine Therapy."[18] I recently found this definition, and it helps me understand. That opportunity with Hal and Betsy was eighteen years ago. At that time, I had only heard the word but had no understanding to go with it. It was unusual eighteen years ago for people to be talking about the benefits

---

[18]   Richard Rohr, *What the Mystics Know: Seven Pathways to Your Deeper Self* (New York: Crossroads Publishing Company, 2015), 79.

of meditation. I did not know many of the people, and it was a bit scary to attend. But they lived in my neighborhood, and I was searching for new experiences. It was convenient. It took me a long time to settle in! We chose a phrase to use as a mantra. I chose, "Be still and know that I am God." We read passages from the Bible or inspirational literature and then sat in silence for about twenty minutes if I remember correctly. Within four minutes, I was squirming! My mind kept thinking of the day's events, the work I had to do before I could teach in the morning, what I was going to serve for dinner tomorrow night, how I was not a good enough mother or Anne would not have died (irrational, I know), and so on. My mind was anything but quiet. But I did keep sitting with my eyes closed.

One of the techniques they taught was to think of a river flowing gently, with a boat floating down the river. I was to put the thoughts in the boat and let them float away. It worked for two seconds until the next thought came. I said my mantra. Along the way, I also began to concentrate on my breathing. The time seemed like an eternity. But after about three months of practicing at home and attending the gathering once a week, I found that I was looking forward to the quiet times. They introduced me to a book called *Psalms for Praying: An Invitation to Wholeness* by Nan C. Merrill.[19] I had used the Bible and daily prayer resources before, but this was a contemporary version of the Psalms that I have really enjoyed. I was looking for "something" to happen—a sign I guess that I was connecting. But there was not any sign. I experienced some resistance. I would be faithful each day enjoying the quiet for weeks, and then I would let it go. I kept asking myself why I kept giving up this time with God even when it was so meaningful. After meditating in the early morning, I hopped in the shower, and while the water was pouring over me, an insight would pop into my head. As I was finishing up preparations for my teaching day, I felt calmer. Or an idea would come that had eluded me for days that helped a student who was having difficulties. I now recognize that

---

19   Nan C. Merrill, *Psalms for Praying: An Invitation to Wholeness* (New York: Continuum International Publishing Group, 2007).

the process of listening within for guidance heightens my creativity and problem solving. That is God at work. I was becoming *aware* of spiritual presence. One day while meditating with the contemplative group a year or so later, I had my first experience of the darkness, while my eyes were closed, turning a beautiful color of purple! I kept encountering new-to-me meditation possibilities over time.

During a conversation, the parent of one of my students mentioned very excitedly her discovery of Dr. Dharma Singh Khalsa's book and CDs on medical meditation.[20] It sounded intriguing. I bought the book and CD set and started to use the meditations. It was a whole new form of meditation for me, using chanting. With chanting, it vibrated my whole body. I loved it! Since I had never done anything like this, I was very self-conscious, so I secluded myself in the basement, and I found it very helpful.

Next, I was sent an e-mail introducing me to the Healing Codes. Alex stated, "We believe the Healing Codes are what has been predicted by the greatest minds of our time as the future of medicine. Only its scope encompasses more than medicine. It heals relationship problems, mental health issues, career problems, peak performance issues—you name it—because it all has the same source, which is stress caused by destructive, painful cellular memories in our unconscious minds."[21] In the book, there are many stories that are unbelievable. Dr. Ben Johnson's was one of them. Over time using the Healing Codes, he had healed his Lou Gehrig's disease! What was most helpful for me was *The Healing Codes Manual.*[22] It gave me a step-by-step guide for healing the things that I did know and unconscious things I carry around with me that affect my life. Alex

---

[20] Dharma Singh Khalsa, MD, and Cameron Stauth, *Meditation as Medicine: Activate the Power of Your Natural Healing Force* (New York: Fireside (registered trademark of Simon & Schuster, Inc.), 2001).

[21] Alexander Loyd, ND, PhD, and Ben Johnson, MD, DO, NM, *The Healing Code: 6 Minutes to Heal the Source of Any Heath, Success, or Relationship Issue* (Peoria, AZ: Intermedia Publishing Group, Inc., 20010), 167.

[22] Alexander Loyd, ND, PhD, and Ben Johnson, MD, DO, NMD, *The Healing Codes Manual* (Dr. Alex Loyd Services, LLC, 2004–2010).

Loyd's questions helped me dig deeper. Positive statements the manual provided helped me be more articulate.

Along the way, I discovered Wayne Dyer's work. I started my reading with *Wisdom of the Ages*. I feel that I grew along with Wayne himself. Year after year, new books, CD sets, and videos of live lectures came out. I read and listened multiple times, gaining understanding. He had a way of taking complicated life issues and spiritual insights and putting them into words and examples that were very clear and usable. You can find a list of these items on our website, www.thelightgap.com. The first meditation CD that came out is called *Meditations for Manifesting*. It too uses chanting. Again, I found it very helpful. More recently, he produced the CD *I AM: Wishes Fulfilled Meditation*. He explains the nature of the words I AM by saying it relates to Genesis, where Moses asked God what his name was, and he responded I AM. Wayne Dyer suggests that what you put after I AM is a creative statement. The CD is designed for relaxed meditation. I usually sit quietly with this music playing as I meditate.

One of the last tools I added for meditating was tapping. A friend recommended it to me quite a while ago, but I did not intuitively say, *Oh this is something I need to investigate,* as many of the others were. I am not sure why this was, but I think I just did not understand the process. When I discovered Nick Ortner's website, tapping (also known as EFT) came to life. In 2013, he published his book, *The Tapping Solution: A Revolutionary System for Stress-Free Living,*[23] which gave me a guide for zeroing in on a particular issue or feeling. It is a technique "… based on the principles of ancient acupuncture and modern psychology. Tapping uses specific meridian endpoints while focusing on negative emotions or physical sensations."[24] It looks funny, but it really works. I love the way it can be used right as an issue comes up that is upsetting. When that happens, I can go

---

[23] Nick Ortner, *The Tapping Solution: A Revolutionary System for Stress-Free Living* (Carlsbad, CA: Hay House, Inc., 2013).

[24] Nick Ortner, *The Tapping Solution: A Revolutionary System for Stress-Free Living* (Carlsbad, CA: Hay House, Inc., 2013), back cover.

off by myself and start tapping. Sometimes during quiet meditation, an issue comes into my consciousness. I begin right then tapping on healing that issue. At first, I needed the guidance his book provided or specific wording on a theme, which his website gives away often. Once I understood the principles, I began to free the process up, using exactly what thoughts were coming to my head, making it *me* specific. When I got in touch with leftover grief related to Anne's death, I had a tool to overcome the emotional pain. It was something to physically *do*, and it worked! Here is an example. When my computer recently got a virus, I was calm—until I wasn't. For a variety of reasons, I became almost hysterical. I had not had that happen in years. I began tapping and sobbing all at once. The fear of losing all the work that had gone into writing this book came out first. Every frustration I had encountered in "the book" process and more came out. Next, all the self-defeating thoughts about not being good enough came out. Who wants to read what I have to say anyway? Then railing at the world for creating computers that I just don't know what to do with when something goes wrong. This was probably frustration leftover from the beginning of computers. The requirement to use a computer to write student reports was daunting at first. When a mistake was made, the text disappeared for good, and you had to start over! Personal stuff came out that I had been working on and had thought I was rid of long ago. I was definitely in distress at a level of ten! I was just hitting the tapping points with no regard for what I was saying. The negative was coming out. No nicely worded statements for each tapping point. And then ... I began to calm down. I began to state the positive, how thankful I was for my son Michael who knew what to do with the computer. Next, I could reject the thought that I did not have anything important to say in our book ... Soon I was not crying. I was calm, unbelievably calm. Wow! I felt healed! This entire process took place in about fifteen to twenty minutes.

As you can see, my tools increased over the years. Terry has taught me how to combine both the physical tools and the silence of going within. I have always found walking very helpful. Terry Patten's Integral Spiritual Practice Workout and Yoga are practices that use my body and heart in meditative ways. The use of the Healing Codes, tapping, music, reading, journaling, and inspirational guides combine well to create an integrated meditative experience. Marianne Williamson's *A Year of Miracles,* Wayne Dyer's *Living the Wisdom of the Tao,* Jonathan Star's *Tao Te Ching,* the Common English Bible, and Willis Barnsone's *The Poems of Jesus Christ* are some of the books I use regularly. With so many options for practicing awareness and silence, my insights have increased. I am more aware of my experience of the gifts of the larger cosmos, and I have a more encompassing understanding of this world and how it is put together. Worship is enriched. My excitement and thirst continues.

******

Terry's Voice

I was reading authors from every walk of life, including conservative Christian thought to challenge my thinking. I also read about the life of Buddha and found his philosophy of life to be incredible. Dr. Wayne Dyer introduced me to the life of the Chinese philosopher, a God-realized being named Lao Tzu, who lived five hundred years before Christ. This is not a religion but a way of life aligned with nature. The classic text with these verses, called the Tao Te Ching or the Great Way, offers advice and guidance that is balanced, moral, spiritual, and always working toward good. Dr. Dyer studied and lived the Tao Te Ching and eventually wrote a book called *Change Your Thoughts—Change Your Life: Living the Wisdom of the Tao.*[25] So many different books helped me realize that my experiences in nature were an important part of my life. There are many authors now writing about the fact that our bodies are actually connected through nature to God. We may be hardwired to exist in the natural

---

[25] Dr. Wayne W. Dyer, *Change Your Thoughts—Change Your Life: Living the Wisdom of the Tao* (Carlsbad, California: Hay House, Inc., 2007).

discoveries and insights into the mysteries of life on our planet. It is a place of infinite possibilities.

Before my LIGHT experience, I had not thought of spiritual without religion. As I became aware of new ways God was acting in my life, I realized that my background did not include what I had experienced with the LIGHT consuming me. In the LIGHT, the power of the love and joy was all consuming. It is hard to put into words!

My God experience became central. I certainly could read about such experiences in the Bible. Examples might be Moses and the burning bush or Mary being visited by an angel. Or closer to my experience, Saul experiencing a blinding light and, as a result of this experience, becoming Paul and changing his whole life, traveling and speaking to continue Jesus's ministry. But no one I knew was saying they had such a dramatic experience of God until Terry told me about her NDE. This probably reflects what I was willing to read prior to this time. Earlier, I would have been very skeptical of someone who was talking about such an experience. I would never compare my experience to these biblical people. However, *I did have an experience* that I had thought impossible! And what do you do with that experience? I began to read books that I probably would have never read without my LIGHT experience. The books just presented themselves to me. Friends gave them to me, friends recommended them, and I looked them up. Or I went into a bookstore, and just the right book was there on the shelf in front of me. They caught my eye. I was reading nonstop. This process continues currently. I began asking new questions. I couldn't read fast enough. I would hear scripture read in church, and I began to say to myself, "Oh, I know what that means!" I paid attention to what I was feeling and experiencing. Thanks to the cassette/CD player in my car, I listened to books as I traveled each day back and forth to the school where I was teaching. I excitedly talked about the books I was reading when I gathered for social occasions. I began telling others of my experience. I was afraid at first of what people would think, but most did not question or reject my story. They were interested. People told me their stories. Puzzle pieces were fitting into place.

New experiences helped me redefine my beliefs. I was much more open to new ideas. I was hungry for new connections that would help me understand what I had experienced. All this was going on at the same time I was going through the process of grieving the loss of Anne. Talk about opposites—a mountaintop experience while in the depths of despair daily. That was my experience for months.

The summer after Anne's death, I spoke earlier of the experience of going to the rain forest in Peru. My experience changed the direction of my thinking and feeling again. Somehow in my education or in my interpretations of what was being taught, I had the idea that we were more intelligent, more "with it" scientifically, than the indigenously connected peoples in the rain forest. They are still part of a hunter-gathering culture. Not so! I had unexpectedly found a hidden misunderstanding within me—that I, from the Western world, was somehow better. What I found were wonderful people! People more in tune with nature, more in tune with communication with the spiritual parts of life. For these people, *all* of life seemed to be spiritual. They had so much to teach me. I was experiencing more of the spiritual. I found that I needed to define the difference between spiritual and religious before I could again decide what I *really* believed about God and how that relates to living life.

Wisdom from a Rainforest by Stuart Schlegel helped me define spiritual versus religious. Terry found this book while attending a rain forest conference and gave it to me as a gift.

The direction of Stuart Schlegel's life was changed by his work in the Philippine rain forest. He went to the Upi Valley as a missionary, but after three years of work, found that he was being called to understand the way of life of the "forest people," the people whose way of life had not been disturbed by the American influence in the Philippines after WWII. He decided to go back to the United States, to the University of Chicago for a degree in anthropology. He returned as an anthropologist instead of clergy. He spent two years documenting the way of life of the Teduray people of Figel. These people lived in the mountainous forest on the Island of Mindanao in the Philippines. He found this community had a tolerant, gentle, egalitarian way of life. His experiences transformed his own values and beliefs profoundly. His distinction between spiritual and religious helped me to understand the difference. Schlegel spoke of spirituality as "… whatever path we choose to journey toward wholeness and meaningfulness … our vision of what will make us whole and well. All people are on a spiritual quest, whether aware of it or not; to seek meaning in our lives is a part of being human." He is talking about the experiences and feelings of the divine within all of us. There are unlimited forms, infinite possibilities. Religions are groups of people who have developed words and ideologies, theologies, to institutionalize the experiences of spirit, Creator, God. "The term religion … is best applied to the traditions and institutions that have developed to protect and promote some particular historic version of spiritual understanding."[17]

For now, I have defined spiritual or spirituality. It will be an ongoing process. It is difficult for us to grasp in this culture because, until recently, we did not use the term often. Spiritual is speaking about our spirit or our soul. It is a way that we talk about the mystery that animates all life. It is about the opportunity to explore the various ways of being in relationship with our self, with other human beings, and with God. It is knowing that *God is within us*, not just out there somewhere.

- Spirituality is like water to a fish. It is the environment we live in.
- Spirituality is both a worldview and a process of development.
- Spiritual experience is like snowflakes, as unique as each one of us.
- Spiritual growth is an ongoing process.

---

[17] Stuart A. Schlegel, *Wisdom from a Rainforest: The Spiritual Journey of an Anthropologist* (Athens, Georgia: University of Georgia Press, 1999), 192–193.

- Spirituality causes us to ask questions as we find the motivation and creative power to be something new.
- Spirituality brings community and interrelatedness and balance to life.
- Spirit calls us to explore the mysteries. There are infinite possibilities.
- Spiritual experiences are something out of the ordinary. We *feel* the difference as we *feel* love or joy.
- Spiritual connections with a friend or a stranger bring a knowing that the conversation was meant to be, which can enable healing.

One of the belief changes for Terry and me was a strong interest in understanding all_religions, including those of the indigenous peoples. We believe that no one way is the only way or has all the answers. To me, it just does not make sense that God would leave out millions of people by choosing one particular religion. We say God is love; saying that one religion has all the answers is not congruent with an all-loving God. I compare it to a jigsaw puzzle. If you do not have the picture on the cover of the box, it is difficult to see what the finished puzzle will look like until many pieces have been put together. Each religion has beliefs and traditions that provide very helpful insights into the true nature of God. Respectful dialogue is a key to better understanding. Finding the common threads that produce love and respect will lead to peace.

Another change that I see beginning to develop, which will provide growth for the future, is the *weaving together of religion and spirituality* into a life fabric that brings balance to our everyday lives and the everyday lives of our immediate communities and our countries. Being a part of a religious community gives me a way to celebrate God's constant presence in my life. It gives me a framework to think and rethink the mysteries of life. The opportunity to attend meaningful worship on a weekly basis renews my spirit. Living brings each of us insights. Community provides support as we examine our particular beliefs and the beliefs of the historical

Christian path. We grow in our faith and understanding as we share the ordinary ups and downs of life, as well as the tragedies of life. Where two or three are gathered, there is God also. As we really take seriously that *we are all one*, it will give us a better way to put beliefs into action. I hope religions will begin to look at the doctrines and their theological constructs and realize that there are inconsistences in the belief systems they are teaching. They will no longer try to control but will provide for a collecting of the wisdom we gain from our individual experiences of God. The picture being made in this new puzzle will provide a wider view. Our imaginations will be freed up to provide a vision of a better way of life that supports all.

Before Anne's death, I had never thought to meditate. Upon returning from my first rain forest experience in Peru, I was ready to sit quietly, ready to listen for the voice of God within me. Prior to this, I had never thought of meditating. But I didn't know how to go about it. I continued to be the one talking via prayer. I thought most of the answers came from the "experts." Studying the lives and suggestions of authors was helpful. It inspired me. Could I figure out the process of meditation? Communication, via what I was calling intuition or coincidences, was going on, but I was feeling there must be more.

Within that second year after Anne's death, I learned that a couple I had met at church, Hal and Betsy, were inviting people to their home once a week to teach and practice the monastic tradition of contemplative meditation. Richard Rohr, a current theologian and writer, defines contemplation as the "… deliberate seeking of God through a willingness to detach from the passing self, the tyranny of emotions, the addiction to self-image, and the false promises of the world." He calls contemplation "The Divine Therapy."[18] I recently found this definition, and it helps me understand. That opportunity with Hal and Betsy was eighteen years ago. At that time, I had only heard the word but had no understanding to go with it. It was unusual eighteen years ago for people to be talking about the benefits

---

18   Richard Rohr, *What the Mystics Know: Seven Pathways to Your Deeper Self* (New York: Crossroads Publishing Company, 2015), 79.

of meditation. I did not know many of the people, and it was a bit scary to attend. But they lived in my neighborhood, and I was searching for new experiences. It was convenient. It took me a long time to settle in! We chose a phrase to use as a mantra. I chose, "Be still and know that I am God." We read passages from the Bible or inspirational literature and then sat in silence for about twenty minutes if I remember correctly. Within four minutes, I was squirming! My mind kept thinking of the day's events, the work I had to do before I could teach in the morning, what I was going to serve for dinner tomorrow night, how I was not a good enough mother or Anne would not have died (irrational, I know), and so on. My mind was anything but quiet. But I did keep sitting with my eyes closed.

One of the techniques they taught was to think of a river flowing gently, with a boat floating down the river. I was to put the thoughts in the boat and let them float away. It worked for two seconds until the next thought came. I said my mantra. Along the way, I also began to concentrate on my breathing. The time seemed like an eternity. But after about three months of practicing at home and attending the gathering once a week, I found that I was looking forward to the quiet times. They introduced me to a book called *Psalms for Praying: An Invitation to Wholeness* by Nan C. Merrill.[19] I had used the Bible and daily prayer resources before, but this was a contemporary version of the Psalms that I have really enjoyed. I was looking for "something" to happen—a sign I guess that I was connecting. But there was not any sign. I experienced some resistance. I would be faithful each day enjoying the quiet for weeks, and then I would let it go. I kept asking myself why I kept giving up this time with God even when it was so meaningful. After meditating in the early morning, I hopped in the shower, and while the water was pouring over me, an insight would pop into my head. As I was finishing up preparations for my teaching day, I felt calmer. Or an idea would come that had eluded me for days that helped a student who was having difficulties. I now recognize that

---

19   Nan C. Merrill, *Psalms for Praying: An Invitation to Wholeness* (New York: Continuum International Publishing Group, 2007).

the process of listening within for guidance heightens my creativity and problem solving. That is God at work. I was becoming *aware* of spiritual presence. One day while meditating with the contemplative group a year or so later, I had my first experience of the darkness, while my eyes were closed, turning a beautiful color of purple! I kept encountering new-to-me meditation possibilities over time.

During a conversation, the parent of one of my students mentioned very excitedly her discovery of Dr. Dharma Singh Khalsa's book and CDs on medical meditation.[20] It sounded intriguing. I bought the book and CD set and started to use the meditations. It was a whole new form of meditation for me, using chanting. With chanting, it vibrated my whole body. I loved it! Since I had never done anything like this, I was very self-conscious, so I secluded myself in the basement, and I found it very helpful.

Next, I was sent an e-mail introducing me to the Healing Codes. Alex stated, "We believe the Healing Codes are what has been predicted by the greatest minds of our time as the future of medicine. Only its scope encompasses more than medicine. It heals relationship problems, mental health issues, career problems, peak performance issues—you name it—because it all has the same source, which is stress caused by destructive, painful cellular memories in our unconscious minds."[21] In the book, there are many stories that are unbelievable. Dr. Ben Johnson's was one of them. Over time using the Healing Codes, he had healed his Lou Gehrig's disease! What was most helpful for me was *The Healing Codes Manual.*[22] It gave me a step-by-step guide for healing the things that I did know and unconscious things I carry around with me that affect my life. Alex

---

20 Dharma Singh Khalsa, MD, and Cameron Stauth, *Meditation as Medicine: Activate the Power of Your Natural Healing Force* (New York: Fireside (registered trademark of Simon & Schuster, Inc.), 2001).

21 Alexander Loyd, ND, PhD, and Ben Johnson, MD, DO, NM, *The Healing Code: 6 Minutes to Heal the Source of Any Heath, Success, or Relationship Issue* (Peoria, AZ: Intermedia Publishing Group, Inc., 20010), 167.

22 Alexander Loyd, ND, PhD, and Ben Johnson, MD, DO, NMD, *The Healing Codes Manual* (Dr. Alex Loyd Services, LLC, 2004–2010).

Loyd's questions helped me dig deeper. Positive statements the manual provided helped me be more articulate.

Along the way, I discovered Wayne Dyer's work. I started my reading with *Wisdom of the Ages*. I feel that I grew along with Wayne himself. Year after year, new books, CD sets, and videos of live lectures came out. I read and listened multiple times, gaining understanding. He had a way of taking complicated life issues and spiritual insights and putting them into words and examples that were very clear and usable. You can find a list of these items on our website, www.thelightgap.com. The first meditation CD that came out is called *Meditations for Manifesting*. It too uses chanting. Again, I found it very helpful. More recently, he produced the CD *I AM: Wishes Fulfilled Meditation*. He explains the nature of the words I AM by saying it relates to Genesis, where Moses asked God what his name was, and he responded I AM. Wayne Dyer suggests that what you put after I AM is a creative statement. The CD is designed for relaxed meditation. I usually sit quietly with this music playing as I meditate.

One of the last tools I added for meditating was tapping. A friend recommended it to me quite a while ago, but I did not intuitively say, *Oh this is something I need to investigate,* as many of the others were. I am not sure why this was, but I think I just did not understand the process. When I discovered Nick Ortner's website, tapping (also known as EFT) came to life. In 2013, he published his book, *The Tapping Solution: A Revolutionary System for Stress-Free Living,*[23] which gave me a guide for zeroing in on a particular issue or feeling. It is a technique "… based on the principles of ancient acupuncture and modern psychology. Tapping uses specific meridian endpoints while focusing on negative emotions or physical sensations."[24] It looks funny, but it really works. I love the way it can be used right as an issue comes up that is upsetting. When that happens, I can go

[23] Nick Ortner, *The Tapping Solution: A Revolutionary System for Stress-Free Living* (Carlsbad, CA: Hay House, Inc., 2013).

[24] Nick Ortner, *The Tapping Solution: A Revolutionary System for Stress-Free Living* (Carlsbad, CA: Hay House, Inc., 2013), back cover.

off by myself and start tapping. Sometimes during quiet meditation, an issue comes into my consciousness. I begin right then tapping on healing that issue. At first, I needed the guidance his book provided or specific wording on a theme, which his website gives away often. Once I understood the principles, I began to free the process up, using exactly what thoughts were coming to my head, making it *me* specific. When I got in touch with leftover grief related to Anne's death, I had a tool to overcome the emotional pain. It was something to physically *do*, and it worked! Here is an example. When my computer recently got a virus, I was calm—until I wasn't. For a variety of reasons, I became almost hysterical. I had not had that happen in years. I began tapping and sobbing all at once. The fear of losing all the work that had gone into writing this book came out first. Every frustration I had encountered in "the book" process and more came out. Next, all the self-defeating thoughts about not being good enough came out. Who wants to read what I have to say anyway? Then railing at the world for creating computers that I just don't know what to do with when something goes wrong. This was probably frustration leftover from the beginning of computers. The requirement to use a computer to write student reports was daunting at first. When a mistake was made, the text disappeared for good, and you had to start over! Personal stuff came out that I had been working on and had thought I was rid of long ago. I was definitely in distress at a level of ten! I was just hitting the tapping points with no regard for what I was saying. The negative was coming out. No nicely worded statements for each tapping point. And then ... I began to calm down. I began to state the positive, how thankful I was for my son Michael who knew what to do with the computer. Next, I could reject the thought that I did not have anything important to say in our book ... Soon I was not crying. I was calm, unbelievably calm. Wow! I felt healed! This entire process took place in about fifteen to twenty minutes.

As you can see, my tools increased over the years. Terry has taught me how to combine both the physical tools and the silence of going within. I have always found walking very helpful. Terry Patten's Integral Spiritual Practice Workout and Yoga are practices that use my body and heart in meditative ways. The use of the Healing Codes, tapping, music, reading, journaling, and inspirational guides combine well to create an integrated meditative experience. Marianne Williamson's *A Year of Miracles,* Wayne Dyer's *Living the Wisdom of the Tao,* Jonathan Star's *Tao Te Ching,* the Common English Bible, and Willis Barnsone's *The Poems of Jesus Christ* are some of the books I use regularly. With so many options for practicing awareness and silence, my insights have increased. I am more aware of my experience of the gifts of the larger cosmos, and I have a more encompassing understanding of this world and how it is put together. Worship is enriched. My excitement and thirst continues.

******

Terry's Voice

I was reading authors from every walk of life, including conservative Christian thought to challenge my thinking. I also read about the life of Buddha and found his philosophy of life to be incredible. Dr. Wayne Dyer introduced me to the life of the Chinese philosopher, a God-realized being named Lao Tzu, who lived five hundred years before Christ. This is not a religion but a way of life aligned with nature. The classic text with these verses, called the Tao Te Ching or the Great Way, offers advice and guidance that is balanced, moral, spiritual, and always working toward good. Dr. Dyer studied and lived the Tao Te Ching and eventually wrote a book called *Change Your Thoughts—Change Your Life: Living the Wisdom of the Tao.*[25] So many different books helped me realize that my experiences in nature were an important part of my life. There are many authors now writing about the fact that our bodies are actually connected through nature to God. We may be hardwired to exist in the natural

---

[25] Dr. Wayne W. Dyer, *Change Your Thoughts—Change Your Life: Living the Wisdom of the Tao* (Carlsbad, California: Hay House, Inc., 2007).

world around us. Scientists are researching the possibility that our bodies are actually made of elements of the earth and that the more we lose this connection, we might be losing our health along with it. As we all watch cancer, heart disease, obesity, diabetes, and so many illnesses overtake loved ones, it does make us all ask why this is happening in such great numbers now. The concept of nature being involved resonates with me because there have been so many of my spiritually connected moments that happened in nature. Perhaps you can identify with times in your own life when nature brought an amazing experience in your life. There are parallels with increased health problems on our planet and the disconnect many people have with nature today. We should all start listening as we see our world disconnect through technology-filled lives where many individuals may never see any natural growing spaces, let alone walk in grass. Are you aware that our feet have receptors connecting with meridians, the pathways for energy in our bodies? Putting your bare feet into grass, sand, dirt, and mud can send healthy messages into your body. But only if you are barefoot!

I have connected with Gregg Braden as a human being, brilliant scientist, and writer trying to link science, spirituality, and the real world. His books are deep in content, but they have made their way into my heart in so many ways. Some of his earlier works such as *The Isaiah Effect, The God Code,* and later *Deep Truth* were challenges as I read them but significant in my growth. Second readings in later years revealed messages I missed. As a speaker, he is fascinating as well as challenging to understand. I feel that he is trying to help Christians, Jews, Hindus, and Muslims understand all of the lost books that could have been included in the Bible but were discarded in the fourth century by writers for various reasons. He also helps us understand how translations put up barriers about words that we take for granted as we read the Bible. Different translations and meaning of words may present a very different picture, both in the Old Testament as well as the New Testament. He presents findings from the Dead Sea Scrolls that perhaps we need to read and digest before we decide what we believe. He presents findings as they relate to history we might not know. His travels to far-reaching places to research included Israel, Egypt, Europe, India, Tibet, and South America. His research is fascinating and might provide some incredible insights to all of us. I am realizing that he is a voice that will keep me listening.

Gregg Braden's website is full of very thoughtful and intriguing information.[26] I especially connected with a segment he wrote in August 2015 after traveling to Cusco, Peru, and to the Inca ruins of Machu Picchu. I found his writing very significant for me. I also spent ten years going into the area and could identify with the changes that were experienced each year I traveled. I had several very powerful spiritual experiences in the Andes hiking the Inca Trail as well as in the highly spiritual feeling received in Machu Picchu, standing within the amazing Incan culture. The Incans were likely asking the similar questions about life and death. While many travelers chuckled when the guide said to touch this huge, massive stone and feel the energy from it, I *could* feel it, and it was amazing. I shared that I could feel the energy. I got this kind smile, and it was always followed by a questioning look.

I realized after hearing Gregg's stories, time had changed the area even more since my travels. The indigenous people of the Andes Mountain region are changing and adapting. Change is inevitable. Are they perhaps adapting better than we have? I was shocked to hear that the city of Cusco hosts McDonald's right down the road from the historic four-hundred-year-old cathedral in the city's central square I visited numerous times. How often I walked that square, and I can't imagine a McDonald's restaurant there. He shared that the Big Yak Burger that has replaced the traditional Big Mac at McDonald's in the Tibetan capital of Lhasa at an altitude of 12,000 feet.

In the Andes, in Peru and Bolivia, Gregg Braden experienced people wanting to preserve their way of life and yet become part of positive change as our planet grows in understanding. He talked about a type of power that's often overlooked today, the power of

---

[26]   www.greggbraden.com.

beauty. I experienced the same awe, seeing beauty in God's natural environments that are amazing yet recognizing that change is inevitable. He talks about beauty being a "force" in nature that we overlook. He is speaking about a beauty being a force, a scientifically based force. I can identify that it is a power and not just something we seek out to enjoy. He released a book called *Secrets of the Lost Mode of Prayer* based on our North American Navajo people who find and accept the beauty in their lives. He wrote about his journey to Tibetan monasteries in his book *The Isaiah Effect*. Tibetan monks shared with him a similar lost mode of prayer. It is a prayer activated by *visualizing* and *feeling* the request has already been received, not by asking. The Incan, Navaho, and Tibetan people all have a common mode of prayer. It is visualizing and feeling the outcome already in place. Gregg Braden is a refreshing voice saying that as a collective species of loving, caring people, we can change our thoughts to the positive and away from doom and gloom. Too often I hear people asking why is God allowing natural disasters, starvation, violence, and disease. God gave us free will to make choices. As a planet, all of us *on* it are responsible for what is happening *in* it. I am responsible; we all are. The oneness that we share, culture, music, art, and beauty bring us closer to God as human beings. It is also inevitable that tragedies and big problems in one part of the world will affect the lives of entire communities in other parts of the world. Oneness means that we can no longer separate spirituality from our everyday lives. Science is our everyday lives, and so is spirituality. They are intertwined through God's design for our universe.

******

Marj's Voice

A discussion of my spiritual growth over the years, building on my LIGHT experience that "broke me open," would not be complete without discussing Neale Donald Walsch's book *Conversations with*

God: Book 1. The recommendation to read this book was another one of those God-inspired coincidences.

One evening, we had invited a good friend over for dinner. He had been part of my husband's youth group years ago. When he was in high school, we often invited Steve over for dinner. After dinner, he would sit at our piano and treat us to a concert while I put the kids to bed and Jim went off to his meetings. This night, I was telling him about my LIGHT experience at Anne's death and my journey in trying to figure out what I had experienced. In the conversation, he asked me if I had discovered *Conversations with God* by Neale Donald Walsch. I had not. "Oh you *have* to buy that book!" So I did.

What a find that was for me! I could not put it down. It contained answers to all of the questions that I had piled up to this point in my life. Did I understand it all? No! I am still working on that. I stayed up well into the night, many nights in a row, just to be able to continue reading the conversation that Neale was having with God. He asked every question that you and I would ask if we had a chance to sit down with God. I was very intrigued with the story of how this conversation came about. His book was the result of his voiced frustrations related to his life not working! His relationships had fallen apart, he had lost his job, and he was homeless. He had a habit of writing his thoughts down in letters to vent his frustrations but usually did not send them. This particular time, he grabbed his yellow legal pad and asked "… a pile of angry questions … to the greatest victimizer of them all. I decided to write a letter to God." As he looked at what he had written, he soon realized that he was writing a dialogue. "Before I knew it, I had begun a conversation … and I was not writing so much as taking *dictation*."[27] Eventually there were three books produced in the Conversations with God series. Many other books followed. As Neale Donald Walsch published his conversations, he began lecturing around the world.

---

[27]   Neale Donald Walsch, *Conversations with God: Book 1* (New York: G.P. Putnam's Sons Publishers, 1995), 1–2.

I know that this method of communication sounds impossible. It did to Neale too. He asked, "Is it my imagination? Why me? I have messed up my life." After reading the first book, I decided to just "hold and ponder" his statement on how the book came into being until I was ready to make a more definite decision. I do not see how anyone could write these books without having had a direct experience with God. I had heard of automatic writing from our artist friend Sally years before. That probably helped. But I too had had my LIGHT experience, which was an unexplainable experience given the beliefs I had once held. Neale took hold of the creative seed and produced the books. I took hold of the messages and began to put them to work in my life. Processing the information in the book took time. I had no desire to go off into some crazy fantasy world. But the information hit me with an intuitive knowing that I chose to accept. Often what I was reading made so much more sense than beliefs I had been taught over the years. The conversation also produced excitement and energy within me! I could hardly wait until the next book came out. Some ideas took two or three years of contemplation before I decided what I really believed. I even went to Oregon to be part of a group that discussed putting information from Conversations with God into practical educational use. In 2015, Walsh published a book called *Conversations with God for Parents: Sharing the Messages with Children.*

In our book, I cannot put down all the ways that these books have helped me understand life, God. They have provided a reference point from which I began to grow and change. Neale Donald Walsch, in his book *Conversations with God, Book 1*,[28] states that feeling is one of the languages of the soul. "Hidden in your deepest feelings are your highest truths." Other ways God communicates with us is through thoughts and ideas and through direct experiences. In college, this was one question that kept coming into my consciousness. Where do ideas come from? I didn't have that idea yesterday, or even an hour

---

[28] Neal Donald Walsch, *Conversations with God, Book 1* (New York: G.P. Putnam's Sons, 1995), 3.

ago. Where did it come from? Somehow I never connected it to God communicating with me—me personally! Now I know that happens. I also know that it happens for *all* people. God is communicating with *everyone*. I now know that God does not judge and that takes me into the freedom to be *me*! I thrive when I do not have to take someone else's view of who I *should* be. Imagination becomes very important. For the purpose of life is to remember who we really are—souls who have a body right now. Life continues in another form when we leave this life, this realm. We call it dying, but really we are just going on in another form. That helped me heal from the loss of Anne. *She is alive in some form.* So my job is to continuously recreate who I am into the next, better version of myself. Each day becomes an opportunity to start over if I choose to. I am not stuck with my "bad" choices. What is the goal? The goal is to reflect love in all that I do. Each of us has gifts, talents, passions, and things that we do well. I can use these to create who I choose to be. I use my imagination to create a vision of what I can contribute to make this world a better place. Putting it into action is the next step. But I don't have to go to some distant place, unless I choose to. There are always opportunities right where I am. If I make a mistake, I can just start again and again until my life reflects the vision I have for myself and the world I want to live in. Thoughts are tools for creating. So I am in a process of deciding which thoughts are not serving me well and using more positive thoughts to create what I do want to experience. It is hard work unlearning, recreating, and renewing. It takes a lifetime … many lifetimes perhaps to really understand. It is a start-and-stop growth pattern. But I have grown by leaps and bounds.

Neale Donald's work has spread all over the globe. He has written many books, traveled the world speaking, and cofounded an organization called Humanities Team. The team's goal is to embody the Oneness of All by responding to the world's most chronic issues in order to bring sustainable peace and harmony. His work has inspired the work of many other authors and organizations. In his book *Tomorrow's God*, he talks about the "New Spirituality being the civil rights movement for the soul."[29]

******

Terry's Voice

I had been reading information on spiritual growth for so many years. A simple book that didn't make the best-seller list produced an amazing happening in me. It is called *The Jesus Seeds*.[30] I was flying home to Michigan from Ft. Lauderdale, Florida, where both Marj and I attended the Hay House I Can Do It! Conference and Writing from the Soul Conference. At the conference, I saw a book lying on a table and was drawn to it for some reason. I did not know the author. I began reading it on my flight home.

By this time, I was ready to tell my story and begin writing this book. Laurel Geise's own experience was one of a vision that appeared to her during an evening meditation. She was transported in the vision to Qumran of many thousands of years ago. It happened while she was still in her easy chair meditating. She eventually journeyed to the Holy Land and found the scene from her vision. It changed her life, leaving the business life to get her doctorate in spirituality. She was driven to gain insights from world religions and belief systems. Her style of writing and the ease with which it spoke to me settled in right away. She was giving me pause to think about Christ in the scope of history, affecting lives in every culture and religion. Her understandings about our soul's ability to guide our lives matched what I had learned in my NDE and research. She put into words what I had experienced over the years that followed my NDE. "At the core of every soul, the seeds of truth and grace await

---

[29]   Neale Donald Walsh, *Tomorrow's God: Our Greatest Spiritual Challenge* (New York: Atria Books, a trademark of Simon & Schuster, Inc., 2004), 387.

[30]   Laurel Geise, *Jesus Seeds: Igniting Your Soul-Guided Life* (Bloomington, IN: Balboa Press, a division of Hay House, 2013).

the right frequency of light to awaken them. With this activation, they burst open, allowing wisdom to flood the soul and rise to the cognitive level of the mind. In this awakening comes access to the cosmic encyclopedia of life."[31]

I read the last word of *Jesus Seeds* as my plane touched down three hours later in Chicago. I had closed the book, closed my eyes, and thought maybe I could meditate as I processed thoughts presented in her story. All of a sudden, my ears blocked, and I had excruciating pain in my ears. Instinctively I pushed my ears with my fingers and without thinking began to do my Healing Code meridian points and then began tapping! I only mildly became aware of the wonderful couple next to me looking at me with wide eyes wondering if I was okay. As we landed, I just pointed to my ears, and they quickly nodded their heads in understanding, I'm sure wondering if I was for real. I had this sense that perhaps while I thought I was saying the words inside of me, I might have said them out loud. I don't actually know. I had experienced pressure from planes in my ears before but nothing like this! I was no longer hearing the high-pitched sound. I was not in silence, but I was hearing wind and the rustle of leaves from outside with no doors open. (And no trees in sight!) Once inside, everything around me was totally normal by sight, but my hearing was definitely in an altered state. Nothing I tried was changing anything.

I found the gate for my connecting flight was near an eating mall area with McDonald's. I sat away from the crowd to eat and was fascinated by the sounds I was hearing. Where was the sound coming from? I could hear outdoor sounds of wind, blowing leaves, birds, and voices that seemed distant. I looked up and over at McDonald's, which was a long ways away, and I realized I heard the workers' voices. *Really* odd—I was too far away. And I was hearing silence all around me with all these people in an airport right by me! The outside sounds were clear and in nature ... not the sounds of an airport. I was

---

[31] Laurel Geise, *Jesus Seeds: Igniting Your Soul-Guided Life* (Bloomington, IN: Balboa Press, a division of Hay House, 2013), back cover.

fascinated and wondering how I could be hearing this because I was still seeing the sights normally in the airport.

I finally thought, *Wow ... I better just go sit at my gate*, even though I still had another hour. I got to the gate, and there were no people, just the man at the counter. I went up and asked if the plane boarded early, and he said, "Are you Terry Larkin? We've been paging you!" I had lost a complete hour. And I never heard anyone paging me. He told me the doors were closed and they had given away my seat, but they had another seat way in the back. They reluctantly let me on the plane, and of course everyone glared at me as I boarded. Oh wow, I was so embarrassed. I walked to the back and sat down next to a very nice African American man who smiled at me, thank goodness, and said welcome! All of a sudden, my hearing cleared, and I was fine all the way home. I was introspective with wonder.

The man next to me smiled and pointed to my book. "I see you are reading about Jesus. Do you believe all of that? I don't know if I believe in a God. I am rather lost myself." He looked lost and began telling me he was on a flight to go see his dad, whom he had not seen or spoken with in twenty-five years, and he had great fears. I found just the right words to tell him about my near-death experience in ten minutes or less, hoping I might open a window into a belief in God. I told him about Wayne Dyer forgiving his father after hating the man all his life and how it totally changed his life. And I told him that frankly, I was just "processing" the information in *Jesus Seeds*. This flight from Chicago to Grand Rapids, Michigan, is barely twenty-five minutes long. For the first time, I had openly shared my story from my heart, sending love to a man that I had never met. When he got up, he said just a simple, "Thank you, you've made it easier for me to face my Dad." I have no idea what happened to the man or if I changed his thoughts in any way, but I suspect I made a difference.

I had been searching for the sounds I heard in my NDE, but never in my wildest imagination was I expecting to have "sound" moving in from another realm. I know that had to be the explanation of birds and nature sounds. Was the altered time part of my experience, or was I just *lost* in thought? Nothing that happens to us is a coincidence.

Perhaps I was simply to meet a man in need of some encouraging words. I was in a very humble state while I was with him, still feeling emotions that overcame me as I processed my experience after reading words in a book that was meaningful for me. Thank you, Laurel Geise. I enjoy her very wise words on her website, "Only you know your path to God. Choose it, and never look back."[32]

Both Voices

Our book is called *The Light GAP*, a forest term for the area opened up to the sun by fallen trees, bringing sunlight onto the forest floor so that seeds can germinate. This is the process by which regeneration of the forest occurs. Sometimes seeds have been waiting hundreds of years for the right conditions for this process to occur. Our human lives follow this pattern. As forests make use of sunlight in a gap, human beings make use of hard times and tragedies. When these challenging times come, they are a reference point to help us decide what we want our lives to look like. We are never alone, but we have to be *aware* that we are not alone. Divine guidance is available to help us. The amazing thing is that this guidance appears in every form you can imagine. Often we call them coincidences, intuition, synchronicities, luck. It doesn't matter what we call them. These "events" can be seeds to new growth or to the feeling of joy. They can be a song you hear on the radio, or an unexpected meeting of a friend, that in the words or conversation gives you a message you needed to hear, or an idea or an answer that has been struggling to be birthed. These times are a gift. It is the grace of God acting in our lives. These events are "quick starts" to the creative power within us. Our lives have had such events. They have activated the seeds of new life. They have sprouted and are growing.

---

[32]   www.laurelgeise.com.

Chapter 6

Health and Healing
Serious Decline in Health

Love is all there is, learned from my NDE in 1982, is a powerful message. Knowing that fear did not need to be part of my life changed the person I was becoming. We are all connected through God. I learned this during my NDE and internalized it in the Amazon. "We have the ability to heal ourselves" took longer to absorb, understand, and become part of me. I was learning from God's amazing beings placed in every corner of our world. God's grace facilitated my journey to understanding health using the power we have within our soul. Human beings have part of the divine right within them. I needed to understand the power of God within to heal.

—Terry Larkin

"Therefore I tell you, whatever you ask for in prayer, believe that you have received it and it will be yours" (Mark 11:24).[33]

Jesus told us that *belief* was powerful. Every major religion around the world tells us the same thing. It would be many years later that

---

[33] *Holy Bible,* New International Version, NIV.

my belief in my own body's ability to heal began. There was so much more. I had many old paradigms that had been internalized as beliefs. I had to learn how to let them go because they were translating into disease in my body. Doctors and well-meaning friends would say, "Your body is aging; your mother had serious heart disease, and you too are at risk; your mom and dad had high cholesterol; your mom had uterine cancer; you had two serious brain concussions; the fracture line is leaking a fluid, causing unknown symptoms." This is a very short list of so many negative statements I heard, and I thought all of these would happen to me! My belief system led me to believe that all I had to do was follow the doctor's orders, pray for healing, and have faith. I thought at the time, *God will decide. We have no control over the outcome.* My belief has changed.

We have a piece of the divine that lives in our soul, but I found out the hard way that my whole belief system was holding me back. I had not yet let go of some limiting beliefs that were no longer part of me. Intellectually, I thought I had love for all. I let go of anger and resentments resulting from childhood events and difficult adult situations. I knew that all people were God's amazing creation, living the best they knew how, given the circumstances at the time. Had I forgiven myself for actions? I had not, and I was very surprised once I uncovered them. I had relegated to my subconscious my own imperfections along with deep-seated emotions and feelings that had become part of my body memory. I always kept striving for perfection. If only I do what is "right," all will be well. The problem came when everyone around me had a different idea of what doing right meant!

My health decline story is like falling down a winding stone staircase in a very tall castle, one step at a time, and landing at the bottom with a thud. As I relate this story, I will help you visualize my pitfalls. Then I will show you the long, slow haul back up that staircase and into the beautiful sunshine. You may recognize yourself. We not only can heal ourselves, but we can bring diseases to ourselves as well.

My life began changing in 2002 after having traveled abroad leading student workshops for the past ten years. Planes crashing into the Twin Towers in New York on 9/11 changed so many lives. My life changed as well.

I took my last workshop group into the Amazon in 2002. After the most profound spiritual experiences came into my life during those ten years, I should have realized there might be a downward spiral for my body due to stress and sadness. My current body was in a linear world, still trying to make sense of time. I had returned to this reality. My life was unraveling in a lot of ways. CET had to close, which brought sadness and heartache to both of us. I was growing and expanding spiritually in ways that were very "unusual," so I was still tucking all of this inside of me. How terribly unhealthy that turned out to be! But I never even considered any of this at the time.

Our role as a parent changes as our children move into the adult world. I somehow thought we were handling situations okay, but I realize now how difficult that transition was for me. Our three sons were grown, marrying, and leaving home. Each child was unique. Their choices for their lives were equally different, and we celebrated their diversity. There were amazing highs and devastating lows. Emotions and feelings creep into everyone's lives. Our youngest son served a year in Iraq. He was burned and flown to Germany. Trauma embedded into my body then. Jacob is a success story now, working through PTSD in very good ways. But I tucked away a few more negative emotions into my subconscious, and yet I still kept saying, "Life is good." This was a *big mistake* for me not to recognize and pull these emotions out, not place them within. Recognizing this was significant later during healing.

At the same time, changes were happening within the school district where I was teaching, which launched me into a new environment, with new stresses. I *loved* teaching. I had great success as a teacher learning how to use my own energy field to help children relax their minds enough to learn how to read and de-stress from their own traumas in life. One can learn so much from first graders. Their intuition could match mine! I also wanted to share knowledge and techniques freely with other teachers, so my life became stressful with long hours volunteering to help the district. I was having trouble with the balance of family and work. I wanted to keep teaching the important lifelong learning concept of the *love* of learning. I wanted to help them embrace better self-care through positive emotional experiences. However, schools in Michigan were in trouble financially, and new concepts such as No Child Left Behind were making life *worse* for the children left behind! New ways to teach to the test were eating up valuable learning time. State school funding shifted, forcing the closing of schools and the moving of classrooms. I had to leave my treasured classroom of eighteen years in 2005, moving to a new building. I watched the neighborhood school concept disintegrate. I had worked so hard to help my students love school, learning in a stimulating environment. I internalized the failure of the system to change in positive ways. I felt responsible. I should have realized my lack of control over it. We had such a talented teaching staff at Holland Public that was trying to hold it all together. My emotions brought more traumas into my body.

My health declined slowly in the beginning. I didn't even recognize that it started in 2002, but by 2006 my health declined at a very rapid rate. Internal trauma began back then. Diagnosis ideas ran wild. It was probably MS they decided. But through a synchronistic event, I found a doctor familiar with complex migraines—hemiplegic migraines. Little was known about them. Mayo Clinic collected my tests and helped my neurologist because they had started complex migraine research. My migraines started in the head and then moved down into the body. They hit my chest, causing heart difficulties. Later they struck my abdomen, causing unusual bleeding, requiring a hysterectomy. I had way too many trips to the ER. Each episode brought stroke-like symptoms, numbing one side of my body. It was very frightening because every test made it look like I was having a heart attack or stroke. These episodes caused nerve damage and weakness on one side, with muscles declining rapidly. These events were happening daily. Within about four to five months, my health was very poor. My neurologist worked amazingly hard to help but warned the nerve damage was likely permanent. Upward progress was *slow.* I worked hard with physical therapy, but lots of drugs were required.

I was determined to keep teaching. I loved teaching. There were times that work was not possible, and I missed a lot of days. But I began a rapid search into medical meditations. Basic meditation that I had begun in 1993 actually helped a lot, but I needed more. My spiritual mentor was my sister Marj. She was always finding just the right book for me to read. All of us need a mentor like her! I hope all of you realize you have people out there provided through the universe to help you. You find them if you ask and watch for a person to show up. Migraine episodes kept happening. Each time, I was losing strength as well as muscle control. My body was becoming weaker. I was lucky to be able to walk down our street. But I made it through the school year by coming home every day and using meditation. My kids and husband were respectful of the sign on my door, "I'm meditating. Get a snack. I'll make dinner soon!" My wonderful husband began to cook and do the shopping and laundry!

It was summer 2008. I was not sure I'd be able to return to teaching in the fall. Relax, sleep, meditations, sleep, walks on the beach, sleep, sunsets ... that was my life. My husband and I took many trips into nature. In the privacy of our home and camper, I tried *Meditation as Medicine* by Dharma Singh Khalsa, MD.[34] I really connected with the book. His voice on the CD was facilitating my understanding about why it was going to work. His life inspired me to integrate his material into my life. As an MD from California, he furthered his training in India. The CDs included music and meditations. I was chanting foreign words that he had translated. There was music, hand motions, and words used for specific purposes. It was very different, and I thought surely my friends and family would think this was *nuts.* Not Marj. As I told her, I found she had read it and was using it too! Coincidence? I think not. We were able to help each other. I was

---

[34]   Dharma Singh Khalsa, MD, and Cameron Stauth, *Meditation as Medicine* (New York, NY: Fireside, 2002).

comfortable because I recognized and experienced similar chants with hand and body motions used by shamans in the Amazon. If chanting and hand motions worked for them, why not? The local indigenous people in the Amazon had amazing success stories to tell. If you are looking for a fantastic explanation why self-healing works in the body medically, Dr. Dharma Singh Khalsa explains it extremely well on the CD of his book.

Marj then suggested I try *The Healing Code* by Alex Loyd, PhD, ND, and Ben Johnson, MD, DO, NMD. I started immediately adding this to my already established medical meditations, available at that time only in notebook form. I began to experience times when my energy would return. Wow, there was progress while I was using both of them. I was still having migraine episodes every day then, but they began to spread out and were now only about once a week, after a month moving to every two or three weeks. It was progress, enough that I thought I could start another school year. I know now that *The Healing Codes* and *Meditation as Medicine* were working because I was training my mind to become a healer. I was combining spirit with action through God's grace. At the same time, I was also *letting go* of limiting beliefs. I was *letting go* of negative embedded emotions one at a time.

I found that I could combine the techniques from *Meditation as Medicine* and *The Healing Code* into my own unique daily practice using music, yoga, and movement that spoke to my soul. My spiritual knowledge was growing in ways that were helpful. Dr. Wayne Dyer's books, *There's a Spiritual Solution to Every Problem, You'll See It When You Believe It*, and *Wisdom of the Ages* were especially inspiring. There were many other authors contributing to my growth. In meditation, I found God within myself. I was gaining strength.

I experienced a huge change when I realized, and knew beyond any doubt, that we not only have a piece of God existing inside of us from birth but that we *are* a piece of God. Inside of us, there is an amazing power, and most people rarely tap into it. I know that I did not. Wisdom has been passed down through literature as well as legends from ancient civilizations, but churches brought in their own differing interpretations, causing confusion. Wisdom was inside of me? I was beginning to realize that yes, it is true, and we all have that gift given to us at birth. I began to *ask* God a lot of questions once I realized answers arrived in so many ways! Whatever pathway you have to God, stick with it! God gave us free will for a reason; we can celebrate the differences in people! *Seek and ye shall find* took on a whole new meaning for me.

I was also realizing I needed a change from our large family home. I started using the techniques I learned in meditation for other things as well. We wanted to move out of our large family home where we raised our family. I wanted light, open spaces, and a more reasonable size. I needed to let go of a lot of *stuff*. I started meditating and visualizing my husband, Doug, and me in our new home space. I was visualizing us sitting at the closing on our house. Houses were not selling well at the time. We took a leap of faith and bought our place, a pile of dirt at the time! It was no accident that we sold our house, closed, and moved into our newly built home the same day. I know that many would say it was only a great coincidence, but I knew by then I was experiencing how thoughts could change my life. I began to *believe* that I could change my thought about health as well! I was getting healthier, but overwork and stress continued. I was still on beta-blockers, anxiety medication, blood pressure medications, cholesterol medication, and many drugs to control my migraines.

I began to find new authors and new music for meditation, and I kept reading new books written by authors I had been reading for years. I think one of the most significant changes in my meditation practices came when I found Dr. Wayne Dyer's Meditation CD called *I AM, Wishes Fulfilled*. I found the CD first but then quickly needed to make sure I read his book by that name as well to understand it all. I found what I had been searching for since 1982. I found sounds that would *take me back* into my white LIGHT experience. After using it for about a week, I understood how to "feel" the vibrations in and around my body. I felt them before, but understanding them was thrilling. Using these sounds, I could visualize myself in white light. I went back to research. I understood how Carolyn Myss had taught me about chakras and how significant they were to my healing. Her work has become profound as I proceed in understanding healing.

I also had learned that *any* person has this same ability to experience healing through meditation. I am not special because I had an NDE. But it did jumpstart my ability to find vibrational energy. Every human being on the planet has the ability to learn these techniques. I've since found a lot of information about others who have studied and found that vibrational levels can help healing! It was so affirming when I began to find more physicians saying the same thing.

I healed little by little. *No* quick miracles like we too often expect. I was using prayer in a whole new way. The more I combined everything, the easier healing became. Getting myself into a deep meditative state was the key, but so was the belief that I *would* heal. It was not just my mind saying, "You can heal." It was changing my belief one step at a time and letting go of negative emotions that I uncovered during my meditations. My body was experiencing the letting go. I was using the vibrational field around my body to channel healing to specific places in my body. I was removing stored feelings attached to memories and surrendering them to God. Making a connection to our supreme being through energy is critical. Shamans figured out long before modern medicine that a connection to spirit, an absolute belief they could heal, and letting go were critical pieces of healing. We can enhance traditional medicine with *spiritual wisdom.*

Then I gathered the courage to tell my neurologist what I had been doing. I informed him that I had been able to stop several migraines as they began and have it slowly dissipate without using any medication. He had never heard someone say they could do that. Instead I was using positive belief, *The Healing Codes* and tapping right away, and the attack would slowly stop. Meditation was also giving me strong messages that exercise and diet were critical ingredients in health as well.

I had informed my neurologist I wanted to go off my medications. He was a little reluctant at first, saying I could land myself right back to repeated complex migraines and if that happened, it would likely be a lot worse for me. I agreed to wait three more months. My neurologist had been astounded with how quickly the healing had taken place. He was very open to hear all that I had been doing; he admitted there is a lot of research that would support what I was saying. He wished he had the time to read more.

I am drug-free now. With my doctor's help, I had a lot of drugs to discontinue, which took time to accomplish safely. I kept medical meditations going every day, my designed yoga routine, along with the Healing Codes adapted now into the music in meditation CDs. In the next two years, all of my blood work numbers normalized, surprising and satisfying my general doctor as well. I have normal cholesterol, hemoglobin, and my red and white platelet counts were back to normal.

I am in fantastic shape now, and I am using my routines daily for maintenance. Good health has to be maintained. It is not a place to arrive but a place to appreciate by keeping good habits in place. Many people say that I look ten years younger than when I retired from teaching. I'm off all drugs. I even went back to guest teaching and have retained energy with no migraines now for several years. They are gone. Now I'm concentrating on healing and letting go of my body's allergies. It will happen! I also fully know and realize I still *need traditional medicine* in my life! I need a balance of both the spiritual world and the world God designed to help all of us, including medicine when vital for health.

So, why did my health decline?

I understand now that I sent emotions and feelings from events over time deep into my subconscious mind. It took years of meditation and searching for understanding to let them surface so I could *let them go*, surrender them, and heal. I first needed to recognize them! But before the healing could take place, my belief had to move into *knowing* I could heal myself. I also realized that I had work to do. God is a constant companion in this process, but for most of us, it is not going to be an instant miracle, nor is it the voice of God talking out loud. In meditation, ask God for guidance.

1. Listen for the answers from within.
2. Watch for information arriving from people that match your intuition.
3. Ask for understanding from God.
4. Put the answers into action.

I needed to solidify my own beliefs to bring inner peace to my soul. It was the realization that God is within each and every one of us waiting for us to *ask* for understanding how to heal. I never understood that concept. Listening for the answers within was *new* to me. Instead I was letting everyone else provide the answers for me. I had to change beliefs in order to heal. I had to first ask for guidance from God and then have a knowing I was getting direction.

Guilt piled on again when I began to ask why I had not shared my experience with others in order to help them. I recognize it was lack of self-confidence in the belief that I had something worthwhile to share. It was *critical* for me to surrender this guilt. And I had finally learned that I needed to accept unconditional love from God for myself as well. I was not perfect, and He's okay with that. Loving myself was the last gift I understood. I lifted huge, heavy emotions over days of meditating and saying, "Here it is God! I'm surrendering these to you." There were a lot of tears. When I forgave myself, I was a lighter, healthier, and more loving human being. We have to love ourselves before we have enough love to give away to all those we care about! Now, I still remind myself with the beautiful painting of a tiny baby sloth sitting in my meditation space that life is a *slow* journey to become more loving to *everyone*. I no longer question that I moved out of the continuum of time, looking into the incredible eyes of a very tiny baby sloth. And he still reminds me that we were meant to have fun and enjoy everything life has to offer, not spend time in fear and doubt. Good health holds a key to enjoying the world we create for ourselves.

I witness many people experiencing *fear* of God. Sometimes churches emphasize a judgmental and vengeful God. If you believe in God, you go to heaven, but *only* if you act and do things a certain way. *That was not in my belief system any longer.* The God I met in my NDE was nonjudgmental, wanting us to be the love that He shared. Love greeted me and enveloped me in a total unconditional love. I can feel that love every time I meditate, read, sleep, and live freely.

I have never been afraid to die again ... that released me from so much fear! For years, I still had fears of other types and phobias. I am now able to take note of them, make use of any messages they might bring, but then let them go free of judgment. I uncovered huge emotions that resulted from the trauma of my car accident that produced my NDE. Those took time to release and let go. I have taken judgment of others out of my life now, and it has freed me to bring compassion and understanding to all people, including myself. I learned compassion through forgiveness. I am frequently in tears over real-life news clips or sappy movies where people help other people! These are tears of love, not sadness, knowing and understanding how connected we are to each other.

It took my own failing health to help me *remember* that I am *not* my body. I liked the way Dr. David Hawkins helped me in his book *Letting Go: Pathway of Surrender* by saying that, "The body is not the real self; it is like a puppet controlled by the mind."[35] *From my NDE, I knew my mind was not my body*; my mind was operating, remembering and reasoning when I was not in my body at all. Our soul does not die. My body was not present. I began asking the question, does one life include the past, present, and future? Death is an illusion. In recent years, Dr. David Hawkins, Dr. Norm Shealy, Dr. Joe Dispenza, Dr. Wayne W. Dyer, Dr. Deepak Chopra, and so many others helped me put together pieces of my life puzzle. I began to understand some of the mystic events that happened in my life that I could never express to people because I did not understand the

---

[35]   David R. Hawkins, MD, PhD, *Letting Go: The Pathway of Surrender* (Carlsbad, CA: Hay House, Inc., 2012), 295.

science behind what was happening with my body. My health story was a journey that brought deep understanding to the words *mind, body, and spirit*. We hear these words often, but do we incorporate all three in our daily life? We cannot separate them even if we try. Science proves more and more that the spirit or the divine by any name exists. All of us are caught in a shift of human consciousness; science is our pathway to understanding ourselves connected to God and all humanity.

Following my NDE, I was profoundly changed, but in the early years, I was struggling to understand healing. In the beginning, I just assumed that "healing ourselves" meant that somewhere on earth there were medicines that would cure any of our illnesses. I still believe this is true. I also thought it meant that with enough research and learning, the medical profession would come up with cures for every disease. This is becoming a reality, and history is showing the tremendous progress that has been made in this field. But I now realize that my NDE message meant so much more.

I remembered the amazing things from university professors teaching our workshop students in the Amazon about science and life with our groups. I was searching for truths that put the pieces of the healing puzzle together. The spiritual key proved critical to the whole process.

I experienced unique mind-expanding truths during deep meditation over a period of years listening to shamans demonstrate their healing techniques. I never understood completely where this knowledge was coming from until the past three years when I realized it was coming from within me, connecting with the universal mind through God as my consciousness level was expanding. Growth came through making connections to experiences in my life I could not explain at the time they happened. The more we learn, the more we are *able* to learn!

A shaman uses not only medicinal plants but musical sounds and chants to go into a deep subconscious state. He is considered a spiritual guide, teacher, and doctor. In Amazonian culture, they are called a *curandero* or medicine man. Even in the 1990s they referred to themselves as shamans. These ancient traditions from indigenous people are embedded in one form or another all over our world, including our own Native American culture. I was looking and listening for their healing wisdom. I began to grow in understanding as I traveled worldwide to experience other cultures and hear their stories and legends about healing. Kenya brought new and different stories. But when I listened carefully, they contained the strong spiritual connection and mind control to open communication with the divine. Each used various music, chanting, and hand motions to help engage their mind. All of them used a deep meditative state to receive their information. I began reading from experts in the field of spirituality, science, psychology, neurology, and medicine. Experts in all of these fields were helping me form a picture in my mind of healing. Going to the Amazon for ten years gave me huge insights into the world of shamanistic healing, which was validated by stories from around the world. It's only in recent years I began reading and hearing about professionals who believe these ancient traditions are a *very* valuable resource. I began making connections with my NDE experience as I realized the altered state the shamans put themselves into could be achieved in different ways besides mind-altering plant substances. It was the deep meditative state. I had learned how to achieve this deep state, as have countless others worldwide.

Spirit is a very important, vital part of their success, actually providing answers to the shaman about which plant to use and how. I now realize they were asking God for help and receiving answers. Though their methods were different, they were putting themselves into a deep meditative state using plants and using the same universal mind through God! But plants were only one part in three. Plants helped the body, but what about the mind and spirit? They were not successful without all three. Our mind only appears to be part of the body. I already knew from my NDE, our minds work independently of our body. Spirit or God was critical in shamanistic healing; it is *just as critical* for us as individuals trying to heal. Another step in my understanding was that every one of us has the ability, but very few people actually believe or recognize it. It is only recently that shamans are sharing the same thought. For centuries it was believed that only the shaman could contact the spirit for guidance. But now they are helping others realize that the power is from within each person. Their methods may be different, but there is a lot in common. An individual can achieve the same results.

I now use meditation every day to help keep my body in the best shape it can be. Any of us can have a life-challenging event in a heartbeat. I'm working hard to make sure I can take on any challenge sent my way with a positive, proactive practice! We *need* medicine at critical times, and we are so fortunate for modern medical practices in trauma and life-threatening disease. But we might not realize the harmful effects of many often-prescribed medications. Modern medicine has made amazing progress, and we need to listen to it all. But I have opened my mind to new paths to health and healing. We have found there is incredible information out there for us but only if we are willing to trust in our intuition and not let limiting beliefs get in our way. Read something that expresses new thought! Neuroscientists tell us it stimulates our brain's waves, alters the pathways, and creates new ones. We are all on a journey to better ourselves as human beings. Why not be healthier while we do it! Are you convinced that the epidemic of heart disease, cancer, diabetes, asthma, arthritis, and others is caused only by environmental catastrophes or poor diet? Is it possible that our own minds can be causing disease too? If we add environmental issues and poor diet to that mix? Not a great thought.

Marj and I imagine a world filled with happy, healthy, loving, and peaceful people. We can start with ourselves, letting our loving and caring ways ripple across the world. It sounds so simple, "Don't let ourselves fall into the negativity around us!" Our thoughts are *real vibrational energy.* Science has proven that we catch these vibrations from people around us, and we share ours with others. Which vibrations do you join? We can join the millions of people interested in world peace and harmony through love and understanding God's planned diversity, or we can choose to dwell in the negative and find lots of company there.

Many others in our world share this same vision, one individual at a time *connecting* and spreading knowledge with others in every corner of our world. The biggest question for all of us is, *how* do we achieve our goals using love and compassion? When our health is wonderful and the sun seems to be shining in our lives, we love our lives. Then some part of our world comes crashing down upon us, or we lose our health one way or another. The way to cope with our life challenges and still maintain health has been a challenge for people all over the world ever since man arrived on the planet. *Health* is all encompassing. We need *health* in our bodies. Our emotional *health* is critical. Marj and I believe our spiritual life holds a key to *health*, opening doors for us as humans living an earthly life in a vessel we call our body. We need *health* in our spiritual lives to work together with our mind and body. Our soul is guiding us in ways we never understood years ago, even though we always had a strong belief in God. What changed in us to bring peace, better health, and understanding? We opened our mind to all possibilities and kept on learning!

Over years in my teaching career, and in my search to understand my NDE, I was also studying and absorbing literature written by medical scientists explaining brain function. Marj and I had the privilege of hearing Dr. Joe Dispenza talk during Hay House's I Can Do It! Workshop in Ft. Lauderdale, Florida, in 2014. In his book, *Breaking The Habit of Being Yourself,* [36] he provides a very understandable view of brain function and what happens in our brains when we meditate. He uses neuroscience and quantum physics to show us how our brain functions and how we can change old patterns! Here are some concepts that helped us process and understand healing.

- The total brain is made up of about 5 percent conscious mind and 95 percent subconscious mind.

---

[36] Dr. Joe Dispenza, *Breaking the Habit of Being Yourself: How to Lose Your Mind and Create a New One* (Carlsbad, California: Hay House, 2012).

- About 5 percent of our mind is trying to use logic and reasoning to form our intentions!
- Our subconscious mind (95 percent of our brain!) holds our positive and negative emotions building since childhood. Layers of emotions of unworthiness, anger, fear, shame, self-doubt, guilt, and fear are trapped inside this mind.
- Our brains move from the beta state (fastest and highest) to delta state (slowest and lowest).
- Meditation can take us out of the beta state and into the alpha and theta brain wave states. It is there we can uncover negative emotions "stuck" in our subconscious.
- Once we recognize and release these emotions, our brain functions can become balanced and highly integrated. Imbalance facilitates disease.

Dr. Dispenza now has a new book, *You Are the Placebo*, suggesting scientifically we can change our health through thoughts. We all harbor fear, anxiety, and painful emotions in our bodies. Do we know how to remove them?

Dr. David Hawkins, MD, PhD, in *Power vs. Force*, uses a table to show us these same emotions explaining our various levels of consciousness. He was an amazing and brilliant mind helping to explain these same brain functions and why many people operate in the beta state most of their lives, often through ignorance, poverty, and hunger. The anger that breeds in this state brings violence to so many places in our world. Marj and I have studied and read his work for years. He has another book titled *Healing and Recovery* in which he offers *knowledge* helping us understand how and why our brains can help or hinder our physical health. His last book written before he died is called *Letting Go: The Pathway of Surrender*. He tells his own story of healing from extremely complex and devastating illnesses. It is one of the most powerful accounts of self-healing we have ever read. He also shares how very difficult it is to change our behaviors to bring about healing. It is one of the most powerful guides to letting go. I had not read this book until after I healed and after we began writing this book. He helped me understand it was my letting go continuously that most likely helped most during my healing. Dr. Hawkins has touched our lives in incredible ways. His writing can be very difficult to understand, but it is always worth the effort. Dr. Dispenza, in his book, *Breaking the Habit of Being Yourself*, gives us the very practical step-by-step process to help all of us do the work.

As you read our NDE research in chapter 8, you will find Dr. Eben Alexander and Jill Bolte Taylor, PhD, brain researchers, who are paving the way for new ideas to emerge and be scientifically proven. Dr. Eben Alexander was an atheist whose NDE changed his life, bringing him back to share his incredible knowledge of the brain threaded with a new spirituality in his life.

There are amazing people out there releasing new books every day! Look up Dr. Lissa Rankin, MD, in a book called *Mind Over Medicine: Scientific Proof That You Can Heal Yourself.* [37] You can visit *Norman Shealy's* website to read about the curing power of energy and spirituality, or buy any of his many books. He's an icon that started his studies back in the sixties when alternative medicine was not so popular. Carolyn Myss and Norman Sealy wrote a book together called *The Creation of Health*[38] that is excellent. They are both very well respected in the field of health. Dr. Dharma Singh Khalsa, who wrote *Meditation as Medicine,* wrote a newer book called *Food as Medicine* that combines spiritual health with healthy eating habits. Dr. Alexander Loyd, who wrote *The Healing Codes,* has a newer one as well called *Beyond Willpower: From Stress to Success in 40 Days.* If your interest takes you into current shamanistic thought, you might look up *A Shaman's Miraculous Tools for Healing* by Alberto Villoldo. And be sure to go to our website, www.thelightgap.com. We are keeping our Health and Healing section up to date with new resources available to you.

---

[37]   Lissa Rankin, MD, *Mind Over Medicine: Scientific Proof That You Can Heal Yourself* (Carlsbad, California: Hay House, Inc., 2013).

[38]   Caroline Myss, PhD, and C. Norman Shealy, MD, *The Creation of Health: The Emotional, Psychological, and Spiritual Responses That Promote Health and Healing* (New York, NY: Crown Publishers, Inc., 1993).

Through experience, study, and personal knowledge, Marj and I have developed a workshop to help participants understand the healing process through shared stories and information about how to let go of our emotional attachments that are damaging our health. We work with the group, teaching basic meditation techniques along with practice, guiding the participant to try energy medicine. There are many resources and opportunities for classes available in most any community. We encourage you to just take *one step at a time* and just *begin*! Health is an ongoing process. Start with something that appeals to you; your own guidance will begin to take over, and you will have put yourself on a path leading to quality health, and perhaps prevent future illness. You might start simply by having a mind that is open to new possibilities.

I opened my mind many years ago. Daily I am amazed when new learning literally falls into my lap. I *did not* recognize that I still had a piece of healing that was yet to come as I was finishing the writing of this book. What happened next took me totally by surprise. Within three weeks of closing the notebook on our final manuscript, I decided to return to Shelbyville, Tennessee, where my NDE occurred, to reconnect with friends and see if any details or feelings had been placed in my subconscious that were important. Another piece of the healing puzzle occurred! It was mid-April, 2016. There were details I wished I could remember ...

I felt drawn to make this trip. I was hearing that internal voice saying, "Go!" But I had no idea it was going to be wrapped in days of amazing "coincidences" providing lost information and lost memories, all gently guided through amazing people in a town I had left years ago. I had wonderful memories of living in Shelbyville prior to the accident and the years that followed. Details filled themselves in easily as I talked with people, walked the streets, sat in the First Presbyterian Church that was my church home back then, and visited familiar places. The NDE itself was already "crystal clear," complete with even the tiniest details. But the days following the return into my body and being rushed to a second hospital were a total blank for me. I had not even *one* detail in memory of the eight days I spent in

Baptist Hospital in Nashville following emergency surgery. I couldn't even remember coming home, which always bothered me. And I had only very faded memories of the three- to four-month period following my return to my Shelbyville home, a home we loved.

Through amazing synchronistic events, the stamina of special friends, and a lawyer who was a personal friend as well, I uncovered a file I never knew was significant in my journey to understand my NDE. I had a lawsuit filed against me by the driver of the truck I tried in vain to miss. I had no idea of the significance of this lawsuit until April 2016 as I read the file of my life thirty-four years ago. It confirmed that I was not at fault, but I had forgotten the trauma it brought to me at the very same time I was piecing together memories of my NDE. I couldn't begin to put meaning into the experience at that point because I had no idea people had ever experienced God like I had. As I read my own words in a deposition included in the file, I *remembered* being terrified I would mention that I had been with God in incredible love … allowing all involved to think I was nuts. I had totally repressed *all* of these memories and emotions. I began the process of running away from my NDE, tucking it inside for future thought. I also found complete health records from my accident, which I thought I'd never see again. While I felt the trauma the day I read the file, it quickly turned to peace, which was interesting to me. It took processing over days to understand why I was feeling peace and calm while remembering trauma. I am thankful for the role the driver played in my life, the person who filed that lawsuit, and the lawyer who kept my file. If records of this magnitude had not existed, my memories might have remained buried and my journey very much altered. There are no coincidences.

I was standing in my old home through the kindness of the current gracious and caring owner. The gazebo brought memories of lying in a lawn chair recuperating, watching the kids play as flashbacks of my out-of-body experience kept emerging. What peace and calm I felt as I remembered. Even viewing the accident site brought peace. I met the grandson of the lovely lady who sat under a tree calming my children waiting for their father to arrive to drive them to the hospital to make sure they were okay. I had a visual picture of that scene because caring ambulance drivers made sure I saw it as they loaded my stretcher into the ambulance. I never knew who these people were. I now have names as well as memories. I was feeling peace, not trauma.

I was standing alone early in the morning in front of the old Bedford County Hospital building where my NDE had occurred. I was staring at a beautiful blue sky that outlined the distinct roofline, when I was then able to interweave the God within and the God that is in everything creating a scene. It was a picture put together for me to see that day. God is there for us when we need Him. I was startled as an ambulance drove in right beside me, heading for the side of the building. It was after staring at it that I noticed off to one side right next to the beautiful blue sky was a dark, swirling cloud infused with grays. Right in the center was a huge hole where the sun was shining through, reminding me of the tunnel I went through, reaching the incredible white light and hearing the love-infused sounds I heard that day. My memories were returning, triggered by my emotions and feelings. I pictured the kids running over to my car throwing their arms around me as Doug brought me home, and I knew exactly why there was still a large blank space in the memory that traversed months.

A pattern emerged that morning. I realized that both in the hospital and as I returned home after the accident, part of me was still with God. It was a retreat from the realities of life so to speak. I found amazing *love* and memories *within*. I had to merge back into this realm of my bodily life a little at time. The blanks in my life will stay blank; my method of escape is fascinating and relevant to understanding God and *life*. I had memories of being able to go "back" to God. And yet I had every reason to *live*. I had a wonderful, loving husband and two beautiful children that needed me. In the end, it was my decision. We have free will. I didn't know it at the time, but I was to have another boy, just as treasured and precious as my first two. I was remembering an inability to make the transition.

I realized we are capable of having a piece of our self in each realm, and I believe I did that for three or four months even though no one would have noticed. I was functioning, and in fact my doctor was telling me I was healing with incredible speed. God is with us no matter *where* we are. In deep meditation today, I realize we can all go to that place of love and be with God, and our conscious level can stay with us in the present realm at the same time. This is where *healing takes place, infused in love*. We receive help as we journey in this body, a very necessary, temporary vessel our soul is occupying.

I uncovered the memory of "running away" from my NDE. I thought if I buried those memories, life would return to "normal." I did not recognize any of this in 1982. The history of my growth has now been shared as you journeyed into this book. Did I really think I could run away from God? What a humorous thought now!

Ultimately, every experience I have had since brought me to a very full, wonderful life. It is rich with experiences and has brought me to a better understanding of how life works. All through my NDE long ago! God's plan for sure. Believing that I am able to have a piece of myself in each realm has started a new pathway for me to explore in years to come. I am thankful I followed an intuition, making the trip to Shelbyville, Tennessee. I was being guided by that mysterious force we call God.

Love can bring healing into *your* life. We share our stories and the wisdom that has emerged from events in our lives to help in some small, humble way. We hope you will be open to engage in meaningful dialogue with a friend who just might be looking for you! I have such a friend that encouraged me to tell my story ... to just a few book club friends. And now it is shared with all of you through my writing, which is bringing more healing into my soul. Thank you, Mary.

Chapter 7

Children's Spirituality and Education

I feel so fortunate to have given birth to three precious children. When you look into their eyes, hear their beating heart, and feel their energy, you realize what an incredible miracle they are. All children are a gift. It is new life coming into the world to journey with us. We do not own these children. The children that are a part of our family are not just ours. Nothing is more important than giving them a good foundation. As parents, we are charged with guiding them into adulthood, and we will always be connected. A spiritual truth is that *we are all connected, we are all one.* So we are destined to share our children with the world. Children embody our hopes for the world's future, just as we did as children and continue to do with each choice we make each day.

Important to any conversation about the spirituality of children is the understanding that children come to life with a unique set of birthright gifts and talents. They are not empty vessels to be filled; they have potential that is ready to be nourished. *All* children grow and unfold like beautiful flowers, as the "soil" of life is fertile. Each child is as unique as a snowflake. In this time in history, we have become more spiritually conscious. We have new insights into what the rich, fertile soil must contain. Foremost, our children need to understand the spiritual dimensions of the world we all live in. If parents try to make a child into something they were not meant to be,

124

or try to make them bloom faster than they are ready to grow, their life will be more challenging.

Parents naturally want to shield children from harm, and we can do much to create a healthy environment in which they can prosper and grow. We can do our best to keep them safe and to enrich their lives. There is a huge variety of possibilities for creating the "rich soil" for life. What children need is a topic that fills many books! In this book, Terry and I will offer suggestions related to the spiritual part of life. Religious experiences that concentrate on love and not fear offer children very important life guidance. We suggest that no matter what name you give the divine, what path you follow, developing the spiritual elements of life is key.

A Few Spiritual Concepts

So what do children really need to know? What is the end goal children and grown-up children are aiming for?

First of all, *life is meant to be an experience of love and joy.* Life is not meant to be a struggle. Children know this. They smile and laugh very early in life, and they make us laugh. They are full of hugs. They play. They use their imaginations. They are exuberant. These feelings, this instinct for love and joy, need to be encouraged and allowed to grow, not dampened.

Second, *children are three-part beings: mind, body, and soul.* Children are here on earth having a body experience in this life. They need to know that they are not just their bodies. Their soul is their consciousness, their spirit, the source of instinctive impulses. Their bodies are the vessel that contain their soul and are very important. Children need to learn to take care of it so that it stays healthy and strong. As a child, and as a parent, it never occurred to me that I was not just my body. So it restricted my ability to share this insight with my children. Bodies eventually wear out, but the part we call the soul is what lives on.

Third, there is an *inner self that connects us to a guidance system.* Many special people, experiences, and opportunities come to all of us in life. Their *feelings* are a language of the soul, ready to give guidance. How does it feel? becomes a key question. Children can learn to ask and listen for suggestions. It is an inner support system. They can learn to become *aware*, to pay attention to that inner talk where new thoughts, new ideas, and dreams come into their consciousness. I believe that God put all we need into place at the time of creation. Our children require our love, attention, guidance, and our ability to listen for *their* wisdom coming from within them, and they need to learn to follow their instincts. Yes, all children will experience difficulties. With a shift in perspective, these challenges can help them make new choices that keep them closer to their built-in experience of happiness.

Fourth, *no one is perfect, but ultimately, all of us are perfect in God's eyes.* We are here to remember that this is so. God is love, and love is always offered, no matter if we succeed or fail. We make judgments; God does not. We are accepted just as we are. Humans are not always able to give this kind of unconditional love, but God does. We are never alone. The pressures are great in our society to be the smartest, to be the best, to own physical things. Children need to know they just need to be themselves. When they are truthful and responsible, others around them will trust them. Forgiveness is always possible. The goal is for children to know unconditional love. Children need this message spoken and experienced often so they are free to try new things and try again if it does not work out. Failure can act as a frame of reference, especially for older children, teens, and young adults. If the young person is doing their best, it is not failure. It is something that didn't work. It gives them an opportunity to try another way. Are their choices working? If not, they have the power to make new choices and cocreate what does work for them.

Fifth, *thoughts are very creative tools.* Things children think and say are powerful. In order to make life full of joy, we need to have the tools to help us change our perspective, to try out new insights, to listen to our intuitive built-in guidance system. Knowing how powerful our thoughts are is such a tool. Children benefit greatly by understanding that thoughts carry energy. It is like the children's book *The Little Engine that Could* by Watty Piper. The little, less powerful engine kept saying, "I think I can, I think I can," and he was the one with enough energy to get the train up the mountain. What we think about all the time draws it to us. Louise Hay talks about this in her children's book *I Think, I AM!* "When a child says something over and over, they begin to believe it is true. What you believe creates what you do and what happens to you."[39] Children can learn to create what they want with their thoughts as well as their actions. Louise Hay's book calls them affirmations and teaches children how to use them. Examples: "I love myself just the way I am. I learn from my mistakes and move on." They have to learn too that negative thoughts keep what they don't want coming to them! Positive thoughts are a higher vibrational energy than negative thoughts. When children are peaceful, they radiate peaceful energy. When they are stressed, angry, or depressed, they radiate a lower vibrational energy. Understanding this use of thoughts, combined with their power of choice, children can begin to have power over what they experience.

Sixth, *begin to ask, and the doors will be opened. Use your imagination to visualize* what you want to create. This is the message of a biblical text that is found in all four gospels and other places in the Bible. Since Anne's death, I have been trying to understand what I experienced and why I had a LIGHT experience, dreams, and so many coincidences. I was reassured by these experiences that Anne was living in some form. All of these events over time kept me growing instead of giving up. At the publishing of this book, I will have been working on this question for twenty years. Ultimately the answer was easy. I *asked God* for help, and I received it! For some reason, I was not angry with God but leaning on Him for dear life. He provided good support. In my research, many authors spoke of the law of attraction and helped me to believe that this Bible passage is solid information. I have experienced the results of asking. However,

---

[39]   Louise L. Hay, *I Think, I AM! Teaching Kids the Power of Affirmations* (Carlsbad, CA: Hay House, Inc., 2008), 2.

it is still mysterious. It seems that not all requests are answered, but perhaps it comes in a way we are not expecting. I was not expecting to be consumed in LIGHT and told I would write a book. So, help children learn to ask for what they can imagine or envision, through prayer, meditation, mindfulness, or just while being quiet. God communicates with all people, and that definitely includes children. The child's job is to listen for God's voiceless voice. It comes in many forms.

I feel that "ask and you will receive" is related to the use of our imaginations. The two need to be put together. Children have such freedom as they use their imaginations freely. It is a built-in system. It is another example of children knowing, when we have forgotten. I have always believed that the continued development of our imagination is so important. It is what we use to create! It is what we use to envision something new. It is what Thomas Edison used to create electric lights. It is what the Wright brothers used to build the first flying machine. J. K. Rowling's commencement address to the students at Harvard University was put into a book, *Very Good Lives: The Fringe Benefits of Failure and the Importance of Imagination.* J. K. Rowling says this about imagination: "I have learned to value imagination in a much broader sense. Imagination is not only the uniquely human capacity to envision that which is not, and therefore the font of all invention and innovation; in its arguably most transformative and revelatory capacity, it is the power that enables us to empathize with humans whose experiences we have never shared."[40]

There will always be mysteries we do not understand. We observe that many children have severe challenges all of their lives. They may be physical, mental, or situational. We cry out with anguish at the unfairness. We ask God why this is so, but some life mysteries defy answers. I do believe that *everything* has a purpose in *life*. I do not know or understand the purpose of challenged children and adults.

---

[40] J. K. Rowing, *Very Good Lives* (New York: Little, Brown, and Company: Hachette Book Group, 2008), 41.

As I often do, I turn to *Conversations with God: Book 1* for help in understanding. I found an interesting discussion that helped me work through the whys of children born with such mental and physical limitations. If this question is on your heart, I think you would benefit by reading *Conversations with God: Book 1.*[41]

However, as part of understanding, let me introduce Marshall Stewart Ball, author of the book *Kiss of God: The Wisdom of a Silent Child.* He has great physical challenges and is amazing. He is a child who is spiritually guided. At three and a half, Marshall began to communicate by pointing his head at a homemade alphabet board. At age five, he spelled out on his alphabet board: "Altogether Lovely. God is altogether good and merciful because He is also bright and intelligent. Seeing, feeling all that is true. Clearly He feels listens to all our hearts and desires. Clearly he has everybody's dreams in mind. I see a God altogether lovely."[42] Does this sound like a five-year-old you know? As Marshall grew, he continued to talk about God pouring out love and acceptance for all. He can neither speak nor walk, but his wisdom abounds.

There is a spiritual connection here. These wonderful children are family members; they come through our schools, churches, synagogues, and temples and often show amazing resiliency and birthright gifts. The challenged children often call forth in us unexplainable feelings of love, compassion, patience, and understanding. Our devotion to them inspires the doubtful people who observe from a far. God's energy is pulsing through them. The presence of imperfection forces us to trust in the interdependent needs of us all and to trust that the universe knows what it is doing. All children are valuable. We are harming the whole community when we do not make sure that all children get what they need. It is like the Shawnee tribe's version of the golden rule I found in the book *The Golden Rule* by Ilene Cooper, "Do not injure your neighbor, for

---

[41]   Neal Donald Walsch, *Conversations with God: Book 1* (New York: G.P. Putman's Sons, 1996), 45–47.

[42]   Marshall Stewart Ball, *Kiss of God: The Wisdom of a Silent Child* (Deerfield, Florida: Health Communications, Inc., 1999), xvii.

it is not he or she that you injure; you injure yourself."[43] *We are all connected. We are all one.*

Photo by Carol Miller

I had an amazing experience during a guided art meditation. I was spending a week at the GilChrist Retreat Center in Michigan writing social-emotional curriculum for children. During the meditation, I had a vision, but I had trouble clarifying my vision. It was bothering me; somehow I knew I needed to know what was in this vision. As I was having a meaningful conversation later in the week with a woman I met at the community building, I mentioned my struggle to clarify my vision. She responded, "Was it a web?" I immediately had a clear picture of the web. That was it. It was another of those amazing coincidences ... a gift. It gave me a visual picture to use with children to explain the concept: *We are all connected. We are all one.* What we do affects the people around us. Recently after meditating, I wrote this: Spiritual life is like a spider web. God is in the center, and all is woven into a beautiful, interconnected web of life. There are connection points, there are common paths, but each of us is part of the whole. Each of us is unique and essential to the integrity of the

---

[43]   Ilene Cooper, *The Golden Rule* (New York: Abrams Books for Young Readers, 2007), 15.

web. A few anchor the web. All is a delicate but extremely strong, interdependent, whole. Within what appears to be chaos is an elegant pattern, which includes *every* soul. I share this photo that my friend Carol Miller allowed me to use. She is an amazing photographer. This whole experience is an example of how God's great web works in our lives.

Scientific Research

One of the oldest debates in the history of the field of psychology is nature versus nurture. Is it the child's environment that is the strongest influence in children's development, or is it the child's genes? Bruce Lipton, PhD, is a cell biologist, researcher, and lecturer. His work is current and important. He has worked on cloning and examining the principles of quantum physics related to understanding the cell's processing systems. Research into the cell's membrane shows that each cell has a "chip" that is equivalent to a brain. A new scientific discipline called epigenetics has developed out of Lipton's work. Other researchers have verified his concepts and ideas. Also, he is on the leading edge of connecting mind-body medicine and spiritual principals.

Lipton put out a DVD called *Nature, Nurture and the Power of Love*.[44] This DVD is an experiential lecture, friendly for those with little science background. I appreciated the models he used to make the information clear. He states that what drives the body system is *not* the genes. New findings have shown that we are personally responsible, giving us control. Cells work as a community. This research emphasis points out the importance of people working together in community also. Biologists have discovered that each cell has all the intelligence of the body. Our community of cells comes together *to share*. It has to do with proteins and amino acids and genes working together. If we are experiencing stress and fear,

---

[44] Dr. Bruce H. Lipton, PhD, *Nature, Nurture and the Power of Love: The Biology of Conscious Parenting*, DVD (Murfreesboro, TN: Spirit 2000, Inc., 2002).

the connections made between the proteins and amino acids are misshapen. When we are experiencing love and calm and love, they form correctly. Bottom line, the control of our biology is from the outside, not the inside of the body!

Why is this important? Because it is our perception or *awareness* of what we are experiencing in our environment that is the biological switch or signal that turns the genes off and on. *Your perception of your environment is controlling your body functions.* The choices we make related to what we are experiencing matter. Providing life's essentials for our youngest members, our infants, toddlers, and preschool children, increases their mind and body's healthy growth. Providing inadequate forms of care and learning environments puts our children at risk right from the start. Their biological systems will go into survival mode, producing *inadequate growth*. His work helps us understand how important loving environments are to children— and for all of us. Angry and toxic faces and experiences for children slow their growth. Positive involvement in family and the broader community provides healthy growth. The spiritual implications are extensive. Love is an actual energy, a high-frequency energy. Love makes a difference no matter what the life circumstances.

David Hawkins, MD, PhD, was a psychiatrist and researcher. In his book *Power vs. Force: The Hidden Determinants of Human Behavior*,[45] he talks about a scale of vibrational energy that he researched and created. The development of computers enabled him to deal with huge amounts of data, which was key to his research. "It became clear that the calibrated levels correlate with specific processes of consciousness—emotions, perceptions or attitudes, worldviews and spiritual beliefs."[46] Terry and I find Hawkins work fascinating. It helped me understand *why people act the way they do* and why children act the way *they* do. It also helps me understand why it is so important to help children understand the spiritual concepts

---

[45]   David Hawkins, MD, PhD, *Power vs. Force: The Hidden Determinants of Human Behavior* (Carlsbad, CA: Hay House, 2002), 68–69.

[46]   David Hawkins, MD, PhD, *Power vs. Force: The Hidden Determinants of Human Behavior* (Carlsbad, CA: Hay House, Inc., 2002), 67.

that undergird the life we live here on earth. This chart is based on the knowledge that everything emits energy, either positive or negative. We intuitively know the difference between a positive and a negative person. Another concept that Hawkins explains is that like energy clumps or collects. I believe these are two very important concepts. It is why, when we are in a group of people for a meeting, the positive ideas and actions being given to a topic can change to negative as the result of one or two negative responses. The same happens when children are working or playing together. It is worthwhile viewing his chart and reading the background information. If you find this interesting, you might be interested in his last book before his death in 2012 called *Letting Go*.[47] I find this book easy to read and a review of much of his earlier work. He has a CD set called *Realization of God*.[48] It is a lecture that Terry and I attended in 2003. It was a joy listening to this man. He laughs spontaneously throughout his lecture.

Helpful Ideas and Connections

Parents, teachers, coaches, and caretakers need to recognize the *whole child* as they are working with children. Often they are inviting the brain and skill set of the child to show up and inviting the spiritual part of the child to stay dormant. Children also need the *whole adult* to show up as they are working with them. Parker Palmer talks about adults living a "divided life." This process of dividing our lives usually begins as children go off to school. We feel that we need to keep our spiritual lives separate from our secular lives. "We hide our beliefs from those who disagree with us to avoid conflict, challenge, and change. This dividedness can become pathology, a problem hard to solve."[49] I was invited by the Winnetka Public Schools, where I

47   David Hawkins, MD, PhD, *Letting Go: The Pathway of Surrender* (Carlsbad, CA: Hay House, Inc., 2012).

48   David Hawkins, MD, PhD, *The Realization of God* (Chicago: CD set presented at Transformations Learning Center, 2003).

49   Parker J. Palmer, *A Hidden Wholeness: The Journey Toward an Undivided Life* (San Francisco: Jossey-Bass, 2004), 6.

was teaching, to take part in a two-year experience of Courage to Teach. The creation of this opportunity was sponsored by the Fetzer Institute, and is the work of Parker Palmer and others who became facilitators. Those who chose to participate formed a circle of trust that met for a two-and-a-half-day retreat each season. It is important work. It has helped me be "divided no more." Our spirit and role belong together. Later work with Courage to Lead helped give me the courage to write this book with Terry! All that we can do to help children keep their life passions (role) and their souls working together will make a significant difference in our world.

My teaching experience tells me that children often begin to hide their truths and beliefs during the primary grades. It appears to happen as a protective act, to keep themselves free of teasing and as an attempt to fit into the culture. Unfortunately, this discourages spiritual growth. When Anne died, one of her college-age friends told me that she used to believe in the significance of her nighttime dreams until she began high school. At that point, she was studying science, and those studies convinced her to let go of believing in the substance of her dreams. Let me share a couple of stories from children in my first-grade classes that illustrate this point.

> One day I became frustrated with the two girls in my first-grade class who were best of friends and were always talking when they should be listening. We were in the process of gathering at the rug for a math lesson. "Helen, why do you have to talk to Judy all the time?" "But, Mrs. Steiner, we were in heaven together before we came here. We used to play together in the clouds."

I have to admit her comment stopped me in my tracks. This wonderful, full-of-life child was talking about heaven. It just "fell out" naturally. So why didn't I just as naturally return the ball of the conversation and say, "Tell me all about that. I would love to hear more about your life before you came to this life." Why didn't that happen? I was

134

definitely very interested! Another day, I had more wisdom. I tried hard to help Rebecca stay with her truth.

Our first-grade class was sitting on the rug together ready to listen to Rebecca's "published book." She sat excitedly in the author's chair and began to read her story about her imaginary friend. The kids were excited too because she was such a good artist and storyteller. They loved her drawings. She was the go-to person if someone wanted help with their drawing. Rebecca began to read. The story told of her imaginary friend who came to see her every Monday. They would jump on the bed and talk and have a wonderful time together. She went on with more details. It was so well illustrated. The braids on the imaginary friend were flying up into the air. The joy both children were experiencing was drawn in their faces. The class was getting restless. One of her classmates raised his hand. He asked if this girl was real or imaginary because the experience she was sharing was so real. She turned around and looked at me. I was sitting right next to her. Her facial expression told me that she was looking for guidance, reassurance … and perhaps the courage to tell the truth. I encouraged her to tell them what she believed. She turned back to the class and spoke her intuitive knowing. "My friend is real. She comes every Monday, and we play." She continued to read. There were more details, more excitement in her voice. Another child's hand went up and asked again, "Is your friend really real?" She looked at the kids, she looked at me, back at the kids, then back to me. Finally, she looked back at the kids and said. "It's my imaginary friend."

What is going on here? The spiritual part of these young children is active and spilling out. I am willing to believe that imaginary friends are real. Rebecca needed extra love. Her two-year-old brother had died unexpectedly the year before. We need to remember that spiritual experiences are *normal* for all of us. Sometimes we as parents, grandparents, teachers, or religious leaders think that teaching is the only way that children are going to know about God. This is just not true. They are telling us about the memories they have of the place of pure *love*—their source—the place or realm that they have left to join us here on earth. They may be being helped in a difficult time. What I know is that children are not empty vessels that need filling up. They are full of passions, personality, and possibilities at birth. And there is more to their young lives than you might think. I say again, all that we can do to help children keep their life passions (role) and their souls working together will make a significant difference in our world.

Luckily there are many books and other resources that have been written for children that help them interpret and understand spiritual concepts. They are great conversation starters. This will be just a short list to get you started. There is a full list of the books we have used on our website www.thelightgap.com. Wayne Dyer has written quite a few. I have often used his books *Incredible You! 10 Ways to Let Your Greatness Shine Through, Unstoppable Me! 10 Ways to Soar Through Life,* and *I am: Why Two Little Words Mean So Much, No Excuses! How What You Say Can Get in Your Way* and *You Are Not What You've Got.* Deepak Chopra has a helpful book for children in the elementary upper grades called *On Your Way to a Happy Life.* Recently I discovered Mike Dooley's books *Dreams Come True ... All They Need Is You!* and *Your Magical Life. I Think, I AM: Teaching Kids the Power of Affirmations* by Louise Hay is a very helpful book for understanding affirmations and examples of them. We adults can inspire children to use them. Remember, picture books also help older children (or even adults) understand unfamiliar spiritual concepts. The more the adults surrounding children grow their spirits, the more likely the children close to us will learn to do the same. Older children and teens are ready to take on more ideas and information and often are asking questions. Neale Donald Walsch has recently put out a book called *Conversations with God for Parents: Sharing the Message with Children.* It is a very helpful resource. It is a book for you to consider investigating if you and your children are ready to go deeper.

There is always hope. One of my favorite musicals is *Man of La Mancha.* The character Don Quixote, Knight Errant, can only see the beauty in a barmaid and prostitute he names Dalcinea. It is like God, who only sees the good and beauty in us. The award-winning song "The Impossible Dream" really defines the task we have as parents and educators and spiritual beings. Some of the words encourage us to keep going, even when the going gets rough: dream, fight, run, not hopeless, reach, question, love, quest, heart, peaceful, calm. Keep evolving!

Educational Insights

Terry and I have many years of teaching experience with primary children. I worked alongside my husband often as he worked with junior high and high school youth in the church. Terry and I both took junior high and high school youth to the rain forest in Peru, Terry to Costa Rica, both of us to Kenya, and I took a group to Tanzania. Working with children is rewarding work. With our combined experience, we could write a whole book on what we feel is important in education. Here, I am going to highlight possibilities related to integrating spiritual concepts into educational settings. We are aware of the controversies. The issue is how we can support the *whole child,* allowing their hearts and spirits to be nurtured, without violating family beliefs or separation of church and state. Terry's and my answer is, how can we afford *not* to support the whole child!

Looking at indigenous cultures inspires our thinking. Anthropologists help us understand that North American tribal cultures had different ways of looking at children.[50] The Lakoda tribe considered children as sacred beings. Therefore, they treated them with respect and gentleness. To say that someone was acting like a child, for the Lakoda, meant you were acting like a sacred being. They had childrearing practices that reflected democratic principles. Their goal was to teach courage, not submission. The Europeans that settled our country believed that Native American children were little primitives in need of socialization. Many settlers of European descent considered their children inferior to adults, so that same comment that an adult was acting like a child would be an insult. They brought with them the idea that children had to be punished to bring them into submission. These settlers used a hierarchical, coercion pattern of discipline. We continue to this day the struggle related to our view of who children are.

Children are sacred beings. We all are. They have more recently arrived from a place of pure love, which gave them unrestricted freedom. The adjustment can be difficult. That is one of the reasons babies cry. Our children will thrive when given love, when they are treated in their homes and educational settings with respectful communications and gentle guidance.

In chapter 5, I mentioned *Wisdom from a Rainforest*[51] by Stuart Schlegel. He discovered as he studied the ways of the Teduray people of Figel in the Philippines that they had a "custom" for helping children *be* themselves as well as serve the needs of their community. This society had family groups called "pots," the same as our individual family units of mother, father, and pre-puberty children. They were eating from the same pot. Extended family members, grandparents, great-grandparents, aunts, uncles, and grown cousins were known as the "kindred." The kindred were responsible for watching the children in their growing years to see what talents and passions developed from within each child. When they were old enough, they

[50]   Linda Lantieri, ed., *Schools with Spirit: Nurturing the Inner Lives of Children and Teachers* (Boston: Beacon Press, 2001), 40.
[51]   Stuart A. Schlegel, *Wisdom from a Rainforest: The Spiritual Journey of an Anthropologist* (Athens, Georgia: University of Georgia Press, 1999).

were given tasks in those specialties, first playing the skills, then practicing and developing them into what they liked to do best. They grew naturally into the jobs they did best. Each chose a specialty, such as basket weavers, legal sages, farmers, conflict negotiators, shamans, and so on. Specialties were *not ranked*; they were *valued equally* for their part in *creating success and harmony*. All specialties were felt to be equally important and valued gifts to the community. They worked for their own enjoyment and the well-being of the community. In this forest area, respect was valued, and competition was considered unhealthy.

I suggest that it would be possible in educational settings to observe children on a regular basis as part of evaluating children's progress. It could be a "specialty" staff person's job to observe their school's children over time to record evidence of each child's birthright gifts, passions. It could be a part of a child's running record that followed the child through school. This process would include regular, one-on-one conversations. When it was time for them to begin making decisions about what kind of career they were going to pursue in life, they would have a better idea of their "specialty." It is a good model for creating a world that displays understanding of the uniqueness of each person. It would go a long way to foster resilience and courage in children becoming adults. *The inner life and outer life, the role and soul of children would be more likely to stay together.*

With the spiritual nature of human beings in mind, we plan for children with the goal of helping them make meaning and find purpose in their lives using the child's natural inclination for pushing their growth. This process proceeds from the spiritual inside of each child, rather than just the outside, physical aspects of life. Who they are with others, how they interact in everyday situations, is more important than what they do or what they have. From a spiritual standpoint, we choose to help children be a partner, not a dominator. The adult also does not dominate but is a facilitator, encouraging the wisdom of the children to come out. In educational settings, adult leaders choose experiences and ways of teaching where competition is downplayed. A child's competence is measured by his or her own progress, not by comparison. Everyone's achievements are celebrated, not just the top few. By human nature, we are meant to be a part of communities. We need each. Children need to learn to be interdependent, not dependent.

Characteristics of a School with Spiritual Concepts Embedded

Reggio Emilia from Italy developed an infant and preschool system of daycare/learning centers that has become known worldwide. They developed many methods that take into account the spiritual nature of children. It is a model that can be adapted for all age learners. The school was developed by the community after WWII as they began to rebuild their lives and town. Destruction and tragedy were everywhere. But the spirit of the people was not broken. The theme of our book, *The Light GAP,* uses the analogy of the forest, where the floor of the forest is quite dark. When a tree falls, it often takes others with it, opening up the area to sunlight. New growth comes from seeds planted by nature, waiting in the soil for years for the right conditions to produce new growth. Reggio Emilia had experience great tragedy, but out of that tragedy came new ways of thinking and hope for the children of this town. With God's promise, "ask and you will receive, knock and the doors will be opened," combined with the community's imaginations, the town was rebuilt. All of the children were blessed with excellent care and secure passage of the values of their culture, while both the men and women worked to get their city operational. Information can be found at www.reggiochildren.it. Many YouTube videos are also available showing their work. You immediately are stunned at the quality and complexity of the children's work. A view of their work tells you immediately that the children's work is well beyond what is usually seen in "normal" schools.

Infants and toddlers are hardwired to take in everything around them that they see, hear, and feel. The Reggio approach honors the inside-out approach to learning. It gives even the youngest members freedom of movement and exploration. The teachers are not pouring information into the children; they are drawing the children's observations and reflections out. Children are building their knowledge through experimenting. With the preschoolers, the ideas for projects come from the children. Teachers ask well-developed questions that stimulate their exploration or project. They observe the children's progress and document their reflections, theories, ideas, and opinions. Children can follow an interesting idea for weeks, even months. Each school has an art center at its center, where the children's explore their ideas by drawing, painting, and sculpting. Artwork becomes a tool for communicating their thinking. Reggio's buildings are a form of beauty, constructed to invite discovery. The environment is an essential third teacher; child, teacher, and environment. Rich, large windows provide sunlight. There are art studios, "interesting" objects for inspiring inquiry, materials for expressing their ideas, and nature spaces. The environment invites children to discover explanations for the world around them. Play is the children's mode of work.

Why is this approach to teaching children a form of spiritual expression? It honors the *uniqueness* of each child. It encourages the children to *develop self-knowledge*, out of which they learn to love themselves. When we love ourselves, we can give love to others. There is a strong emphasis on community and cooperation. Dependence is not life giving. God gave us free will. The children make decisions on how they will spend their time, engaged in exploring their ideas and questions. The children are becoming interdependent, able to share their solutions and adjust to new solutions when they see the value of doing so. The children's imaginations thrive. Children's *imaginations and visions* ultimately create a better way to live together and the next best versions of themselves. *Joy, peace, and love* are the vibrations of God. This type of environment allows these energies to thrive.

My hope is that these learning concepts and methods will be brought into schools for all ages. Schools would again be full of windows to bring in light. They would be beautifully designed.

Various learning spaces and workshops would be available within the school. Many forms of materials—scientific lab equipment, mathematical models, computers, building materials, art supplies, and musical instruments—would be available for young people to explore their talents, ideas, and inventions. The practice of documenting their thinking and gathering to share ideas would be part of each day's routine. Essential skill development, such as reading, writing, literature, social studies, math, science, and the arts would be integrated with related projects and discussions. Interest groups would form. Facilitators and students would "dig out" the facts on a topic chosen by the students and teachers together. With the facts presented, the students would use logic and critical thinking skills that had been encouraged for years to begin to express *their opinions* and *their solutions to issues*. How often are children asked what they think? The art of asking questions would be developed and valued. Knowledge would be applied to the important issues of the time. Their intuitive feelings would be honored. All voices would be heard. Students, teachers, and facilitators would work together to come to consensus on the rules of the community. Students' "specialties" would determine children's contributions to the whole. The governing of the school would be decided as needed by the students and adults together.

Does it sound like too much of a dream? I think not. We need to go where often we dare not go. Anything is possible when new ways of thinking are used. We have to ask ourselves, are all of our present-day schools really working? Yes, some are, but many others are not. Rethinking from the bottom up may be needed. The Reggio Emilia schools show us what is possible. Their ability to engage the minds, hearts, and spirits of the children lets us know we are on the right track. I am reminded of Wayne Dyer's book *There Is a Spiritual Solution to Everything.* He suggests that we have to ask the question of what generates life, because that is where the solution lies. So I suggest that we trust in the spiritual nature of our existence and go for it! There is a spiritual solution to education.

Chapter 8

Near-Death Experiences
Death Brought
Understanding of Life

*All Earthly wisdom is but a rehearsal for that great
awakening, an awakening that takes place upon death.*
—Plato

This life is a continuous journey. My life continued even though I
died that day. The International Association for Near-Death Studies
(IANDS) defines an NDE as "a *lucid* experience associated with
perceived consciousness apart from the body occurring at the time
of *actual* or *threatened* death or medical compromise."[52]

Throughout documented history, all religions have shared one
common deep-seated belief: there is life after death. Plato described
Greek soldiers who "died" on the battlefield and then came back.
Every war has stories of dead soldiers who returned to life. Literature
is full of stories of people termed "mystics." Many stories of near death
in early history resulted in persecution because people were thought
to be heretics. So most likely, many NDE accounts were destroyed.
I would find out in my own life, these experiences involving the
divine couldn't be kept inside. I was a shy soul and kept my learned
information within, sharing only with a few. But this was not without

---

[52]   IANDS www.iands.org.

serious consequences. I was literally sending messages of fear to my body rather than love. That was a serious mistake, as you read in my chapter on health and healing.

I have since read countless NDE accounts from published books and on websites spanning twenty-three years. In 1975, Dr. Raymond Moody released his best-selling book, *Life After Life.*[53] Newer versions of his book were released in 2001 and 2015. It was Moody who actually coined the term "near-death experience." Dr. Moody recorded and compared experiences of 150 persons who died, or almost died, and then recovered. His findings are fascinating. I read so many NDE experiences, and each one was unique. I was searching for why they would be so different. For many years, most people expressed a reluctance to tell others of their experiences. They were expressing what I was feeling. Were there appropriate words to describe a physical beauty not found on earth and brilliance wrapped in a coat of pure love? I had a "window" into the afterlife, but would people believe me if I shared my knowledge"

I was talking to myself constantly and maybe not in good ways. Who was *I* to know anything? My thoughts were expanding with knowledge. I did not "fit" into a society that kept science and medical research going but put religion into a box with a lid that was already closed. Inside that box, culture trapped the collective idea that religious institutions already have all the answers. Really? Then, they defied each of us to find the *right* answers. *Close* the lid. They were asking us not to question. And I wanted to know *why* I could only find near-death experiences in libraries or bookstores under sections labeled New Age, Mystic, or Paranormal, all other words for "weird." Did paranormal mean my experience was *not* normal? I didn't think it was very common until I started reading the research. Perhaps you have had these same thoughts and have stayed away from reading books if they were not labeled "Christian." I had grown

53   Raymond A. Moody Jr., MD, *Life After Life: The Investigation of a Phenomenon-Survival of Bodily Death* (NY: Harper Collins Publishers, 1975; San Francisco: Harper San Francisco, 2001; NY: Harper Collins Publishers, 2015).

up in a Christian home. I had experienced events that had expanded my Christian views.

For me, my experiences sent me right to new thought and into those books. I wanted to know what prominent scientists were saying about our universe and how it worked. Did they find God? I wanted to hear stories from prominent physicians who were also beginning to open their minds to new thought. Were they hearing these NDE stories? Did they believe them? I wanted to hear information shared by spiritual leaders across the globe. "God created the heavens and the earth." I had experienced a *oneness* that helped me know that God created *every* human being in love, unconditional love, all across the globe.

Almost all NDE accounts I read expressed the love and peace they found in that realm. Even if a person experienced something negative, they always related the love they felt. NDE experiences happen in every walk of life. It's not an inclusive group of religious people. In fact, every religion in every culture children, atheists, agnostics, and spiritual people with no religious affiliation have shared NDEs. You will see in the literature to follow their experiences have common traits that are not exclusive to any religion or culture.

Let's step into the world of research. You might be unaware of how prevalent NDE experiences have become. Especially in the past fifteen years, modern medicine has allowed doctors to resuscitate individuals in cardiac arrest from heart attacks, strokes, diabetic comas, and serious accidents much worse than mine.

There are terms often used in conjunction with near death. It is only recently that research is beginning to separate NDE accounts for various reasons. It's important to note that a person does not have to die physically with cessation of the heart or breathing to experience an NDE. Some show clinical death; some do not. Our world loves acronyms; here are a few for you.

NDE: near-death experience—leaving the body, encountering the divine

OBE: out-of-body experience—leaving the body but not necessarily into another realm

STE: spiritually transformative experience—visions and/or experience with a being of light

NDLE: near-death-like experiences—intense experiences during meditation, sleeping, or even ordinary states of consciousness

Physicians began compiling research in earnest in the 1970s, including some earlier accounts that were verifiable. Websites began in the 1990s as computer technology expanded that capability. Today there are literally thousands of sites to explore. As we all know, we need to be cautious and discerning when reading on the Internet. I will only share the two most *widely respected* research sites. Dr. Jeffrey Long was the founder and creator of NDERF (Near Death Experience Research Foundation), which now includes two newer but independent sites: ADCRG (After-Death Communication Research Foundation) and OBERF (Out-of-Body Experience Research Foundation).[54]

NDERF is devoted to the study of NDE and support of those experiencing NDE and related experiences. NDERF has nothing for sale and does not solicit donations. This is refreshing in today's web culture. Because Dr. Long began his studies in the 1970s, this site includes accounts dating from prior to 1970 all the way to new accounts they receive daily. Many newly reported NDEs are from people like me, sharing after many years of silence. They have also posted eleven original NDE research papers. The research is completely fascinating and time-consuming to read. Currently NDEs and NDE-related material is available in twenty-two foreign languages. Readers from over seventy different countries access this website.

The first and probably the most highly respected website is IANDS,[55] the International Association for Near-Death Studies.

---

54   NDERF, www.nderf.org; ADCRF, www.adcrf.org; OBERF, www.oberf.org.
55   IANDS, www.iands.com.

Dr. Raymond Moody is most widely known and credited with the beginning of this website. But Dr. Moody tells us that it was his friend John Audette who was the conceiver, originator, organizer, and founder of IANDS. John asked him to endorse his project, which he did. There was actually a team of many psychologists and medial doctors, which included Dr. Moody. Dr. Moody was interviewed recently about his thirty years of NDE research, and it is posted on YouTube. He talks about how important these NDE experiences are as people reflect on their potential bearing on the biggest question of human existence, is there an afterlife? Thus far, the question of an afterlife has been a conceptual question. That is, it requires logical *reasoning* about concepts, not scientific methods. He feels that people will be waking up to this idea pretty quickly and that it will transform the landscape of rational study of life after death.

This website is very comprehensive and is currently able to report some startling statistics. They share that NDE belongs to a larger family of experiences that go beyond the usual limits of space and time and can transform a person's life and beliefs. They may be called spiritually transformative, conversion, mystical, religious, or transpersonal experiences. Many of these experiences can at times be confused with NDEs, but IANDS refers to these as "near-death-like experiences" or NDLEs. Approximately 75 percent of actual NDE accounts on IANDS are by individuals close to death or they were believed to be clinically dead. They are separating NDLEs from NDEs now, citing the statistics separately. Early research put these together.

Plato, in his "Myth of Er,"[56] Book X of the *Republic*, recounted the earliest known description of a near-death experience. Er went to battle where many Greeks soldiers were killed and placed in a pile upon a funeral pyre to be burned. After sometime, his body revived. He described watching many spirits leave their bodies along with his own. But he was told he must return to inform other men in the physical world what the world after death was like. After seeing many

---

[56]   Myth of Er, www.wikipedia.com.

sights, Er was sent back, but he had no idea how he got back into his body. He merely woke up and found himself upon the funeral pyre. Plato did not doubt the survival of bodily death in a different realm. But he thought that human language was inadequate to express the ultimate realities. He felt that words concealed the true inner natures because a body's physical senses could not adequately experience the complex whole. I found Plato's writings from so many centuries ago to be very insightful for myself. I had experienced expansion of my senses, as I described in chapter 1 of this book. I too found the English language totally inadequate to describe the feeling of this expansion.

Accounts can be found in the folklore of European, Middle Eastern, African, East Indian, East Asian, Pacific, and Native American cultures. According to NDERF research, every day in the United States, 774 NDEs occur. Non-Western near-death research has been conducted in China, India, Thailand, Tibet, and in native cultures in Australia, Chile, Guam, the continental United States, New Zealand, and Hawaii. It is only in recent history that Eastern ancient texts have been released for reading by Western researchers. Finding the Dead Sea Scrolls and continued efforts to translate and understand the ancient texts is expanding thought, especially expanding what we think we know and understand about the life of Jesus. This sharing of ancient writing expanded with the ousting of the Dalai Lama from Tibet. Many have now travelled into Tibet and have begun writing about their findings. I believe that in sharing our thoughts of life and death between Eastern culture and Western culture, we will find more similarities than differences. This is an area where my own research is expanding still today.

Dr. Raymond Moody Jr. in *Life After Life*[57] discussed some important thoughts about death taken from *The Tibetan Book of the Dead*. This amazing work compiled long-told oral traditions handed

---

[57] Raymond A. Moody Jr., MD, *Life After Life: The Investigation of a Phenomenon-Survival of Bodily Death* (NY: Harper Collins Publishers, 1975; San Francisco: Harper San Francisco, 2001; NY: Harper Collins Publishers, 2015), 116–118.

down through countless generations but recorded and written in the eighth century, CE. This had been hidden from outsiders for centuries. I found it fascinating that the authors of this text were writing it to help people who were dying. They felt that dying was a skill, something to be done artfully if they acquired the necessary knowledge to do it well. So the book was read to an individual as part of a funeral ceremony or during the dying person's final moments of life. This would serve two important functions. One was to share a wondrous phenomenon at the same moment the dying person was experiencing it. The second was to keep the emotional, grieving family thinking positive thoughts, not holding the dying person back by their emotions. It was important so that the dying person could enter into the other realm in a positive state of mind, not worrying about the physical realm. In the Tibetan account, they told of being outside their bodies, able to see and hear their relatives but not able to communicate as they were greeted by beings of pure light. In death, they would experience what they called the "shining" body. They would have the ability to travel anywhere by thinking themselves where they wanted to go, where their senses would be extremely heightened. The book describes feelings of immense peace and contentment. These findings are very interesting to me. There are such striking similarities in NDE accounts to the experience the Tibetans were describing to help the person dying and their grieving family. These similarities suggest to me that NDE knowledge was being used to help the dying in Tibet. We should be able to do the same to help our loved ones die peacefully, letting them know they will be greeted by a being of light in pure love.

Similarities between Eastern NDEs and Western NDEs include the belief that there is an afterlife, a profound sense of peace, being in an otherworldly realm, meeting deceased relatives, and meeting spiritual or religious figures usually in keeping with one's cultural background. I have personally read accounts of people meeting Jesus, Mary, Abraham, Moses, Buddha, Muhammad, Krishna, and figures like Michelangelo or Archangel Michael. I met a spiritual being I have always called God. My inner meditations might refine that some day. As I write these words on my computer, my body vibrates with a presence I will begin to call my spiritual guide that God has sent to help me. I know he/she exists. I have many experiences to draw on. I'll break for one story before more fascinating NDE statistics.

I was in Rome with my husband in the fall of 2014. We had been to St. Peter's, the Vatican, the coliseum, and all of the usual sights, and while I am always open to anything spiritual that might happen to me, there was nothing out of the ordinary. We went on a walking tour of less traveled sights. We entered a cathedral that dates well before Christ called Basilica di Santa Maria Maggiore. Pagan signs were pointed out in the architecture. I was standing in front of the tombstone of Raphael. I wanted to *know* ... are spirits of people here that are pre-Christ? *Are* they in heaven somewhere? I closed my eyes in quiet meditation, asking this question. I can only explain what happened in my limited words. My body began to vibrate at a level I haven't experienced since my NDE. Many people experience this vibration that can only be described as "the vibrating willy's"; they go up and down the meridian line throughout our bodies. It's a warm, wonderful feeling that no one wants to stop. I experience it often when I am asking significant questions, or it "springs" itself on me at the most unusual times. I hear the significance of it as I stop to realize what I was just thinking about. As I reflect on those thoughts, I realize it's either an answer or confirmation of a true thought. In this Roman cathedral, the vibration was at least quadrupled in me and enveloped my whole body. Spirits all shouting *yes* to me. I could tell it was many spirits. They stayed with me the whole time in the cathedral. I was overtaken but in an amazing joyful way. I uttered no words to anyone, just taking it all in. As we went out the door, I said to my husband, Doug, I need to tell you what just happened. His words before I could say anything were, "I know. Do you have any idea how you clutched on to me that whole time ... I could see it in your face."

There are elements or characteristics that have shown up with consistency as reported by people experiencing an NDE. Numerous research studies are available on both IANDS and NDERF that confirm the consistency and accuracy. All researchers comment that no two NDE experiences are identical, but within a group of experiences, certain patterns become very evident. Researchers are sharing their conclusions.

Common elements, as reported by NDERF and IANDS:
- separation of consciousness from the body with a sense of peace, virtually never discomfort
- perceiving their body from an outside position, often having the ability to see and hear details of events
- a sense of movement through darkness or a tunnel
- intensely powerful emotions—most reported peace, joy, and love
    - 8–18 percent (depends on study) report fearful events
    - all report difficulty finding words to describe
- heightened perceptions—hearing beautiful distinctive sounds
- encounters with a bright light with intense feelings of love, joy, peace
- perceiving a spiritual realm—may include vividly memorable landscapes
- encounters with others—deceased loved ones, animals, deceased pets, spiritual beings, or religious figures
    - 74 percent saw spiritual beings, deceased loved ones, or religious figures
- knowledge of the nature of the universe—a sense of alteration of time and space
- a life review
- a sense of oneness and interconnectedness
- decision to return or stay—encountering a boundary of no return
- a sense of having knowledge of the future
- messages regarding life's purpose
- returning to the body—usually feelings of pain associated with the cause of NDE

I found the correlations IANDS and NDERF discovered in research to be very significant as they were filtering through my own mind. I can identify with others how difficult it is to find words to describe this kind of experience with understanding. Other NDE accounts talk of disappointment hearing that some people obviously got way farther into the realm than others! It's interesting. I am fascinated but not disappointed. I will be there again. Death is no longer a worrisome event, and I am able to visualize perhaps farther than most what these accounts are describing. What a treasured gift, and I am hoping all of our words might be a gift for you in some small, humble way.

Correlations, as reported by IANDS and NDERF:
- No correlations have been found between religious beliefs and the likelihood or depth of the near-death experience.
- No significant correlation has been found between age, race, sexual orientation, economic status and the likelihood, content, or depth of the near-death experience.
- No correlation between the life history, beliefs, behavior, or attitudes of a person and the likelihood of having a radiant or harrowing NDE has been established.
- There is no evidence of a correlation between the means of coming close to death, including suicide, and likelihood of having a distressing NDE.

I had to spend a bit of time reading through and understanding any of the low percentage of "harrowing" or dark NDE accounts so I could process them. I found another acronym that is very new to research called dNDE—distressing near-death experience. I found the information interesting. Most of these accounts talk of feeling "out of control" of what was happening as they traveled through a tunnel, experiencing features that they viewed as frightening. An even lower percentage of people describe it as "hellish." Even these negative accounts describe a loving touch. Most people find after returning to their body, their lives are made incredibly better. Their lives become more loving. Their details of what they saw are all very similar to any of the positive NDEs. These NDE accounts emphasize they were not personally tormented. And they *all* came back with the ability to add *love* to their lives, which they seemed to recognize upon their return. The IANDS website suggests that people who are in a distressed frame of mind at the time of their NDE and those who were raised to expect distress during death may be more prone to distressing NDEs.

These two websites also contain very valuable information for mainstream physicians to read and digest. A person experiencing an NDE first encounters a medical person. It can be devastating to hear right away, "Oh, that didn't really happen." It doesn't matter how kindly it is said or the explanation. I believe spiritual damage occurs. Some physicians still hold on to the idea that NDEs are not real. If you are one of them, I encourage you to read these websites and study what the new research is saying. All of us are subject to beliefs that have been embedded into our minds for various reasons, like medical knowledge, scientific knowledge, religious training, or parental misunderstanding. There is a section called Explanations for NDE on the IANDS website. The studies are explained in detail in medical terms. The thoughts contained there might help any medical professional have a greater understanding of what happens during an NDE. If you hold on to any of the following beliefs, you might want to open your thoughts to new research. These are the questions answered, but they are in detail on the site for all readers.

Answers, as recorded through research reported by NDEF and IANDS"
- Aren't NDEs hallucinations? No.
- Aren't NDEs the result of anoxia (lack of oxygen) in a dying brain? No.
- Haven't locations in the brain been found to produce an NDE? Complicated answer. Mystical experiences, yes. NDE, no.

- Haven't certain drugs been shown to produce an NDE? Mystical experiences, yes. Not NDE.
- Can an NDE be induced through meditation, shamanic drumming, yoga, or other spiritual practices? Mystical experiences similar to NDEs, yes.

IANDS is stating that the research has shown there is no such relationship between apparent life deeds and type of NDE! We can only interpret this to mean even people who have committed atrocities have had a positive NDE. The most saintly person we know might have had negative images in their NDE. There is no relationship found. Mankind might assume that if you were a horrible person in life you would experience a negative NDE. That is not what they found. This matches the knowledge I understand. God accepts you for what you *are*, a human being making mistakes that we try to make better during each earthly life we live. Pure *love*. Through all accounts of life reviews that I read, they all involve learning about their mistakes in a totally loving way.

Is it possible that God sent his son, Jesus, to let us know that *love* is the most important ingredient in life? I can only share one person's lowly message brought back from my NDE. I am an ordinary person sharing what God shared with me. *Love is all there is.* Because I was raised in a Christian home, I read the Bible with new eyes upon my return. My eyes were opened to a global picture of God's unconditional love, shared by Jesus so long ago. After much reading, it becomes obvious that NDE experiencers are telling this same message of God's unconditional love. They are sharing this in every culture and religion. That is good news. It can and will make a difference globally.

What does unconditional love mean to you? Do you find yourself saying, "God will love me *if* I do something particular or say particular words"? And we can all fill in the blanks. Processing unconditional love may be easier for someone who has experienced it firsthand. Being in agony in an accident was not a gift, but experiencing God's love was the most precious gift I have ever received. I now realize that once you see divine love, you cannot un-see. Once you feel divine love, you cannot un-feel. Once you hear divine love, you cannot un-hear. Perhaps this sounds strange, but when processed, it is powerful. No one has to nearly die to receive that love! It's there for each and every one of us. There are no strings attached.

Many of us had loving parents or grandparents. My childhood was far from perfect, but I did feel loved. Not all people had love in their childhood. Experiencing hate or cruelty breeds more hate and cruelty. We hear it on the news all of the time. There's only one counterforce for hate, and that is love.

Life moves on, generation after generation, guided by a God that gives each of us unconditional love always. We say those words as Christians, Jews, Muslims, Buddhists, and Hindus. There are those that have only found hate in their lives, and they can't imagine a God of unconditional love. Unfortunately, people like that live in every culture. The news reports their stories and deeds us regularly. That's when we say, "Heaven help us all!" Well, heaven is there to help us all if we allow it to happen. *Love. Unconditional love.* We have the ability to put our bodies into a vibrational level to emanate love throughout the universe. Send it. Show it. Be it. Our *collective* vibrations together can make a difference for peace in our own homes, families, and communities. That love can spread globally.

Dr. David Hawkins spent his entire life working with people's emotions and how they affect us personally in our own bodies, as well as how emotions affect all of us globally. He was a brilliant man. Marj and I have read his books and heard his lectures. We continue to digest his work. He is an invaluable resource for all professionals who work in the areas of mental health, psychology, medicine, self-help, addiction recovery, and spiritual development. His work is also for the everyday seeker of peace and love. We highly recommend looking up his vast collection of audio lectures and books![58] It took years to fully understand him, but I found his last book written before he died in 2012 very valuable reading. This book was easier to grasp.

---

[58]   David R. Hawkins, Veritas Publishing, www.veritaspub.com.

It is *Letting Go: Pathway to Surrender.*[59] I credit his knowledge with finally helping me understand why I was able to heal myself, as you read.

Another common trait shared by NDE experiencers is an insatiable drive to gain more knowledge about the world. I have certainly experienced that in my life since 1982, and it is with me all the time. I can't stop reading, listening to, and hearing the work of scientists, medical professionals, and spiritual leaders. My bookshelves are overflowing.

I cannot begin to list all of the books I've read of individual accounts of NDEs. I learned from them all. There have been a number of medical professionals writing recent accounts of their own NDE experiences. They have made a profound difference in my understanding.

Dr. Eben Alexander was one of those scientists who argued that near-death experiences were impossible. He is a highly trained neurosurgeon of twenty-five years. He spent fifteen years at Brigham and Women's and Children's Hospital and Harvard Medical School in Boston. He knew that NDEs felt real, but he thought they were fantasies produced by brains under extreme stress. He also did not believe in God or an afterlife. But his own brain was attacked by a rare illness, sending him into a coma in 2008. In his words, "during my coma my brain wasn't working improperly—it wasn't working at all … In my case the neocortex was out of the picture. I was encountering the reality of a world of consciousness that existed completely free of the limitations of my physical brain. I was in a better-than-average position to judge not only the reality but also the implications of what happened to me. Those implications are tremendous beyond description. My experience showed me that the death of the body and the brain are not the end of consciousness that human experience continues beyond the grave. More important, it continues under the gaze of a God who loves and cares about each

---

59   David R. Hawkins, MD, PhD, *Letting Go: The Pathway of Surrender* (Carlsbad, CA: Hay House Publishing, 2012).

one of us and about where the universe itself and all the beings within it are ultimately going … the place I went was real."[60]

Dr. Alexander's story is told in his book *Proof of Heaven: A Neurosurgeon's Journey into the Afterlife*. This book became a number-one *New York Times* best-seller in 2012. He has since written a second book titled *The Map of Heaven: How Science, Religion, and Ordinary People Are Proving the Afterlife*.[61] It was published in 2014. I did not read either of these books until after Marj and I began writing our own book.

As a scientist and neurosurgeon, Dr. Alexander had incredible insights into his experience in another realm. When I read his first book, I devoured it from start to finish. His experience was very different from mine. He experienced dark moments, which I did not. Many might read the details and find it too hard to imagine it could have been real. I never had a moment's doubt. Even in his dark moments, he never felt frightened or

threatened in any way. He also tells of meeting beings, animals, and finding incredible love in God. The knowledge that he absorbed from his experience is astounding. I had no trouble understanding any of it. I was amazed to read in print all of the same thoughts that were shared with me and so much more as well.

He too talked about how long it took for him to process it all. Meditation was very profound and necessary for him to be able to allow his brain to retrieve and process the information learned during his NDE. He credits Robert A. Monroe, founder of Hemi-Sync, for producing resonating sounds to help him move into a deep meditative state and enhanced state of consciousness. Hemi-Sync uses specific patterns of stereo sound waves of slightly different frequencies in each ear to induce synchronized brain activity. Dr. Alexander is able to explain with precision how and why this works in our brain. He talked about how Hemi-Sync enabled him to return to a realm

---

[60] Eben Alexander, MD, *Proof of Heaven: A Neurosurgeon's Journey into the Afterlife* (New York: Simon & Schuster, 2012), 9.

[61] Eben Alexander, MD, *The Map of Heaven: How Science, Religion, and Ordinary People Are Proving the Afterlife* (New York: Simon & Schuster, 2014).

similar to that which he visited deep in coma but without being deathly ill. Eventually Sacred Acoustics emerged from Hemi-Sync and has produced CDs available for listening with purpose, some for meditation and some for everyday listening.[62] I had previously found a similar type of acoustic music from Jim Oliver as well as in Dr. Wayne Dyer and James Twyman's work. Using vibrational sounds with the express purpose of bringing the mind into a deeper conscious state has also been used to help those with dementia, Parkinson's disease, and Alzheimer's disease.

Dr. Alexander talks about needing to *allow* the journey to unfold. For me it took learning how to get myself into a deep meditative state, *allowing* my journey to unfold through the help of God and music. I needed to spend years studying the science to understand it! I essentially have "retrieved" that knowledge, matched it with newly published science and medical information, and now feel I can share with others. I feel very blessed to find many of my beliefs matched those of highly educated scientists or physicians. He was willing to share his expertise with the world with the eyes of a physician who experienced a profound NDE, changing his life. I thought you might enjoy hearing some of his statements too.

In Dr. Alexander's chapter "The Enigma of Consciousness,"[63] he helped me realize how important knowledge is to the topic of life and death. God created our world, and through science's discoveries we are beginning to realize the complexities of life. He experienced the same processing of information and remembering, all without his body, the same as I had. He felt he was intricately and irremovably connected to the larger universe and that it was not far away from us at all. He talks about the vastness of it and about it being right here by us. I believe the other realm is right here among us. That's why I was able to spend time with Anne as a spirit, see and talk to people visiting from a past realm in the Amazon, and hear my deceased father in a dream telling me to go get that box. But I had to be open to

---

[62] info@sacredacoustics.com.

[63] Eben Alexander, MD, *Proof of Heaven: A Neurosurgeon's Journey into the Afterlife* (New York: Simon & Schuster, 2012), 149–161.

the idea that life exists around us. Dr. Alexander felt that his journey revealed an immense chasm between our human knowledge and the awe-inspiring realm of God. I believe this is why God is using everyday people to bring messages to the world, like myself. However, God needed some scientists and medical professionals to help us understand the ever-expanding field of quantum mechanics. Even the brightest minds in science are beginning to realize there is something more, turning to the mystical world for answers. Our soul has now been shown that it weighs something. A body has been shown to lose weight as the soul departs. Think of the profound influence men like Einstein have had on our planet. Science is telling us the universe has no beginning or end. I believe God is present within every particle of it. We can learn about the universe from books and lectures. But we can each go deep into our own consciousness through prayer or meditation and access these truths. Dr. Alexander emphasized that he had previously believed that matter was the core reality. His entire view of God and the world changed through his experience. My view has changed as I grew in knowledge and understanding. "I was blind, now I see" has taken on a new meaning for me.

Dying To Be Me[64] by Anita Moorjani is a very powerful NDE account. Hers is a very recent story published in 2012. Marj and I had the honor of meeting her and hearing her speak. She's an amazing, warm, and loving individual. As she signed my book, I had a chance to chat with her briefly about my own NDE. I felt love radiating from her. Perhaps you have had an experience like this. For me, it was powerful because she was a total stranger to me. Her thoughts and mine came together with very few words. It was beautiful for both of us. I also knew instinctively her mind was drifting toward the long line behind me!

Her experience was a lot like mine initially. She was able to see and hear all of the doctors, nurses, and family below. She too felt incredible. "Oh my God, I feel incredible! I'm free and light! How

---

[64] Anita Moorjani, *Dying To Be Me: My Journey From Cancer, to Near Death, to True Healing* (Carlsbad, CA: Hay house Publishing, 2012).

come I'm not feeling any more pain in my body? Where has it all gone? Hey, why does it seem like my surroundings are moving away from me? But, I'm not scared! Why am I not scared? Where has my fear gone? Oh wow, I can't find the fear anymore!"[65]

Her details were very different from mine, but I had grown used to reading unique NDEs. She experienced some very powerful images. As I read her story, I realized how significant seeing her deceased father was for her journey. For me, I had not lost anyone extremely close to me. I began to realize how God orchestrates our experiences for various purposes.

She was dying of lymphoma cancer; she had been battling the disease for four years. In her last stages of life with all of her vital organs shutting down, her family had been told she only had a few more hours to live. She had what sounded like a lengthy time out of her body, but she too talked of expanded knowledge of time and space and how different it was. She talks about the clarity of it all being so amazing. She talks about the fact that the universe makes sense! She finally understood why she had cancer. Upon her regaining consciousness, Anita found that her condition had improved so rapidly that she was released from the hospital in a few short weeks, without a trace of cancer in her body. The medical profession documents all of this. She is now a national speaker and presenter. She talks of self-healing as well as the powerful message of unconditional love.

Anita was part of a traditional Hindu family residing in a largely Chinese and British society in Hong Kong. She lived a life very different from mine, so I was intrigued right away. She was very conflicted, pushed and pulled by cultural and religious customs since she was little. She was sent to a Catholic school, and the confusion and tension was a lot for a young girl. She talks freely about her life. She lost her father just before marrying, which was devastating to her. But she saw him during her NDE. She moved to the States with

---

[65]   Anita Moorjani, *Dying To Be Me: My Journey From Cancer, to Near Death, to True Healing* (Carlsbad, CA: Hay house Publishing, 2012), 3.

her husband. It's a complete story that helps all of us sort through the complexities of life as she explained confusion and conflict causing her cancer. Her story took us from childhood, to sickness, into death and back with a total understanding of life. It reads like a novel but has amazing messages for all of us! I loved her message about not taking ourselves so seriously and to enjoy our life. Love yourself unconditionally and be yourself fearlessly. She states that was the most important lesson she learned from her NDE.

I found I could agree with most everything she said! Our lives are too entrenched in getting ahead and living in fear of what is out there that we are forgetting to enjoy ourselves and be happy! We were meant to enjoy life, and the need to slow down and find the peace within is more important than ever. The good news is that meditation is now being talked about everywhere. I see articles in magazines, newspapers, books, and all over the Internet, even in schools.

Dr. Eben Alexander's second book, *The Map of Heaven: How Science, Religion, and Ordinary People Are Proving the Afterlife,*[66] was released in 2014. It is so readable and brings ordinary people's NDE stories to life. He collected many stories of NDEs, OBEs, and STEs. His style of telling these stories is warm and loving. The stories are meant to help all of us realize that touching the spiritual realm is happening on a regular basis all around us. He infuses scientifically expanded knowledge into his stories. When we allow the divine into our lives, amazing things can happen to change even the most horrible of circumstances that you might call your *life*. We aren't stuck with anything we don't want. We have the ability to change our reality at any moment with our thoughts. His title of *Map of Heaven* threw me off at first. He is using people and their stories as a way God gives *us a map* to understand heaven. Dr. Alexander is also giving lectures now and hoping to make a difference in the medical community who may not yet understand the reality that NDEs are actually happening.

---

[66] Eben Alexander, MD, *Proof of Heaven: A Neurosurgeon's Journey into the Afterlife* (New York: Simon & Schuster, 2012).

Because he was such a nonbeliever himself before his NDE, he is able to relate to doctors struggling to make sense of the topic.

Also in 2014, I had a dear friend, my amazing voice teacher, ask if I'd read *My Stroke of Insight* by Jill Bolte Taylor, PhD.[67] He and I had some very wonderful talks about my NDE. It's not always easy to find a person who already believes what you are telling them before you even start! What a treat and what a wonderful book he recommended! This story should be on the required reading list for anyone told they might be at risk for a stroke or who knows anyone that has had a stroke, or anyone that needs help understanding that our brain has the capacity to heal our body. I had the knowledge from God that we have this capability. But I was still on a very long path to understanding how.

I had been reading many books, trying to learn as much as I could about the brain. I learned more about the brain from Dr. Jill Taylor than from authors who devoted entire books to how a brain works! Her story was like a walk through the brain with a master teacher, a brain scientist. Dr. Taylor was on staff at Harvard Medical School performing research and teaching young doctors about the human brain. She suffered a massive rare type of stroke in the left hemisphere of her brain, from which few people have ever recovered. She was in a coma. After just four hours into this stroke, she could not walk, talk, read, write, or recall any of her life. She surrendered to death, yet her story is one of recovery and what was happening in her brain while she was unable to communicate. She moved into a place inside of her in total silence. She writes with humor and tries to help the layperson understand her feelings wrapped up in the science of our brain functions. She had very significant ideas that were helpful for me. She had gained some spiritual insights herself as she connected and understood that despite her tragedy, there was an unforgettable sense of peace that pervaded her entire being, and she felt calm. I had learned reading the work of other scientists that the

---

[67] Jill Bolte Taylor, PhD, *My Stroke of Insight: A Brain Scientist's Personal Journey* (New York: PLUME Penguin Group, 2006).

vibration level of total peace is the place that healing can take place. She tells of her emotions and helps us understand why she feels she was able to heal by retreating to that silent, peaceful place.

This knowledge related to my NDE by making clear my need to go into silence to reconnect with previously learned information stored in my unconscious mind. I had no trouble remembering every detail because I could always visualize it. It's like an image being implanted in your brain, and it doesn't leave you. But the expansion of that knowledge was lying in wait for me to remember. I don't remember "deciding" that I would come back. For me, I came back with some important knowledge, and I have an important job to do yet. Dr. Taylor didn't want to come back, but she became very excited about what a difference her life could make in the lives of others. She wanted to help all who were recovering from a brain trauma, *everyone* with a brain! She explained that her blessing was knowledge that deep internal peace is accessible to anyone at any time. "I believe the experience of Nirvana exists in the consciousness of our right hemisphere, and that at any moment we can choose to hook into that part of our brain."[68] That place is where we go when we meditate, where healing takes place, where peace and calmness can be found. Imagine what our world could be like if we all found that place of peace and calm. Dr. Taylor explained the title of her book when she said, "My Stroke of Insight would be: Peace is only a thought away, and all we have to do to access it is silence the voice of our dominating left mind."[69] That's the challenge of every meditator! But when you are able to access silence, all you find there is love. God placed that love inside every one of us. Dr. Taylor found that love too.

Dr. Taylor shared forty things she needed most for healing. I internalized this list because it was so significant for all of us dealing with any disease. These are very practical ideas and helpful for medical personnel as well as family members of stroke victims.

---

[68] Jill Bolte Taylor, PhD, *My Stroke of Insight: A Brain Scientist's Personal Journey* (New York: PLUME Penguin Group, 2006), 116.

[69] Jill Bolte Taylor, PhD, *My Stroke of Insight: A Brain Scientist's Personal Journey* (New York: PLUME Penguin Group, 2006), 116.

All of these are suggestions are infused with caring and love. We all need that. If you have any contact with a stroke victim, I highly recommend finding this list in her book or on her websites. Her websites are full of amazing information.[70] I could have used her list of practical ideas during my own healing journey and as I watched my father have a stroke in a restaurant. I did not understand what was happening, and I could have reacted much quicker than I did. I also realized I had used almost all of her suggestions for stroke victims in my years of teaching kindergarteners and first graders! By just changing only a few words, almost *every* one of the forty things are needed for young children to be able to learn to read.

All of our life situations are different. All of our beliefs are different. God created us with free will, and what a beautifully diverse planet has emerged. But what is exactly the *same* in all of us? God is inside each and everyone one of us, waiting for us to go find the amazing peace and calm that dwells within while we search for our own truths. With God's grace, healing also takes place when our belief in healing is strong, supporting our abilities. Our brain begins to provide the channels to our deeper knowing of ourselves.

> In communion with our divine self, we can see and hear God's words. It probably won't be a voice; it's a knowing that you can begin to trust through your intuition. Prayer is talking to God, silence is listening for God, and intuition is God answering back to you. Lots of connections begin to happen. They happen in words from others in books, sermons that inspire, articles online, or a friend that says just the right thing when you need it. Is this coincidence? It is not. It's mind-boggling to imagine how this all is orchestrated, but when you go deep into that place in your heart and believe it is happening, it does! The human spirit is strong enough to push us into a far better and more

---

[70]   www.drjiltaylor.com or www.mystrokeofinsight.com.

harmonious world. Unconditional love has infinite power to heal, whether we are talking about healing an individual, communities, ethnic populations, nations, humanity, life on earth, or beyond.

Chapter 9

Your Spiritual Journey: Balancing Life

All of us have lives that have been challenging in one way or another in the past and/ or present, and we don't know what the future will bring. We are shaping our future with each and every decision we make. Have you thought about what *is* working for you in your life? Have you pondered why there are things that are *not* working for you in your life? Do you find yourself trying to blame circumstances on events "beyond your control" or perhaps blame God, or even say, "God must have His reasons"? We all do this to a certain degree because it's somehow built into our very human existence. But have you considered the fact that you personally have the ability to change your future existence? You can! God created that gift in grace available to all of us.

Mind, body and spirit are *way more than just words*. Because of our experiences and our study, we work hard in our own lives to be fully present in every moment *now*. We try not to dwell on the past or future. But this is not easy on a daily basis. As we began to write this book, Marj and I did find it very helpful to look back on our lives and take a very serious look at what events and circumstances shaped us into the human beings we are today. We began to see patterns of growth and development. We took notice of why and when we put positive practices into our lives to grow in mindfulness, nurture our bodies, and expand our spiritual awareness. The religious path you have chosen can work directly to help expand your spiritual growth into a deep awakening. But if there is disconnection between your religious practices and your spiritual thoughts, it might be causing problems for you physically and emotionally. Only *you* can determine if there are positive changes that will work for you. No one can do that for you. In this chapter, we will share the practical and useful changes we made in our lives to deepen our own spiritual life as we tried hard to balance life. Permanent health and wellness is not a state we can reach, because we are constantly healing. Every moment, our body is absorbing our thoughts, feelings, and emotional experiences. Our lives are a continuing journey, so why not keep them tuned up, ready to go just like we do our cars? We have learned some things that might be helpful for you! We are not experts in any of these fields; we are simply messengers to help you learn and then find the masters that can teach you so much more than we can! We have learned from many masters.

Now that you have traveled our life path of spiritual experiences, we thought it might be helpful for you to see how we mapped our growth. It helped us see and learn from our own histories. Perhaps it can help you find patterns in your own life. Thinking about Jacob's ladder in the Bible, and Abraham Maslow's ladder of conscious evolution using a pyramid shape, we chose the ladder to illustrate our lives. We now know that our journey *never ends*. Ladders can grow taller and taller if we manipulate them, just like our bodies and minds. No two people will ever have the same ladder, just as no two snowflakes that fall from the sky are ever identical. God created each of us in total uniqueness. Wow, can we wrap our head around that knowledge? It's not an easy task! Compassion and love for other human beings and their own ways of life grew in us right along with making sense of God through an NDE and a LIGHT experience. It started with the knowledge that all human beings are connected and that our souls live forever. Death is the illusion, and life is meant to provide a platform for learning and enjoying while earthly years continue.

We are using this 3-D model to show our own *ever-expanding knowledge of our universe* (God's universe). The ladders will never end, as they are only a stepping place for a new one. Because our experiences weave within the spiritual realm, a three-dimensional view into and through our ladders is an important visual.

Terry's Spiritual Ladders of Growth

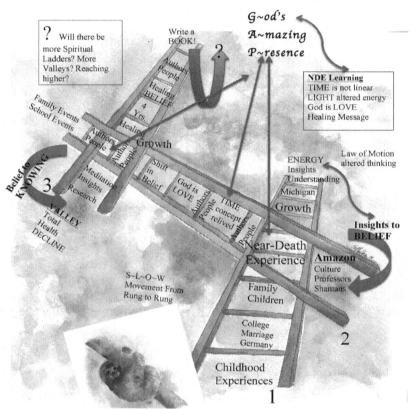

Terry's Spiritual Ladders of
Growth

A word from Terry about her ladder:

All of us begin our spiritual path as we are born into unique circumstances. We take on early beliefs and experience life through the filter of our parents and family life. You will notice that my near-death experience is wrapped into all of my ladders. I couldn't help but change right away, but processing my experience and my NDE took time. I expanded my knowledge traveling internally as well as worldwide. My insights gradually moved into *belief* as God's Amazing Presence continued to come into my life. I was allowing Him to come into my life.

I was hearing messages through meditation, experiences, people, books, and events. Information arrived when I was asking. My belief moved into *knowing*, again gradually, due to my health decline and subsequent healing. *Belief* releases the power within you to make change, both physically and emotionally. Continued movement from *beliefs to knowing* added stability to the beliefs out of which my decisions and actions were made. It was through a very low valley in my life that the most profound learning occurred.

Knowing that this growth took years, God was nudging me to share with others. Maybe I can help shorten someone else's path. I had to overcome great fears to make this happen. And I had to put my learning into action, and my actions changed my life!

My near-death experience will continue to thread through any new ladder as my life's journey creates new experiences. That is because God is with me through every adventure.

Marj's Spiritual Growth Ladder

THE LIGHT GAP

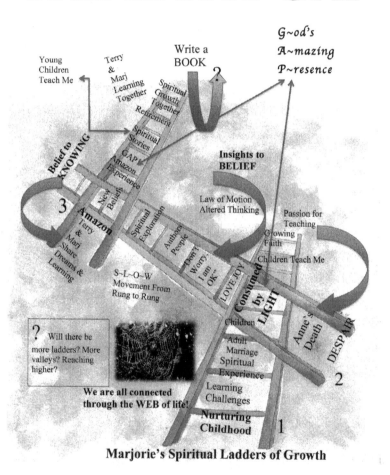

G~od's
A~mazing
P~resence

Young
Children
Teach Me

Terry
&
Marj
Learning
Together

Write a
BOOK

Spiritual
Growth
Together

Retirement

Spiritual
Stories

GAP
Amazon
Experience

Insights to
BELIEF

Belief to
KNOWING

New
Belief

Law of Motion
Altered Thinking

Passion for
Teaching

3

Amazon
Terry
&
Marj
Share
Dreams &
Learning

Spiritual
Exploration

Authors
People

Don't
Worry,
I am
OK~

Growing
Faith

Children Teach Me

S~L~O~W
Movement From
Rung to Rung

LOVE JOY

Consumed
by
LIGHT

Children

? Will there be
more ladders? More
valleys? Reaching
higher?

Adult
Marriage
Spiritual
Experience

Anne's
Death

DESPAIR

2

We are all connected
through the WEB of life!

Learning
Challenges

Nurturing
Childhood

1

Marjorie's Spiritual Ladders of Growth

A word from Marj about her ladder:

Using the ladder to chart my spiritual growth was a very helpful process. Over the years, I had made time lines, but this graphic gave me a better sense of the interrelated movement connecting time to events. Beside our ladder pictures are the questions, "Will there be more ladders? More Valleys? Reaching higher?" Of course there will be! Now we know that everything in our lives is connected to remembering that our job in life is to continuously create new versions of our self that better reflect our understanding of life. On a daily basis, each of us is uniquely interconnected with God. We are included in the process of creation. When we are *all* working together in the creative process, we feel the higher vibrational energy. Out of this new *love* energy, many people make new choices and put them into action, which ultimately has the ability to affect the course of lives all over the globe. We can bring compassion, hope, and peace through this process, both for ourselves and for the world.

My ladder started with childhood experiences because that is where this life starts. It was not perfect, but it was strong enough to support solid spiritual growth. The challenging times, the joyous events, and everything in between make up my journey on this ladder. The most difficult ones are often the best teachers. I have some learning issues, and as a young child, I had a terrible time learning how to read and write. There were many tears. But by adulthood, even in high school, I realized what a gift learning challenges had been. These specific challenges, along with all of my childhood experiences, taught me compassion for others and how to keep working. They made me resilient. I had begun the process of learning to love myself, imperfections and all. That put me ahead of the game.

The ladder took a sharp turn with the death of Anne. Fact is it was the beginning of a whole new ladder extension! I was enveloped in LIGHT with no sense of my physical body and only feeling indescribable love and joy. I needed to understand how this could happen. I was grieving. The coincidences and moments of grace continued in rapid succession for months, jolting me awake. Books, lectures, people-to-people conversations, international trips, and quiet moments solidified my new *beliefs*, which turned into *knowing* over time. I was catapulted up the ladder. During this twenty-year time period, Terry and I have been climbing the ladder together, nurturing and supporting each other in our quest for answers to spiritual questions. It produced balance, excitement, insights, and inspiration.

I am in the process of starting a new extension on my ladder, one that takes me into the third trimester of life. The aging process is at hand. With it may come decisions, health challenges, and loss. Coming too will be new ideas that I put into action, which will bring joy. There are lots of possibilities. A continuous process of following the important threads of my life will continue, interweaving into a beautiful tapestry.

Our two ladders are very different, even as we so often climbed them together! You might say our ladders intertwined along with many teachers we encountered in our lives. Scientists have now given us a mental picture of a holograph so we can visualize our own bodies on the inside! Think of the picture my doctors had in 1982. There was no 3-D picture for them to watch my spleen rupturing, and that was only thirty-four years ago. Look at what doctors see now. I realize doctors could have watched my spleen rupture in 3-D if technology had been more advanced. We can even see the whole structure of atoms, proving that everything that is matter can move and change, even our thoughts! Images of our energy field surrounding our bodies exist. This picture in our heads was not available for people existing in history. And yet they were trying to make sense of miracles and mystical events. We are still trying to do that, but we have more knowledge. Are we expanding our knowledge internally and externally, letting God help us to understand his complex world? Science and spirituality *are* our *lives* in 3-D. New knowledge about our universe can and does include help to understand God if we look and expand our thinking. We shared in chapter 8 how difficult it can be for some physicians to validate a near-death experience until several doctors had one of their own. These doctors are speaking out now and teaching other medical professionals. Is God sending us messages through people? We think so. Are we messengers too? Yes, we are.

Imagine with us for a moment that there is an invisible, thin string that keeps looping *around* each rung on the ladders. That string is too thin to keep us from breaking it as we climb. And yet we keep reaching for it anyway. These breaks produce ups and downs in our progress as we climb the ladders. It is a tricky uphill climb, yet we don't fall off. God will not let us fall, but we do experience interruptions as we try to grow and learn from each experience. We *wish* we had a rope instead. Visualize one strand of the rope for each scientist proving concepts unknown in the past, putting each informational strand together and twisting it into a rope. That rope gets stronger and stronger as knowledge is uncovered. We can now hang on tighter. And yet some scientists have a hard time believing God is part of this picture. We have many on our planet who have no idea what to believe—but not everybody. The number of medical scientists and quantum physicists who believe in God is growing. Thankfully, we have some who are sharing their incredible knowledge with the world and we *need to listen*! We believe God is helping them, as well as each of us who would call our life "ordinary." We feel very ordinary for sure, but *we are* listening, and our minds are closed to nothing. We know God has no favorites; his love is the same for each and every one of us.

Abraham Maslow spent his life studying human behavior. His work is complicated, but he helped us understand that as human beings we are all moving through similar patterns, accumulating knowledge and building our belief systems. Maslow's hierarchy of needs is a theory in psychology he wrote through his research. His work is often shown in pyramid form with physiological needs at the bottom, moving on to safety needs, love and belonging, esteem, and eventually self-actualization. We go through these steps using a brain that bases its life on getting basic needs met first. Then the brain finds a safe avenue through friends and family, achieving self-esteem through them but recognizing some families have not been able to provide positive self-esteem. Then we move on to developing beliefs of morality and creatively solving problems based on acceptance of facts that may or may not be true.

To understand our ladders, it might be helpful to understand in simple terms the type of ladder that Maslow suggests we all climb as we grow in our minds. Dr. David Hawkins talked of similar growth in his books, *Power vs. Force* and *Letting Go*. We found it refreshing that Dr. Hawkins decided to add spirituality to all of his work. More brain scientists are telling us that spirituality is part of the equation. Finally we are getting very practical advice on how to put practices into our daily lives that help us in our search for health. These practices help us emotionally, physically, and spiritually.

Psychologists, psychiatrists, MDs, DOs, doctors of holistic medicine, brain scientists, physical therapists, nurses, and the whole expanding field of natural medicine are working very hard to help us navigate this complicated world of health while emotions often run our lives. It is a world where the mind is intertwined with our physical bodies, and our spiritual self is at times held hostage while we try to figure it all out!

In very simple terms, this is the pattern we most likely followed during our lives as suggested by Abraham Maslow in his work as we climb our ladders of life.[71] These words are our own interpretation of his complex work.

> We *observe* our world, like a video recording in our brain.
> We select *data* from what we observe.
> We add *meanings* from cultural and personal experiences.
> We make *assumptions* based on the meanings we added.
> We draw *conclusions.*
> We adopt *beliefs* about the world.
> We take *actions* based on our beliefs.

---

[71]   Maslow's ladders of conscious evolution, www.wikipedia.com.

Newton's first law of motion states than an object either remains at rest or continues to move at a constant velocity unless acted upon by an external force. The two of us were "acted upon" by an external force for sure! It was God, divine presence, or any of the many names given to belief in a supreme being. We were suspended in time, acted upon by an external force, but remained living life on earth. We couldn't remain the same person. We had to grow even if we didn't act right away. We both reacted differently. No one has to die and come back to have this happen to them. We feel this is a profound message we want to share. We know that human beings have an amazing potential within themselves. It is given in grace by God from birth to develop your soul in your own unique style.

As we move through our very complicated lives, no wonder we don't recognize how, where, or why our beliefs have emerged as they have. Many of us have been taught not to question any of them, to only structure our thoughts based on a faith outlined by someone else. But as we all know, the questions still surface anyway! We all ask them, especially in times of crisis. Perhaps God is making sure the questions surface, so that we structure our lives centered through *love more and more as we grow.* What are we learning from the ups and downs and the tragedies in our lives?

Many spiritual masters tell us that we are doomed to having similar tragedies show up in our lives until we finally get the message that we are meant to grow from each experience in more loving ways. We are not meant to fail, but we were meant to feel and experience God's love every step of the way. Culture around us can give us a very different picture. Think of every ad on TV telling you how sick you are and which medicines you need to take, regardless of the scary list of side effects. Fear is a nasty emotion that brings stress to our bodies in so many ways it is hard to always recognize them. Fear of failure to live up to expectations from God and our fellow man has our planet on stress overload! We fear we are going to get sick. And then we wonder why we get sick. Can you let go of some of these fears a piece at a time? Let love into your mind, body and soul! The message of love in my NDE meant pure love for all, starting with my body and myself. I have learned the hard way that balancing *mind, body, and spirit is way more than just words.* Let's explore some ideas that are working for us. You will find that you can adapt and change any of these to fit your own lifestyle! There is *no* wrong way to make positive changes in your life. And there are many experts ready to help!

I am often asked what the most powerful learning was after years of moving into understanding my near-death experience. I realize now that my NDE healing message and the powerful message of unconditional love are really all one message. This statement sums up why daily life practices used to balance life are so important to us. Deep spiritual awakening can begin any time we choose it!

Health is inner peace wrapped in pure love.
—NDE message reworded by Terry Larkin

Meditation and an Unlikely Companion Energy Medicine

Meditation has been around for centuries. Before modern medicine, the concepts related to meditation were actually *more* widely believed and used than they have been since the nineteenth century began. Advancements in Western medicine brought its decline. It is only recently that our own medical professionals here in the United States have embraced the idea that stress is playing a very big role in disease. Cancer centers are beginning to offer and suggest meditation for their patients. Many of the concepts about meditation used in the Western world have come from Eastern culture. When the term *new age* came out, too many people didn't understand it meant looking back into ancient culture for answers to problems. People backed away, thinking the worst but not at all understanding what it was all about. Instead, my NDE drew me right into genuine *new* thought. Eastern civilizations have used meditation successfully for centuries. Many people read about meditation now, seeing articles and studies proclaiming its benefits, but it is still a low percentage of people who have actually tried it or use it on a regular basis. As you read in our "Health and Healing" chapter, we have embraced meditation along with modern medicine, because it has worked in our lives!

Gradually the idea of meditation is being accepted and even used in schools, calling it Mindfulness Training. As with all new learning related to health, our culture dictates that research is done well before anything can be accepted as true. Research about the effects of meditation is staggering and very positive. An individual's ability to make positive change translates into our body as healing. Prominent research concerning *self-healing* is being conducted in our top universities. It is important for me to point out now that healing yourself does not mean you don't need medical help; it just means that you have more personal power to affect your body's natural healing mechanism. It will take a long time for mainstream medical schools to embrace teaching this reality. Practicing doctors have the research in front of them, and many are now suggesting it to their patients. Luckily for all of us, many resources are now available to us from the web.

Basic Meditation

Getting started can be simple. You can begin by practicing clearing your mind of chatter by substituting loving thoughts for *yourself* and *others*. This is *not* a selfish act! It is a powerfully healthy one. Music can facilitate this clearing of the mind. Concentrating on breathing and thankfulness takes your mind off your "things to worry about list."

To Begin:
1. **Location**: Find a place in your house that is comfortable and gives you a sense of peace and privacy. I have made my own place fit my personality with objects I love and have meaning. The painting of my sloth hangs there, special nature objects, my stack of well-chosen daily meditation literature, and

my rock with three carved holes is my three-candle holder. Sometimes you might want to branch out into nature and find spectacular places and times to make meditation different with sounds of nature.

2. **Pose:** What is comfortable for you? I start on my yoga mat for soft yoga stretching and energy medicine techniques, moving to a sitting position and ready for quiet. A cushion or chair is fine. Sit comfortably straight with feet planted on the ground if you are in a chair.

3. **Tools:** Some people find *relaxing music* enhances the experience. Earphones are helpful. Some find *silence* best. A candle can provide a glowing love feeling to focus on as well as a scent. I also love to have a small flower or plant there for chakra color definition. I believe whatever you *design* for yourself is the most meaningful. Reading and soul journaling can enhance your quiet time. Chances are you will adapt your approach many times to fit your own style.

4. **Breathing:** I prefer to do this standing at the end of my yoga mat. This is an important ingredient. Start with deep breathing. I open my mouth and breath fully and fast for ten in and out breaths. Then I begin breathing in through my nose and exhaling through the mouth. Watch that it is your abdomen filling with air, not your shoulders! Picture and feel the air going all the way up through your body and out the third eye point (between your eyebrows). As you move from very deep breathing to calm, easy breathing, you are able to relax one body part at a time. Start by relaxing your face and neck. Then relax into the heart, body core, and extremities. There are more breathing techniques later in this chapter.

5. **When:** Many experts teaching meditation say early morning and evening are the best. I agree, but if a different time is best for you, do it! People also wonder, "When will I be good at it?" My answer: when you change your belief to "I am good at it." Take away expectations ... simply enjoy your soul's quiet time.

6. **Length**: Twenty minutes is good. Thirty or forty minutes is great when time permits.

7. **What can I expect**? When first beginning meditation, people tend to get frustrated due to a distracted mind. Music, a mantra, and chanting can help. Just say to yourself, "I am better at it than yesterday!" Regardless, you will feel peace, calm, less stress, and a sense of lightness to your body. This deepens with time. Can this bring healing? Absolutely! But be careful about what your mind is concentrating on. Your thoughts create your reality. When your thoughts aren't positive, take note of them and learn from them. But do not dwell on them at this time; release them and let go! I usually tell God, "I'm handing *this* one over to you," and then let go.

You will feel more energy during your day right away, even if you only start with ten minutes. Quickly you become hooked because you realize you have become more calm and peaceful. Soon you no longer want ten minutes, and it easily grows to twenty and thirty. Your body will crave the time, making meditation a habit. The practice then moves into deeper meaning both spiritually and physically. It seems simple, maybe too simple, so people don't try it because they can't really see it could change anything. However, it can literally be life changing. Like anything, it takes a bit of practice to get better at it. We highly recommend you don't worry about whether you are doing it correctly. There are many techniques and styles that serve different purposes. Each unique person reacts differently to outside influences. You will quickly develop practices that suit your own personality. Breathing has proven to be very important in meditation as well as in energy medicine techniques. Oxygen is needed in every cell of our bodies. Forcefully getting it there can and does make a difference in your overall health. I started breathing techniques to get more oxygen into cells as I was healing; it was embedded in Dr. Dharma Singh Khalsa's medical meditation work. Since that time, I have found the practices in too many resources to even mention. But mine have become more refined as I try new techniques and use the ones that really work for me.

There are thousands of meditation techniques with different names around the globe. Today we hear a lot about mindfulness as a method for healing emotional as well as physical health. Mindfulness is paying attention intentionally to the present moment with acceptance in a nonjudgmental fashion. I find *nonjudgment* and *self-love* to be the key to successful meditation. Rather than list names of programs, I believe most all meditations fall into the following five categories: concentration meditation, mind-stretching meditation, reflective meditation, creative meditation, and heart-centered meditation.

Concentration meditation is the foundation for all kinds of meditation. We can make the mind a powerful instrument by developing the ability to focus effectively to enhance and deepen insights into our soul. Like a 25-watt lightbulb, light will diffuse. Use a 25-watt laser beam, and the difference is startling. With patience and practice, you can learn to place your intention on the particular issue for that day and hold it there without distraction.

Mind-stretching meditation helps us stretch and expand our minds. Tune your brain into nothing but be open to *everything*. Turn the wonder of gazing into your soul or marveling in the beauty of nature into listening for the answer to your heart's prayer. Some people begin this type of meditation with prayer or mind-stimulating literature. *If prayer is talking to God, your intuition is God talking back to you.*

Reflective meditation is a more directed or analytical meditation. You can choose a question or theme and contemplate that as you meditate. When your attention wanders, return to the chosen topic. It is sometimes helpful to write down questions as they pop into your head and refer to that list as you sit down to meditate.

Creative meditation is consciously cultivating specific qualities we desire to put into our daily habits. This helps us actively nurture the qualities associated with God's love. Traits such as patience, appreciation, joy, gratitude, love, compassion, nonjudgment, fearlessness, and humility already exist inside of us. Creative meditation can help change locked brain patterns to help us daily to think, speak, and act in a more profound, loving way.

Heart-centered meditation helps us awaken our empathy and forgiveness. Begin with *you*. If we love ourselves, we have a lot more love to give away to others! Channeling that love into your body comes through God's grace. God brought you into this world in total love, and His love is always available to you and through you.

All types of meditation can bring healing, and all of these are interrelated, because they are centered on *you*. Before we share a few techniques that we have used successfully, we need to understand more about energy medicine and how the two practices can be combined to help you on a daily basis. It sounds odd trying to quiet your mind and then trying to boost your energy. I am suggesting boosting your energy first, moving energy that can get stuck in various places in our bodies, and then slow-breathing down, moving into quiet meditation. *I highly recommend you begin first by learning meditation if it is new to you.* Take one step at a time.

What is energy medicine?

Energy medicine recognizes energy as a vital, living, moving force. Energy literally is the medicine. You heal the body by activating and empowering its natural healing ability. Energy is continuously moving all around your body. If life is ideal in our body, energy is circulating naturally and providing the life force needed for every organ in our bodies. We heal by restoring energy that has become weak or out of balance. Understanding chakras in our bodies helps us understand how energy is moved through our bodies naturally if all is running smoothly. Energy medicine is used to complement traditional medical care when a body is out of balance in sickness. Energy medicine can be used as self-care or self-help to maintain our bodies, joining our bodies with our spiritual life to bring balance. By understanding how we change longstanding negative beliefs held in our minds and bodies, we put spirit and wise use of our energy together.

Intention is the field of energy that flows invisibly beyond the reach of our normal, everyday habitual patterns. It's a force we all have within us, and we have the power to draw it into our lives by *being* the energy we want to attract. The power of *thought* is a vibrating energy we use every day to drive this intention for action. It is not enough to engage just the power of the mind, however. We cannot just "think" ourselves well, just as it does no good to say, "I must not have had enough faith in God to make healing happen."

Feelings are critical to the process of meditation in any form. Prayer combined with the use of meditation and the use of energy medicine to enhance your body can be powerful. If the feeling of love and acceptance is felt in your body using your heart, the process of healing takes much less time. That is why spirit is so closely aligned with your body and mind. We have to practice loving. While it sounds so simple, we have been taught that loving ourselves first is selfish. It is not. You need that love sent to your own body in order to heal. I now realize I had to practice love in words and actions for myself so that love would naturally flow to myself and others. Meditation helped put these feelings into my body for healing.

Quantum physics and medical science agree our minds are amazing machines. Let's take advantage of that knowledge and put it into practice along with spiritual beliefs and practices. How do we begin?

Combine Energy Medicine, Meditation, and God
An Active Form of Body, Mind, and Soul

The following practices began years ago when I simply did what seemed to work. When I was healing from complex migraines, information flowed into my mind, so I just did it. I trusted my intuition, and I was listening to my inner mind. My neurologist, cardiologist, and my amazing general practitioner worked with me as a whole person. My GP collected all information from specialists on a regular basis. He is now close to eighty, and while he does not place himself in holistic medicine, he could fit in nicely. Treating the whole person is so important. My practices grew with me as I went off all medications and moved into whole living for myself to maintain health and prevent further serious illness. While meditation, yoga, exercise, and healthy eating practices are a very important part of my life, it is beyond the scope of this book to elaborate in each category. However, we are sharing all that we have learned here in this book and on our website www.thelightgap.com.

We can't *stay* in meditation longer in our day than is practical; we need to get out and live our lives! Love every day; that is vitally important. Daily meditation practices help me be more productive each day with lots more energy. After my NDE, I did not choose to go live a monk's secluded life or devote my life to any particular church. I chose to live and share the gifts I have learned with others and live an adapted Christian life. But all of our materials are designed for anyone.

I designed a thirty-minute energy medicine / meditation routine because in my busy working life as a teacher, I couldn't do more. I have more time now and often choose forty minutes or more instead, but that is a choice I have as a retired teacher. If I could back up the earthly time clock, I would have done this as a young working mom, and I would have modeled it for my kids! I might have prevented experiencing complex migraines in my life. I highly recommend meditation to young working people living busy and productive lives. You will never regret it. Writing this book has brought about new challenges, and I often need my shorter routine once again. It is so much better than letting go of practices my body still craves every day. I do think my body craves this because it brings health, energy, and vitality to my life.

Empower My Belief with Channeled Energy

Energy is your life force. Vibrational energy moves in your body, creating vitality (or lack of it) in your cells, organs, muscles, nervous system, immune system, and every element of your physical body.

Chakras are concentrated centers of energy. Meridians are pathways that carry energy to every part of your body. The knowledge of these seven chakras goes back to ancient cultures. Each chakra is a swirling energy positioned at one of seven points, from the base of your spine to the top of your head.

Aura is the eighth chakra, which emanates energy all around your body. This is energy I learned to "feel" and has been highly developed in me. I am assuming it is because during my NDE my aura came back vibrating at a very fast speed. It took me a long time to come to terms with what it was! But through meditation I began to realize my aura was vibrating at a high level as I began to channel the energy to various places in my body for healing. This aura connects us with and protects us from the environment. Valerie Hunt, a neurophysiologist, spent twenty years at UCLA's Energy Field Laboratory comparing aura readings by people, using EMG (electromyography) wave patterns picked up by electrodes on the skin. Colors seen by aura readers (thought of as mystics with a special talent) matched the wave patterns. Valerie V. Hunt, who wrote *Infinite Mind: The Science of Human Vibrations of Consciousness,*[72] shares these images in her book and on her more updated website, providing insights into her research through UCLA. Valerie Hunt died in 2014, but her work is fascinating and is being pursued by fellow scientists. We can train our minds to release stress, anxiety, and fears. We can instead channel loving energy to very specific places in our body.

---

[72]   Valerie V. Hunt, *Infinite Mind: Science of the Human Vibrations of Consciousness* (Malibu, California: Malibu Publishing Co., 1989,1995,1996).

Chakras: Helping Meditation Become Powerful

In my healing journey, I found it very beneficial to understand chakras. Energy can get caught and stuck, especially in our lower three chakras. Learning how to move that energy allowed healing to take place and enabled me to go deeper into my quiet meditation easily following the exercises. I did not understand in the beginning that I was moving energy! It just worked. Now I have found the science to help me understand why it all works. But, for me, spirit is vital to what the mind and body are doing. God's grace from within guides us if we just simply ask for guidance. My connection with the shamanistic world put some of the pieces together. Shamans have a total belief in God's presence in the process of seeking help as they chant and use music and movement to produce an environment ready to move into deep meditation. If you watch what they are doing, you see that they move energy around a patient as they chant, sing words and use their hands. They achieve astounding results of healing. One of the secrets is *belief* that it works. I added belief to my actions. Another secret is letting go of negative emotions. Shamanistic healers called it taking away evil spirits, but in reality they were helping the patient remove fear and negative emotion. The people literally believed that their healer was taking away any evil spirits that surrounded them causing their illness. We can remove our own fear and negative emotions, realizing that those evil spirits really don't exist, except perhaps in our thoughts. Our human mind has created them.

These chakras are located along the meridian line of our human structure. These same points are used in acupuncture. You will find that energy medicine techniques use these same meridian points with amazing success, but we are able to do them independently. Chakras unite the body, mind, and spirit by amplifying energy that resides in the chakras in our bodies. Balance allows a natural flow through them. Understanding the eight chakra locations and bodily functions in those areas can help us evaluate our daily energy. How do we invest our energy? Each day we can place our energy into fear0020and anxiety, or we can redirect our energy into love, peace, and calm, connecting to the divine. Do we create health or disease, one cell of our body at a time? Using energy medicine and meditation, we can help the flow of energy through chakras. Energy can get stuck in one or more of your chakras, causing emotional swings, physical discomfort, pain, and disease. Giving meaning to chakras can help us take a daily inventory of health and focus on weak areas in our bodies. A short yoga routine combined with sound vibration in music helps to "awaken" chakras daily. Adding simple energy-channeling exercises to meditation helps with fine-tuning and maintenance!

Basic Chakra Guide

This information can help you understand which chakras in your body might need help using energy medicine techniques. Our guide was compiled using many resources. The web is full of resources for more information. You will notice that a sphere around the crown chakra indicates the eighth chakra, or aura. Not all resources recognize an eighth chakra. I believe it is part of the chakra system, as did Dr. Khalsa.[73] I believe that the aura provides an important connection with God, connecting through the universe using our mind.

If you are having a particular physical problem, you may find it listed and be able to know which chakra you need to work on. Or, if you find that you are struggling with a particular kind of emotion, you can locate the word here and see which chakra area it might be affecting. You have the ability to work on a particular area of the body, moving energy in helpful ways.

For a visual to see where your body's chakras are located, a Google search will find many.

---

[73] Dharma Singh Khalsa, MD, *Meditation as Medicine* (New York, NY: Fireside, 2001), 259–267.

Chakra Chart

Number and Name Lowest to Highest	Physical—Body	Psychological and Spiritual Traits
#1 Root Chakra Muladhara Lowest Chakra *Earth*	Base of the spine, bladder, rectum, colon ~ legs	Ego, survival, deepest emotions Attachment
#2 Sacral Chakra Svadhistshana sacral plexus *Water*	Behind lower abdomen, sex organs, bladder, pelvis	Creative expression, guilt, anxiety about money, issues of control and sex Lust
#3 Solar Plexus Chakra Manipura solar plexus *Fire*	Behind the navel, stomach, liver, kidneys	Power, strength, transformation, self-esteem Greed
#4 Heart Chakra Anahata Cardiac Plexus *Air* Important tapping point	Behind the heart, heart, lungs, thymus	Love, grief, forgiveness, willpower Pride
#5 Throat Chakra Visuddhu Laryngeal Plexus *Ether* Healing Code Points: throat and necks	Throat, thyroid, mouth, hypothalamus	Truthfulness, decisiveness, willpower Anger
#6 Third Eye Chakra Anja "sun" Healing Code Points: third eye and temples Important tapping point	Center of the head between eyebrows or third eye point, brain, eyes	Intuition, intellectuality, confidence
#7 Crown Chakra Sahasrara Important first and last tapping point	Top of the head—soft spot at birth, brain, cerebral cortex, pineal gland	Intuition, cognition, spirituality
#8 Chakra Outside of the body Some sources do not include #8. Some combine #7 and #8. Experiencing this energy facilitates healing. I feel it is a very critical chakra.	Aura, bioelectric field surrounding the body, skin	Spirituality, unity with the universe, protective "force field"

Physical Understanding	Color Vibration Matching Flower Vibration
A circuit connects you magnetically to earth. If you are feeling unstable, insecure, or fearful, tap into universal thought. Connect with fears; pull them in, recognize, and let go.	**Red** Roses Hibiscus Poinsettias
This chakra is magnetically powerful. Relationship issues may be bringing messages to you. Feeling financial fears? Turn your thoughts to positive energy. Do *not* focus on what you lack. Go to appreciation.	**Orange** Tiger Lily Hibiscus Marigold Bird of Paradise
Truth resides here to "honor yourself" through your intellect, self-esteem, self-confidence, willpower, and integrity. Face any fears after recognizing them. Turn fear into self-love, and then love for others flows naturally.	**Yellow** Black-eyed Susan Dandelions Chamomile
The heart chakra is a bridge between the lower chakras of matter and upper chakras of spirit. The circulatory and immune system is the chakra of love, compassion, generosity, self-love, love for others, and love for God. If you feel lack of love, begin with yourself. Forgiveness is critical for both self and others. Let it out and take one step at a time.	**Green** Deep green in grass, stems, leaves, and mosses. Heart is also vibrational with red.
Throat chakra includes the neck, thyroid, jaw, mouth, and tongue. This chakra carries the energy of verbal expression. If you are feeling a block in communication with anyone or God, focus on energetics to keep energy flowing up from the lower chakras. Will you fear or love your day? God is *only* love.	**Blue** Hyacinths Bluebells Morning Glories
This is the center of intuition. Your mind creates your reality. Do you create worry? Everything in our lives is designed to bring us to truth. Seek truth within, using your own power of intuition to navigate the universe for information. Do you need to open your intuition? Stay present for each moment of life.	**Indigo** Hydrangea Lilac Lavender Violets Petunias
The crown chakra represents enlightenment and spiritual connection to our higher self, others, and God. As you work on a higher connection within, visualize white light. This chakra is your spiritual center. It is the pathway in and out of the body bringing heaven to earth.	**Violet** Violets Petunias Periwinkle
Spirit gives life to the mind. Mind gives life to the body. Aura is external and is the energy force that surrounds the body. Bioelectrical energy exists in all living creatures. Early religious paintings from the Middle Ages portrayed spiritual people with bright auras. New imaging techniques are capturing these energy fields. Study of auras is new and innovative research. This chakra allows us to send positive healing energy to self and others. Vibration is faster in meditation; think of your prayers as channeled vibrations through God!	**White** Lilies Jasmine Geraniums

Written by Terry Larkin using many resources. Primary information came from Dr. Dharma Singh Khalsa in *Meditation as Medicine*,[74] Carolyn Myss's Guide to Chakras from her CD,[75] and Traci Pederson in "Flowers to Enhance Chakra Energy Flow," *Spirituality and Health* magazine.[76]

[74]   Dr. Dharma Khalsa, Meditation as Medicine (New York, NY: Fireside, 2002), 161–259

[75]   Carolyn Myss, *Chakra Meditation Music CD Guide* (Boulder, CO: Sounds True, 2002), 1–20.

[76]   Traci Pedersen, "Using Flowers to Enhance Chakra Energy Flow," *Spirituality and Health* magazine (June 9, 2015), online edition

Learning anything new takes time and practice. I highly recommend that you take new learning in small steps that work for you. Learn one or two things, put them into practice for at least a week, and then move on to new ones as you see and feel a need. You will find a thirty- or forty-minute integrated spiritual workout on the next page that combines soft yoga, important breathing techniques, a chosen energy medicine routine for the day, and quiet meditation. The design is meant for individualization so that you can change it as needed for your own needs. My own routine developed over many years. I am sharing what has worked the best for me right now maintaining my health, with prevention of disease in mind. If you have a very specific health need that is impacting your life, focus on that need completely!

Your environment is very important. Help your mind enjoy the peace and serenity you create. Ask yourself, "Shall I be inside or outside today? Is there something in my space I need to make new?" Change is good for us, so you might not want to keep your routine identical for more than a few weeks. Make the routine fit your style. Have your loving meditation space ready with a yoga mat and begin with soft music; it can help you focus on breathing and calm your mind while you work through moving energy in your body.

Once you have a private space designed and ready, you might need to simply start with the basic meditation we outlined earlier in this chapter. Here is an order I suggest for learning purposes. Each one of you might be starting in a different place. Keep in mind that if you develop one of these and feel comfortable, you can explore another area by taking only one or two of the suggested techniques at a time. You can incorporate newly learned techniques as the need arises. And as you become more aware of your body and its needs, you will *know* and put into place what works best for you! Each one of us has different needs.

1. Basic meditation—learn first
2. Breathing techniques—add into basic meditation
3. Soft yoga—moving energy—add in a few at a time

4. Energy medicine techniques—channeling energy—learn one or two at a time.

Following is the basic outline so you can see where you are headed. Simply *start* a daily routine. There is no right and wrong. Refer back to basic meditation if needed. Techniques for breathing, energy medicine, and soft yoga can flow into this basic integrated spiritual workout slowly over time as you learn how to do them. Once familiar with the techniques, they are easier to put one after the other in a flow that works. This is simply a suggested time frame. Each individual will be different.

1. Week 1: Put basic meditation into practice (see Basic Meditation).
2. Week 2: Learn one deep breathing technique (Breathing Guide).
   Add prayer pose, cat, and cow in yoga (see Yoga Guide).
3. Week 3: Add more moves from soft yoga routine.
   Learn one simple energy medicine technique (Energy Medicine Guide).
   Learn another breathing technique.
   Begin to teach yourself the tapping points (see EFT Guide).
4. Week 4: Learn one more energy medicine technique.
   Practice tapping. Use our online resources to watch demonstration videos.
5. Week 5: Learn one more simple energy medicine technique.
   Begin to teach yourself the Universal Healing Code.
6. Week 6: As you feel more comfortable with your daily routine, you will begin to design an order, style, and time frame that work for you.

Integrated Spiritual Workout
Thirty- to Forty-Minute Healing Meditation

Always honor your body's limitations! *Growth* will occur.

Purpose: *focus* the mind, *focus* on breathing, *notice* the body, *accomplish* moving energy through the chakras, *surrender* any old belief, and *pray* for healing, moving toward silence for your soul. Well-chosen music for your soul can enhance this whole routine.

5 minutes **Breathing Routine / Stretching**—Think **Self-Love**
Stand at the back of your yoga mat totally relaxed with *insight* in mind. Take note of what you are feeling in your body. As you begin these movements, place in your mind that your goal is to feel love present in your body, thankful for healing that might take place without judgment about your insights.

5 minutes **Energy Medicine**—Think **Joy**
At this point, you can move directly into soft yoga or add an energy medicine technique as you learn them. Most take only a few minutes. Choose what is most important. You will know if adding more makes sense to you.

10 minutes **Soft Yoga Routine** accompanied by music. Think **Grace** pouring in.
    Practice positive self-talk (positive affirmations) while moving.
Soft yoga will facilitate movement of energy through your chakras.

10 minutes **Silence with Your Soul** (20 minutes even better)
    No expectations … just enjoy! End with *thankfulness.*

Always consult your physician before beginning any new exercise program.

Quiet Time with Your Soul: Suggestions

Stand up after yoga, reaching and stretching. Look up and *surrender*. Send love to yourself and the universe by giving yourself a big hug. Take notice of any negative emotions but do not dwell on them and let them go! Your mind and your body are now ready for silence, and you will notice very little mind chatter now that you have completed the first part. You are ready to sit on the mat or in a chair comfortably. Headphones can help to remove distractions. Vibrational soft music or silence can produce an optimum effect. I usually choose Dr. Wayne Dyer's, I AM: Wishes Fulfilled CD, but some days I choose silence. Focus your breathing until it becomes slow and natural. Visualize your body in bright white light; try to visualize any body part that needs attention and send it love. Channel your energy there but then let go and simply enjoy the quiet.

Tapping and healing codes can be used entirely on their own or at any needed moment during your workout!

Breathing Guide Using Stretch and Touch

Energy movement is built into all breathing and stretch techniques.

Instructions will seem long, but once you learn it, these can be done quickly! You will find a few stretching techniques infused into these exercises. I believe they facilitate movement of energy. You will notice I have put these into learning steps. Be kind to yourself. Learn one at a time! Put them into your daily routine slowly as you learn them.
Breathe the power of *emotion* into your life by thinking *love* for your body!

Breathing Exercise 1—Standing

- Begin with a nice deep breath through your nose, exhaling through your mouth.

- Stretch high with both hands, spreading them wide as you move them down to your sides.

- With extended arms, lean deeply both left and then right. Repeat this, only this time as you lean on one side, gently press the side of your head down toward your shoulder as you *breathe deeply*. Repeat on the other side. You should feel stretching in your neck and back. Reach behind your neck at the middle and press on the bony structure you feel. This is another acupuncture point. Press and then massage gently while continuing in and out breaths. Then move one inch to each side at a time and press lightly.

Breathing Exercise 2—Bending and Standing

- Breathe in through your nose and out an open mouth. Reach down to your feet and press in the middle of each foot; this is an acupuncture point. Massage gently. Breathe. With hands in prayer position, push hands together. Breathe. Reach high with one hand, low with the other. Switch several times. End by bending down close to your feet. Breathe.

- Come back to standing. Breathe deeply through your mouth in and out *fiercely* about ten times. Let your stomach muscles pull in your breath each time.

- Breathe deeply through your nose and feel your belly moving outward. This time feel your belly as you breathe *deeply* through your nose and release through your mouth slowly. Repeat as you picture that breath moving from your belly, up and through your chest and out your third eye point (between your eyebrows).

Breathing Exercise 3—Standing

- Place your hands one above the other on your abdomen. Breathe deeply through your nose as you bend forward, keeping your back straight. Open your mouth, putting your tongue up to the roof of your mouth as you exhale.

- Place one hand on the back of your neck and the other on the abdomen. Again bend forward, keeping your back straight. Open your mouth, putting your tongue up to the roof of your mouth as you exhale. Repeat the process with the opposite hand on your neck.

Breathing Exercise 4—Standing

- Press just above your pubic bone with both hands, mostly your three fingers. Feel the energy move *up*. Begin to move those fingers up the middle meridian line from the pubic bone to the middle of your chest, making contact with your heart and how it feels, up across the center of your throat, moving up the Adam's apple and off the end of your chin. Feel the energy moving with you through all of those points. Repeat if you think it is helpful for you on a particular day.

- Press just above your pubic bone again with one hand and just above your tailbone on your backside. Press gently but firmly. Feel the energy moving.

Breathing Exercise 5—Standing or Sitting

Breathing is very important. The following has been with me since early in my healing and has continued as one of the most important breathing exercises that I complete each day. I strongly believe it has brought amazing vitality to my day and relief of any allergy symptoms while I heal them.

- Push one side of your nose closed with your thumb. Breathe very deeply through the other side. Hold your breath for as long as possible while you move your forefinger of the same side to close the other side of your nose. Release your breath deeply out of the previously closed side of your nose. Breathe in deeply through that side. Hold your breath once again as long as possible. Let go and let your breath go through the opposite side of your nose. Repeat several times. I have found this breathing exercise extremely helpful each day to relieve any asthma or allergy symptoms so that no medications were necessary.

Soft Yoga Guide / Moving Energy

You do not need to be an expert at yoga to do some of the simpler moves each day. I highly recommend you take a class, but it is not a critical ingredient. As mentioned earlier, the goal is to move energy daily. The following exercises will stretch and move energy to all of the essential organs. It helps to *think* about these places while your brain is thinking *love*. I suggest using the first three right away. I use music that is soft but invigorating.

Yoga Routine 1

1. **Prayer Pose** arms extended, also called Child's Pose: kneel down on your mat with all fours. Place your hands flat and slide up until you are stretched as far as you are able. The trunk of your body is on the mat. Begin positive affirmations and prayer. I make this as deep as possible, pulling up the energy across my back.
2. **Cat**: Come up on all fours, arching your back and looking downward. Pull your stomach in tightly.

3. **Cow:** Stay on all fours, pushing in the opposite direction with your stomach pushing toward the floor and head arched looking upward as far as possible.

Yoga Routine 2

4. **Prayer Pose** again, and then *leg stretch* outward toward the back one at a time, straight back, stretching the toes and feet as far as you can go.
5. **Crown to Earth**: Come up on all fours and for a few seconds let the top of your head be flat on your mat (connect your crown chakra with the magnetic earth). Try to think gratitude thoughts through mind focus. Bring in *joy* with a huge smile as you bring yourself to a sitting position.
6. **Downward Dog:** If able, lift your body off the mat leaving your hands flat to support you, feet on toes and ball of your foot. Lower your head, let blood flow down to the crown. Deepen by moving your bottom back and doing a walking motion with your feet.

Yoga Routine 3

7. **Body Stretch**: Sit straight up and reach to your toes or as close as you can come comfortably.
8. **Leg Stretch**: Bend one leg in with your foot touching flat against the side of your opposite knee. Stretch again to your feet. Gently massage that foot with your hands. Push on the acupuncture point on the sole of the foot approximately in line with the space between the second and third toes and the corresponding point under your foot.
9. **Leg Stretch Two**: Bend opposite leg in with your foot touching flat against the side of your opposite knee. Repeat foot massage.

Yoga Routine 4

1. **Back Massage**: Lay yourself down one vertebra at a time and then pull up your feet flat so you can grab on to both of your knees. Mind focus—bring in *grace* as you cuddle with your knees rocking back and forth so that the small of your back gets a great massage! Pull your stomach in.

2. **Back Push**: Stay lying down with your feet flat on the mat and knees up in the air close to you. Press the small of your back to the mat using your abs. Hold for a while and then release. Relax. Repeat several times.

3. **Back Arch**: Keep your feet flat and knees up, arching your back up off the mat. Hold. Relax. Repeat several times. Again pull your stomach in as tight as possible.

Change and adapt your yoga routine to meet
your needs on a particular day!
If needed, add healing code or tapping for a specific health issue
(see quick guides for instructions).

Meditation

Going from grace to harmony ... connecting
with God and the world.

Move yourself to an upright position on your mat. Cross your legs lotus style. If you are choosing to stay seated like this for your quiet meditation time, placing a cushion under your bottom and then crossing your legs helps to make you more comfortable. If you prefer to move to a chair, sit comfortably straight with your feet flat on the ground. When I was very sick, I also did my quiet meditations lying comfortably on my mat. It worked. Changing music also helped me go deeper quickly. My breath is usually quite calm and natural after yoga, stretching, and mind control accompanied by soft music.

Realize your body's signals and manage stress by listening to your body! After meditation, I always reach high with both hands stretching outward in a big sun motion and finish with a great big bear hug for myself. Feel the *joy*; I smile big, and on a good day I express the joy by thanking God for all of my blessings with a great laugh out loud and saying, "God, you are awesome!" Remember, you don't have to figure out your problems; release them.

Choices: Silence, Prayer, or add Reading / Soul Journaling: With or without music, this adds to your time in whatever amount you feel is valuable. This could be done either before your quiet meditation, before or after your routine, whatever works best for you. Some of my most valuable insights have come from my soul journal. Soul journaling is writing down feelings and thoughts following meditation.

Energy Medicine Techniques Guide

I prefer doing these on my mat prior to yoga, but
they can be done independently anytime.

Energy Technique 1

- Press just above your pubic bone with both hands, mostly your three fingers. Feel the energy move *up*. Begin to move those fingers pressing up the middle meridian line from the pubic bone to the middle of your chest, making contact with your heart and how it feels, up across the center of your throat, moving up the Adam's apple and off the end of your chin. Feel the energy moving with you through all of those points. Repeat if you think it is helpful for you on a particular day.

- You probably recognize this one; you learned it in breathing exercise #4! It is repeated because it is a great mover of energy. Take note how your abdomen is feeling when you press going up. Notice how your chest is feeling beneath your heart. Take note if you feel stuck when you get to your throat.

- Go back to your chakra chart; you might find some insights that can help you.

Energy Technique 2

- Place both hands on the top of your skull, while one hand overlaps the other. You are on the crown of your head, also a meridian point. Massage your scalp and bone by moving in a clockwise direction. Time can vary, but usually a minute is sufficient. You can have your mind concentrating on a health issue or just enjoying energy moving.

- Place both hands on your forehead, one hand overlapping the other. This position is overlapping with fingers spilling over down the eyebrow line and reaching over into the third eye point. Massage your forehead skin moving over the bone underneath in a clockwise direction. Usually a minute is sufficient. Concentrate on health or joy.

- Place both hands on your chest, embracing your heart chakra, one hand overlapping the other. Massage the heart area, moving first in clockwise direction and then in the opposite direction … eventually just holding and pressing lightly in this area. *Feel* what emotion you might be holding for the day. Breathe deeply and let go. There are times when I want to repeat this particular energy motion; I do what my body seems to want for the day.

Energy Technique 3

- Lower your chin toward your chest. Rotate your head very slowly once in both directions. Lean your head to one side and then the other. With two fingers, touch firmly the bony structure on the back of your neck in the middle. Press. Move about one inch to the right with two fingers, other two fingers to the left. Start low on your neck and move upward to the hairline, feeling the bones beneath your ears. Press and massage lightly.

- Make a decision to learn more about energy moving techniques! *The Small Book of Energy Medicine*[77] by Donna Eden is a book with easy-to-follow directions. She also makes a kit with cards that have many quick and easy techniques.

Channel God's Energy into Your Body Using Energy Medicine

Quick Guide to Energy Tapping

Energy tapping goes by many names. EFT is often used, and it means **E**motional **F**reedom **T**echnique. It started in the 1960s with George Goodheart and John Diamond. It was refined in the eighties and nineties and recently made more accessible to us through the web and books. *The Tapping Solution*[78] by Nick Ortner is a recent, user-friendly version. Their website is full of great things! www. ThrivingNow.com is a website location where you can find easy-to-read instructions as well as scripts and ideas to help specific problems.

Use your middle and index fingers. Tapping three to seven times is plenty. You are tapping on comfort zones, chakra areas, or acupuncture points. Touch is comforting. The idea is to let you speak your truth, choose how you'd *like* to feel, and bring relief from negative emotions that translate to body stress. By tapping on the pain along with the guilt, shame, anger, resentment, worry, or frustration behind it, many people find instant relief and over time great relief. This is just a "sample" script; they are as endless as your mind can create. The nice thing, there is no right or wrong way to do tapping! No one is quite certain why this works, but research shows

---

[77] Donna Eden with Dondi Dahlin, *The little Book of Energy Medicine* (New York: Penguin Books, 2010).

[78] Nick Ortner, *The Tapping Solution* (Carlsbad, California: Hay House, 2013).

it *does*! It has been used successfully with PTSD and recently with Sandy Hook survivors.

To find a very usable image showing tapping points, go to www. thrivingnow.com, and they have a printable drawing you can use.

Here is an adapted script to use:

1. Start with the karate chop point. State the problem. Even though I have _____,
   I deeply and completely accept myself. Chop. Repeat three times.
2. Top of the head. *I wish it would go away!*
3. Eyebrow points near center. *Even though I can't stop worrying I deeply and completely accept myself.*
4. Side of the eye. *All this stress about___ is leaving me drained and upset.*
5. Under the eye. *My _____really hurts!*
6. Under the nose. *Why am I stuck with __?*
7. Chin. *I feel this frustration in my abdomen!*
8. Collarbone. *I don't need _____.*
9. Under the arm. *I recognize _____.*
10. Top of the head. *I ask my body for relief! I deeply and completely accept myself!*

Breathe deeply. Repeat two to three times.

Second and third time around, start telling yourself you have no need for _____. "I replace this fear with love. I release this _____to God. I love and care for _____." Begin to put in the positive and the changes you want. Use the wisdom that comes to you through meditation to find and locate when a particular pain or disease began in your life. Is there an emotional attachment to it that is keeping it in your life? Breathe deeply as you place your hands on your heart. Saying these thoughts out loud can hold a secret to putting an and to it! Pray, surrender.

The Healing Codes

The Healing Code concept was devised and written by Alex Loyd, PhD, ND (who healed himself of Lou Gehrig's disease) along with Ben Johnson, MD, DO, NMD. Dr. Loyd discovered the Healing Codes in 2001 while searching for a cure for his wife's depression. The program originally came out in lectures and was available in notebook form. Eventually he wrote it into a book called *The Healing Code*[79] in 2010. You will find www.thehealingcodes.com has lots more information. The following are the names of the chapters of this book.

Seven Secrets to Life, Health, and Prosperity:
1. There is one source of illness and disease—stress.
2. Stress is caused by an energy problem in the body.
3. The issues of the heart are *the* healing control mechanism.
4. The human hard drive stores our memories—both conscious and unconscious.
5. Your antivirus program may be making you sick. (Stimulus/response sets up a belief system formed early in life.)
6. I believe! (Finding beliefs that are causing sickness.)
7. When the heart and head conflict, the winner is ... *your heart.*

When *The Healing Code* is read, each of these seven secrets to life comes alive in a chapter.

We have been using the Healing Codes for many years. We have found that it works well to place this activity right into our meditation time when it works, but independently is just fine as well. When we first began using the codes, we did them for longer periods of time and went to our manuals to find "specific" codes for specific

---

[79] Alex Loyd, PhD, ND, and Ben Johnson, MD, DO, NMD, *The Healing Code: 6 Minutes to Heal the Source of Any Health, Success or Relationship Issue* (Peoria, Arizona: Intermedia Publishing Group, 2010).

illnesses. These can now be found on their website. We were using them independently of meditation at that time.

It was a monumental leap in belief when I realized I was using my vibrational energy from my own hands to channel this healing energy. My NDE had helped me be aware of this energy. I could *feel* the energy vibration when it was working. And I could feel when the position was wrong. The points used on the body are also part of the chakras and acupuncture points used in many types of energy healing tools. Be sure to send yourself *love* every day while working with energy in a healing code. Many spiritual healers say they are channels for God's energy. We have learned to channel God's energy! We *know* you can too.

"The Healing Codes activate powerful healing centers that can allow the body to heal itself of almost anything. They do this by removing the stress from the body, thus allowing the neuro-immune system to take over its job of healing whatever is wrong in the body."[80]

Dr. Alexander Loyd recently wrote another book called *Beyond Willpower*.[81] This book spends a lot of time discussing energy medicine and why it is a great tool for healing. He introduces some new tools that I have found very useful. He talks a lot about getting to the subconscious and unconscious mind through meditation. Willpower alone cannot heal, and there are many of us trying to use only our conscious mind, and it doesn't work.

Quick Guide to the Universal Healing Code

- Decide on your most pressing issue for healing. The codes suggest doing one at a time. It is great to make a list as you uncover them during meditation (soul journal).
- Memory: Think, when did I feel this? When did it begin or with whom? Meditation can help these memories surface.

[80]   Website quote from www.thehealingcodes.com.

[81]   Alexander Loyd, PhD, ND, *Beyond Willpower: From Stress to Success in 40 Days* (New York: Harmony Books, a division of Random House LLC, 2015).

Just notice; don't add anxiety by overthinking it. Send that experience or person love for helping you.

- Say a prayer for healing, inserting your "remembered" uncovered issue. We use our own words now. A script is found in the *Healing Code* book. We began with that when we were first learning.

> "I pray that all known and unknown negative images, unhealthy beliefs, destructive cellular memories, and all physical issues related to _____ would be found, opened and healed by filling me with the light, life, and love of God. I also pray that the effectiveness of this healing be increased by 100 times or more."[82]

Don't skip this step; you are telling your body to make this healing a priority as well as putting the *feel* of it into your body memory. *Feeling it is critical.*

- Do the Healing Code, holding each position for around thirty seconds or longer in this order, repeating your truth focus statement. Take note of the negative and then focus on the positive.

Repeat sequence. Do the code sequence for at least six minutes.

Universal Positions

Using both hands, put your thumb underneath your four fingers, pointing together toward each position. Hold keeping a space of about an inch between your fingertips and your body.

---

[82] Alex Loyd, PhD, ND, and Ben Johnson, MD, DO, NMD, *The Healing Code: 6 Minutes to Heal the Source of Any Health, Success or Relationship Issue* (Peoria, Arizona: Intermedia Publishing Group, 2010).

1. **Main Bridge Position** is in between the bridge of your nose and the middle of your eyebrow (third eye point). If you need a rest after, place your hands on your cheeks.

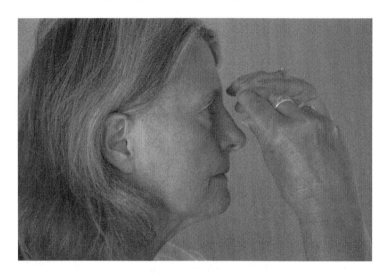

Photo by Doug Larkin

2. **Second Position** is directly over your Adam's apple.

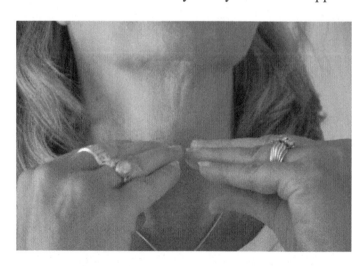

Photo by Doug Larkin

3. **Third Position** is your jaw. Point fingers under the ear at the back corner of the jawbone on both sides of the head. If you need to rest, place hands on the sides of your face down near the jaw.

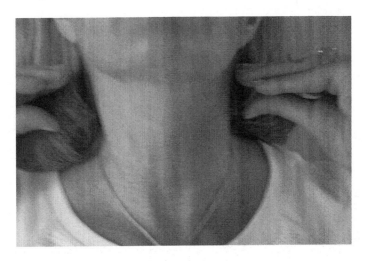

Photo by Doug Larkin

4. **Fourth Position** is your temple. Point your fingers one half inch above the temple and half inch toward the back of the head on both sides.

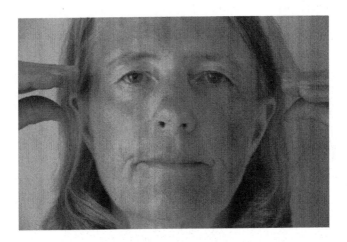

Photo by Doug Larkin

As with any program involving your health, always consult with your physician before beginning any new routine.

Balancing Life

To live a healthy life is something all human beings want for themselves. Balancing a spiritual life infused with a working life is a goal all religions work hard to agree upon. They have guidelines meant to help support the efforts of their believers by putting it into a framework. No real framework exists that will work for everyone. We were given free will by God to design a life perfect for ourselves while living through love existing along with all humanity. As we all know, our tangled world is still trying to figure this all out, and most likely we will still be working toward peace forever, who knows how long! So at best, the two of us as authors can only share what we have learned from countless others and put it into a framework that is always under construction. Our lives move forward each minute, hour, day, and month or years … linear years as we are living in now! We cannot set guidelines for you or anyone except ourselves.

We all are living in this very fast-paced world. We are fighting the clock in some form or another. It's important to step back once in a while and reflect on our routines and see if they are working for us in our lives. If we can find the reasons that we always seem to be in rush, we might be able to figure out how to make sure we have time for all that is important in life. We hope you allow yourself to take control of it all and make choices that will enhance your health and in effect create the life you want for yourself. Asking yourself where stress might be active in your life is helpful to making positive changes. What are your beliefs about what it takes to be in shape and be physically healthy? We all wish for a body that looks and feels terrific! Sometimes we fall into a sweeping fad exercise plan or diet program, thinking it will solve all of our problems. Then old patterns resurface.

So what kind of thoughts do you find yourself having? Journaling can be a helpful tool to find out what a typical week *really* looks like in your life and what thoughts you are having about yourself and God. Most of us who have done this seldom want to share it with another human being! We can find lists of how to balance life. They exist within every expert in all fields of study. We can find countless ones on the Internet. Our list may differ a little. But that's okay. We're not trying to shape your life; we hope you will shape your own!

Tools for Mind and Spirit While Living in Your Body

Creating Balance

You might be looking for something to place in your thoughts while you create health through breathing, yoga, or meditation. Here are some thoughts for you! You can choose just one to think about at a time or take a grouping for a week and see how creatively you begin thinking about positive change.

1. *Love*, live, and laugh. Yes, love is first.
2. *Love* by not taking yourself so seriously.
3. *Love* yourself and others.
4. *Create* a pathway to God.
5. *Create* positive thoughts.
6. *Create* meditation that works for you.

7. *Create* intentions and take action.
8. *Be open* to new thought.

9. *Be open* to energy medicine techniques.
10. *Balance* your energy.
11. *Create* your vibrational energy and use it wisely.

12. *Exercise* daily in some fun way.
13. *Choose* food wisely.
14. *Sleep* at regular hours and do things that encourage deep sleep.

15. *Find* the awesome four: nutrition, water, positive thoughts, and love.
16. *Avoid* the dreaded four: sugar, pollutants, fear, and negativity.

---

17. *Talk* with your physician about proactive health.
18. Use *wellness* to overcome sickness.

---

19. *Create* a life you love.
20. *Laugh,* laugh again, enjoy life, and laugh again!

Don't chase after the past
Don't seek the future
The past is gone
The future hasn't come yet
See clearly on the spot
The object which is now.
—Buddha

Conclusion

Life is the process of awakening to God's unimaginable presence in our lives. For both of us, it has taken years of experiences, study, reflection, and living life to recognize the change in our consciousness levels. Conscious awareness is a steady force contained within all of us whether or not we recognize it exists. We live in everyday reality coping, solving problems, growing in intellect, maturing, and attempting to understand God through the filter of our culture's beliefs. Spiritual awakening begins with a direct connection to God and often an outside force that acts to jolt us into remembering our life's purpose. We talk and think we are learning *about* God. But *being* with God is a whole new direction, and it changed us.

One of us was experiencing a traumatic ruptured spleen and the other the death of a child. A vibrational force in the form of LIGHT followed these shocking events so intense our conscious mind could not easily process the meaning. We can no longer go back to living in the same state of consciousness after the life-changing force first came through shock. When God is experienced, our sensory perceptions are forever altered.

The full circle of understanding our relationship with God could only take place through finding and realizing that *God is in us,* intertwined in a way that has confused man since the beginning of time. We are the ones that need to open the pathway to find our inner God. It is not only a major shock that can get us to this point. Sometimes it is a slow, gradual process. God sends continuous messages, messengers, and experiences to wake us up. All major religions have in their sacred texts a Holy Spirit, soul, divine inner nature, or inner God. The name of the term doesn't matter. It is critical we find God, or whatever term you use, and experience the force that is held within it. While the times and experiences were different, the day each of us realized that our souls could be more than a mere concept, *life* changed! Instead of a concept, we found an actual functioning connection to God that was practical, meaningful, and a useful part of our everyday existence. You would *think* that we learned God was internal on the day of our LIGHT experiences; we did not. Our growth included that climb from *insight*, changing a long-held *belief* that *we* would not hear God specifically talking to *us*. Becoming aware of God's clear message moved us to *knowing* that God is within. Now recognizing that each person is a piece of God, we can say we are cocreating with God the realities of our lives. Truth lives in us. Fear hurts, but love heals.

Perhaps our stories led you into a deeper understanding of being human. Maybe you already knew you were a part of God. Or it might have caused you to challenge some of your culture's most cherished beliefs. Possibly you experienced a disconnection from our thoughts. Even if you didn't find answers, we hope our book served our purpose of helping you discover for yourself new ways of questioning your existence and the meaning of your life.

The information is all around us through countless voices saying the same thing, in literature past and present, on the web, and in every corner of our world. We are part of a huge shift in consciousness on our planet. It is time we used a term called *global spirituality* regardless of the framework you decide to place around your life. This may be a new concept for you to process.

Our lives become easier when we connect with God in a personal way. Many people find comfort bringing their spirituality into their religious practice and thrive. Some are very uncomfortable with religious organizations and also thrive. God loves us all in our unique styles. If you are uncomfortable with the term God, then use another term for the spiritual nature of life.

Science is so interwoven throughout our spiritual lives that each new discovery brings new knowledge about the world God created for us. Science and spirituality started out together. For centuries, humans had various spiritual beliefs and practices that united cultures, villages, and tribes. Ancient religions formed all over the world. Ancient texts may contain a lot more than we think, or have accepted, in our attempt to interpret meaning based on old scientific knowledge. Man lacked the scientific knowledge to pull these two pieces together. Between the years of about 1500 to the 1670s in Europe, what we consider our modern physical science, physics, developed alongside philosophies about our mind-thinking sciences, metaphysics. These early scientists believed that there was a hidden unity all humans were seeking. The first scientists were prosecuted for their theories, and there has been a separation and struggle between science and spirituality ever since.

But currently we are experiencing a new awakening in our world as people digest new religious and scientific theories that begin the debate once again. Evolution of the mind with expanded knowledge takes us right back to the individual person. You and me, all of us, are awakening through God's embedded presence to find love and peace instead of fear and hatred. Knowing you have the power within you to connect to God's divine nature is bringing miracles into everyday existence. Many mystical, God-realized events are being brought into our awareness so we can learn from them. If there is hatred or violence in them, they are from man's inventions and are not from God. God gave us free will. We can use it for love or violence.

You can know yourself at the soul level when you come to a divine spiritual awakening! Any profound spiritual experience brings with it the knowledge God wasn't outside of you. It is finding the divine inside yourself and projecting outwardly the love that is found there. This can happen anywhere. Perhaps it already has happened to you—in nature, at church, in a dream, during a tragedy, watching a loved one take their last breath, experiencing a spirit around you, deep in prayer or meditation. The possibilities are endless. Some experiences are more powerful than others. The vibrations of love are so high we can spread love to others around us, and that has been proven scientifically. We *live* for *life*. Our hope is that you can see we do not *wait* for death to experience ultimate love. We find love within the life we are living. We are bringing heaven to earth, enjoying each moment as we grow in our awareness that God is talking and sharing with us internally as well as through the universe and other people.

The most compelling experience over the past two years has been realizing, and living, that we are really, literally, communicating with God. We imagined this earlier, but it is divine gift to become aware that it is really happening. The great thing is that we know we are no different from anyone else. But we are *aware* of this communication now. Here is an example as we wrote the pages of this book. We have experienced the two-way communication as we follow our guidance while writing in our soul journals. As we meditate, we ask for guidance, write what thoughts pour out that day, then put it away until the next day. It is amazing as we notice the wisdom that comes through our thoughts over the next few days. Words begin to flow onto pages.

This book has taken us well over two years to write. When we began, we had no idea that we would continue to grow in our own spiritual awakening through this writing process. Our consciousness level has expanded even more. We are still opening new pathways to let God's infinite wisdom flow into our lives. We have no idea when experiences might expand into new thought or what form they might take.

We believe our future is not predetermined. Terry's "history" could have been significantly changed through different choices. What if she had chosen to stay in Shelbyville, Tennessee? The circumstances of her life, Doug's life, and her children's lives would have evolved very differently. What would have happened if Marj had chosen to bury her desire to understand life and death, succumbing to her grief instead? What if she had never traveled to the Amazon, following Anne's dream to travel there? The circumstances of her life and those of her husband and two sons would have emerged very differently.

What our expanded knowledge has taught us is that we have choice. We use our thoughts, expressing these thoughts with our words and then putting them into actions that create new possibilities.

We use the reverse process, starting with new actions, to change our unproductive thoughts so that we can get rid of what is *not* working in our lives. We still would have emerged finding these answers but through a very different platform, and perhaps ending life without living our life to its fullest potential. Each day we are cocreating with God, orchestrating our lives in ways we can't fathom. What are the coincidences we have missed in our lives? We have missed many, we are sure. We walked past open doors God provided for us. But we have also walked right into many of them. The outcome may not have changed, but every detail of our lives could have looked different. Our lives are still evolving and changing.

What are the implications for all of us? We can and do change outcomes in our lives by our choices. It's your life and your health; you *can* move *you* into a life you *love*! May you find peace and love wrapped in your life suited to your own soul! A meaningful life will emerge in all of its beauty.

Where there is spiritual unity within your mind and heart, what you do is wrapped in love. You reconcile to the truth of oneness. *I am love*. The presence of the great I AM is with me. Above all, *I am* in gratitude for the miracle of all life, for life is love living itself.

Terry & Marj

In Gratitude and Appreciation

Lois Mulder, our artist. We send gratitude to Lois Mulder, friend and one of life's beautiful souls forever giving to all through her caring and loving generosity. Her talents as our artist, painting the LIGHT GAP, capturing the amazing eyes of our tiny baby sloth, and understanding our needs painting three-dimensional ladders brought beauty into our book, our presentation materials, and our website. We feel incredibly blessed to have such a talented artist as our friend through God's Amazing Presence.

Marianne Novak Houston, mentor and dear friend. A huge thank you for your willingness to read our book and write an endorsement. Your support brought such joy to us. The leadership you provide for Courage to Teach and Courage to Lead has been instrumental in bringing our lives into balance. You have taught and inspired so many people with the Courage and Renewal process that is exceptionally respectful and safe, allowing us to share in a way that our souls show up and gain the courage to step into leadership.

Jason Larkin, our graphics expert. Generous thanks to Jason Larkin, son and one of life's very talented graphic engineers! Always in the background with incredible support and creative ideas poured into our presentation materials. We are forever grateful for another of God's amazing givers of love through his work. Premier Graphics owner: www.mysigndesign.com.

We grew up with loving and incredibly diverse parents, brothers, and sisters. Your support for our thoughts, ideas, and ultimately our book has always been filled with unconditional love. How can we ever thank you for your support? We treasure our unique family all through God's Amazing Presence.

John & Jean Ashby, our parents. We began our lives together with two parents who provided a very creative and loving family life. We lived through life's many trials together and celebrated triumphs. They were always there for us, modeling a giving and caring life for others. Both were loved deeply in life, and now they are hearing us giving thanks to them with grateful hearts in another realm.

Lynne and Bob Krainer, our sister. Lynne and Bob, your infinite wisdom and intelligence has been integrated into our lives and into our book! Your tireless hours of editing were so appreciated. As our sister, we have found a generous, loving, and caring big sister to both of us! Your support of our work is nothing short of miraculous. Your beautiful children and their families are always a source of joy and delight!

Jack and Mary Ashby, our brother. Jack and Mary Pat, your zest for life's adventures drew us into every corner of the earth both in our backyard and around the world. Your model of always nurturing family and friendships brought us to Hawaii to present our Health and Healing workshop and share our book! We are forever grateful for your support. You are such caring people, giving to so many souls struggling in life. Your son has provided us with astounding video to record our presentation. *Thank you, Brian!* You are always inspiring with new thought and tales of adventures too!

Bill and Norma Ashby, our youngest brother. Bill and Norma, your amazing musical talents have put delight into our lives for countless years! Your love of life, God, laughter, and sense of humor, as well as your graceful way of taking in life's challenges, has been a model for our entire family. We are in such gratitude for your support of our writing life, our presentations, and a genuine interest in our lives as our souls developed in unique ways. You always model such amazing listening skills, and we are forever grateful to your generous spirits. Your amazing children and their families continue to bring delight in our lives!

Gratitude for the support from friends and strangers that have become new friends. Our home communities of Zeeland/Holland, Michigan, and Northbrook, Illinois, and Eagle River, Wisconsin, have shown interest and given us support and opportunities to speak. In Eagle River, special thanks goes to Angie and Peter at The Blend coffee shop and Pastor Mary Anne Biggs at UUC Congregational Church for their invitations to use their spaces for presenting. Terry and I gained so much experience by preparing and speaking to our audiences. These opportunities helped redirect our ideas and develop our speaking voices as well as our writing voices. Thank you to all of you who have asked about our progress, are interested in our work, attended presentations, and have requested to know when it is finally in book form.

Terry

First and foremost, my deepest appreciation goes to my wonderful husband, Doug. Thank you doesn't begin to express the gratitude and love in my heart for your unending love and support. You could see deep into my soul when I often could not express myself to others. You were there for me as you heard my ever-expanding experience during my NDE, always listening and hearing with compassion my fears and truths from within. Your talent in photography and business expertise has helped our book, presentations, and website presence. You are amazing as a husband and supporter and are forever in God's Amazing Presence with us.

    My greatest pleasure is in thanking you, Marj, for the privilege of cowriting this book with you, my amazing big sister! Your deep and powerful wisdom has allowed me to share my deepest and innermost truths with the world. Our lives were chosen to be together, first as children and all throughout our adult life—searching to find God's Amazing Presence in both of our lives. You are an incredible soul living a love filled life, a sharing, kind, and caring human being. And to Jim Steiner, Marj's husband, who has always been so steadfast in his unconditional love for me as a person and throughout every step in our journey to create *The Light GAP*.

To my beautiful family, words escape the deep-seated love and gratitude I have for all of you. My children have always been my most significant teachers in my life. Jason, Jeremy, and Jacob, you are so precious to me in every way imaginable. You are amazing and talented men. Each of you is so unique; it makes God's gift of individual lives become very real. You are all living your own dreams, and for that I am eternally grateful. Your incredible wives and families bring delight in my life always, even when time and space keep us apart. I thank you, Michele, Al, and Amanda for giving our sons unconditional love and support. As grandchildren, Jackson, Emma, Cade, and Ellee, you are the continuing delight of my life, bringing the next generation of caring and loving human beings.

My return to Shelbyville, Tennessee, in 2016 brought a reminder of how deep friendships are part of our soul's agenda. To Bailey and Trena Little, I have been so blessed to have you in my life. While distance and time separated us, your love and caring nature brought my NDE experience into the light of remembrance. To Fred Hunt, thank you for being my lawyer and friend so many years ago following my accident! Your incredible file kept for thirty-four years brought together memories that had been missing, facilitating a closure to my NDE. Your recent kindness is well remembered!

Integral to the writing of this book were more people than I have space to mention personally. All of you helped me as I struggled to express thoughts and ideas different from the norm. You helped me grow away from trying to be *like* everyone else and simply be myself in a world that often prefers to keep life's mysteries locked away. Special thanks to you, Mary, my true spiritual mentor and special friend who is always available to listen and support my efforts to write this book. A tribute goes to two dear book club friends, Edie and Jan, who began this journey with me as I first told my story. You were both so supportive. I feel your presence from above where you are free of the ravages of cancer. I miss you terribly. And to Shirley, who has encouraged me from the beginning and keeps encouraging me to tell my story. Special thanks go to all of my delightful book club friends, teacher friends, neighbors, church friends, and fellow singers as they each contributed in countless ways as the complexities of writing a book brought chaos to daily life!

Marj

Deep gratitude to Jim, my husband—you are my hero. You offer love in so many ways. Thank you for spending two and a half years listening to my excitement as well as my discouragement. You are a great resource when I need to wordsmith. Many nights you waited patiently for dinner because "just a minute" turned into hours. "I'll be ready soon. I'm working on the book. I just have to finish this idea." You are a wonderful father, a kind, wise, gentle husband. You have given to the broader community in rich and life-giving ways.

Terry Ashby Larkin, my coauthor and remarkable sister. On a cold winter day in 2014, Terry set out from Michigan to come visit me with a message. The telephone would not do. There was a huge snowstorm that day. The road was treacherous at the bottom of Lake Michigan. You met a huge pile-up of cars on I-94. Seven hours later, you made it to Chicago. Your mission was to convince me that we should write a book together. One of the messages when I was consumed by LIGHT was that I was going to write a book. "Not me! What about?" was my response. Terry's vision and mine has become a reality. Your patience with me has been phenomenal! This twenty-year journey has been extraordinary. We supported each other between discouragement and euphoria, between great writing days and crisis days. You are kind, gentle, intelligent, wise, insightful, adventurous, tenacious, and full of spirit. You live with all of your heart and soul. I am thankful for the practical too. You are much more knowledgeable on the computer than I! Thank you both, Doug and Terry, for the adventures to Peru and Africa. To Doug, thanks for your business expertise on our book project and for the many laughs and hugs over the years.

Always there is love for our sons, Michael and Scott, and daughter-in-law, **Heather**, I am so thankful that all of you chose to

221

come be part of our family. Your laughter and goodness bring joy to us all. Thank you for the love you express, the wisdom you share, and the support you offer. Life was hard at the death of Anne and then Jared, but you have found solid ground, with love in your hearts for these two precious souls.

Anne, we feel you near. We love you! You were a very special daughter. You brought such joy to our lives. Your inner core had nothing but love. What fun we had on our camping trips.

Grandchildren bring new light to the world. I love you, **Ethan and Jonathan**. Thanks for being so wonderful. We are so lucky to be traveling in life together.

Friends are treasured gifts, more precious than gold. I choose not to name all of you, but just know I do recognize the richness you bring to my life. I also know it is a two-way street. We are meant to be interdependent, helping each other celebrate the joys of life, carry each other's burdens, and live fully in the everyday events that make up our days. Sending love to all my winter and summer friends. How fortunate we are.

Love to all who helped us over the hurdles as we were grieving the loss of Anne. In two days, it will be twenty years. Thanks to Anne's high school friends and college roommates who have kept up with us over time. We got to know you and Anne's college adventures in ways we might not have otherwise. Thanks go out to so many. To all of our friends, we thank you for the meals, the guidance, the hugs, the love. To the members of the three churches—Winnetka Presbyterian, Wilmette Presbyterian, and Henry Presbyterian—who surrounded us with love and made God's compassionate heart come to life. To our grieving committee, you listened and let us cry and kept us up and going. Your help carried me for a while and then started me out in new directions. I am very thankful for the support of Sandy Karaganis, principal at Greeley School, and Becky van der Bogert, the superintendent, providing me with compassion and classroom coverage on days I just could not keep going. The school staff and parents were phenomenal, greeting me with smiles and hugs each day, just as all the children in my first-grade class did, along with prior students and parents.

Gratitude to Tim Mahr, professor of music at St. Olaf College, who composed a piece of music for concert band called "Sol Solator," dedicated to the memory of Anne. Continued thanks to **John Thomson, Phil Smith, Bruce Fowler, and Jim Warrick,** music directors at New Trier High School, who began the process. They commissioned the music piece to be written and contacted Tim Mahr, asking him to compose it. How very special it was to hear it performed on both campuses. Anne loved the band, orchestra, and choral music experiences all of these men provided. As I write this, I remember Anne practicing music every night before bed. No one needed to prod her.

Appreciation to Jean Savely who directed the garden and bench project at the Wilmette Beach in Anne's memory. Thanks to all the workers too. We often go down to the lake and sit on the bench opposite a twin bench dedicated to the memory of our friend Skip Uhlemann.

Appreciation to the technology industry. Thank you to everyone over time that has been working to develop technology that helps us communicate. That includes our dad. He worked at the beginning of computers when they were room sized and used cards to tell them what to do. He was called in the middle of the night sometimes to come into the office and find the error so that the assembly line could get up and going again. Terry and I are thankful for the unlimited phone service. We have spent hours talking to each other, editing, making decisions, sharing meditation insights, authors' wisdom, events in our lives … We are grateful for e-mail and messaging also. We could finish a chapter and have the other person editing it within less than five minutes when needed. And then there is the printer, bringing our ideas to print and into physical form. Sometimes my lack of expertise is very frustrating. But not to worry; Michael, Scott, or Terry come to the rescue.

Made in the USA
Lexington, KY
08 February 2017